LEADING PUBLIC SECTOR INNOVATION

Co-creating for a better society

Christian Bason

WITHDRAWN

National Assembly for Wales Library

5400

D0322588

First published in Great Britain in 2010 by

Policy Press
University of Bristol
1-9 Old Park Hill
Bristol
BS2 8BB
UK
t: +44 (0)117 954 5940
pp-info@bristol.ac.uk
www.policypress.co.uk

North America office:
Policy Press
c/o The University of Chicago Press
1427 East 60th Street
Chicago, IL 60637, USA
t: +1 773 702 7700
f: +1 773-702-9756
sales@press.uchicago.edu
www.press.uchicago.edu

© Policy Press 2010

Reprinted 2011, 2014, 2015

British Library Cataloguing in Publication Data
A catalogue record for this book is available from the British Library.

Library of Congress Cataloging-in-Publication Data
A catalog record for this book has been requested.

ISBN 978 1 84742 633 8 paperback
ISBN 978 1 84742 634 5 hardcover

The right of Christian Bason to be identified as author of this work has been asserted by him
in accordance with the 1988 Copyright, Designs and Patents Act.

All rights reserved: no part of this publication may be reproduced, stored in a retrieval system,
or transmitted in any form or by any means, electronic, mechanical, photocopying, recording,
or otherwise without the prior permission of Policy Press.

The statements and opinions contained within this publication are solely those of the author
and not of The University of Bristol or Policy Press. The University of Bristol and Policy
Press disclaim responsibility for any injury to persons or property resulting from any material
published in this publication.

Policy Press works to counter discrimination on grounds of gender, race, disability, age and
sexuality.

Cover design by Qube Design Associates, Bristol.
Front cover: image kindly supplied by www.alamy.com
Printed and bound in Great Britain by CMP, Poole

For Malene, finally

Contents

Preface

This book could not have been written without the energy, efforts and dedication of my colleagues at MindLab and in the three national government departments we are part of: the Ministries of Economic and Business Affairs, Taxation and Employment. Key insights and a number of the case examples in the book are drawn from our experiences there. A special thanks to Niels Hansen, who prepared our internal evaluation research, to Jakob Schjørring, and to PhD fellows Jesper Christiansen and Nina Holm Vohnsen, who have provided much of the input to the chapter on citizen-centred research. I am indebted to my former colleague and co-author Sune Knudsen for showing me the value of design thinking, and to Kit Lykketoft for managing MindLab while I wrote much of the book. Helle Vibeke Carstensen deserves a special mention for constructive critique from the particular vantage point of tax administration.

The wider national and international network of public innovators, scholars and government officials I have drawn on and who have contributed in one way or another to the book are numerous. I think most of you know who you are, and will find your work in some way reflected in the following pages. However, I want to especially mention David Hunter, Martin Stewart-Weeks, David Albury, Geoff Mulgan, Valerie Hannon, John Bessant, Sophia Parker, Brenton Caffin, Stéphane Vincent, Hank Kune, Leif Edvinsson, Tonya Surman and Justine Munro for exposing me further to global developments, for inspiring conversations, and for concrete inputs to the work.

Leading Public Sector Innovation also draws on my earlier work on innovation in government, including a research project that I headed at the consultancy Ramboll and two books I wrote and co-wrote on the topic in Danish, published in 2007 and 2009. Some sections are directly or indirectly inspired from these books.

During my writing, I have noted that innovation in government is gaining momentum. From being an interest mainly of academics a few years ago, public sector innovation is quickly becoming a focus of top public executives and politicians and, more importantly, of the middle managers and project leaders who can get innovation off the ground. From the UK, France and Denmark to Australia, New Zealand and the US, public sector innovation is shifting from a 'what' to a 'how'.

Perhaps it is just a temporary trend. Or perhaps it is a recognition that in times of turbulent change, just doing more of the same won't be even close to good enough. I choose to believe it is the latter.

Christian Bason
Copenhagen, September 2010

Introduction

'In the name of doing things for people, traditional and hierarchical organisations end up doing things to people.' (Writer and thinker Charles Leadbeater, 2009b, p 1)

In the heart of Copenhagen lies *Slotsholmen*, the Castle Islet. It is a very small island, perhaps only one square kilometre in size. In spite of the diminutive area, it houses most of the key public institutions that govern Denmark: the Parliament, the Supreme Court and a string of ministries, including Finance, Justice, and Economic and Business Affairs. Most of these departments are housed in the same interconnected block of buildings, ranging from the red-brick chancellery house from 1721, the country's oldest office building, to the latest addition, a large five-storey modernist property from the late 1960s. It was in that modern building, nicknamed 'Tar Castle' due to its black-green facade, that a group of around 20 senior officials from five different ministries met over two days in early December 2007. Their challenge was to craft a strategy for addressing the seemingly opposing objectives of how Denmark might tackle the climate change challenge while also generating new business creation and economic growth.

Copenhagen in December is a dark place; the group's sessions started in darkness at 8.45am and ended in darkness at 5pm. Those are more or less standard working hours for Danish civil servants (excluding the ubiquitous late evening email-checking). There was, however, nothing standard about the way in which the public servants met during the two days in December. Rather than sitting down around a meeting table to negotiate their various positions, brokering a common approach to the project, they met at MindLab, a cross-ministerial innovation laboratory, which is both a physical space and a research and facilitation unit. MindLab's staff of designers, ethnographers and policy experts had planned and designed their work process in detail, orchestrating it as an open, collaborative workshop. The task description that MindLab had formulated in close dialogue with the Head of Division and project manager from the project lead, the Ministry of Economic and Business Affairs, was the following: how might we help high-level public servants from five very different ministries balance the objectives of CO_2 reduction and business growth while developing a joint strategy that is both innovative, ambitious and realistic? That might have been a tall order even if the ministries had shared interests; however, the

Ministry of Climate Change did not, as a point of departure, hold the same interests as the Ministry of Economic and Business Affairs, which again did not represent the same world view as the Ministry of Science, Technology and Innovation. Add the Ministry of Foreign Affairs into the mix, and you begin to get the picture.

During the two workshop days, the public servants had their world views challenged through a variety of outside inputs, combined with intense work on establishing a common vision and generating specific policy ideas. The sessions were kicked off by a passionate presentation on the aesthetics and ethics of climate change by world-class artist Olafur Eliasson, who once stated that 'art is not valuable because it can be sold, but because it can change the world'. In his contribution, Eliasson gave a very different perspective on climate change than the usual talking heads. He shared selected images of his art, and spoke of topics like aesthetics, perception and subjective responsibility. Particularly, he set the tone for the workshop when he said that he had the impression that Denmark's policy elite seemed to be so preoccupied with securing the right to hold the United Nations' COP15 Summit on Climate Change in Copenhagen that they had forgotten to consider what they wanted to achieve with it.

Other external inputs that provided knowledge and perspective came from a range of technical experts and from the business community. For instance, a young entrepreneur, who had achieved remarkable success by building the entire business model of his design firm on sustainability, shared his vision and practical experience with the policymakers. These inputs served as a common knowledge base that supplemented the extensive policy insight already represented in the room, and gave the participants a collective frame of reference.

The next step was for the group to shape a single vision against which concrete policy proposals could be developed. To stretch the imagination of the public servants, they were asked the following: what is the front-page story of the *Beijing Times* in 2020, relaying what Denmark has achieved over the last decade in combating climate change and simultaneously generating new business growth? The participants were asked to describe not just the headline title, but the detailed journey that had brought the country to this point, *back-casting* from the future to the present. The result was not just an ambitious vision, but also a first sense of what kind of concrete activities and specific events might take the country to that point. As their conversation unfolded, mutual enthusiasm started building, and the dynamics of the group became more focused and creative.

Finally, the workshop applied online collaboration tools for idea generation. Armed with a laptop computer each, the public servants were taken through a process of putting forward new policy and service suggestions across a number of key themes that they had themselves identified. The strengths of the online tools were that the participants could work anonymously side-by-side. No one could see who had entered which idea into the system – but everyone could see all the suggested ideas on their own laptop screen, and everyone was free to comment and build on each other's proposals. Building on a rule of only reacting with a 'yes, and …', not 'yes, but …', to other people's ideas, this generated a tremendous force for exploring what was possible. Rather than criticising suggestions with classical arguments like 'sounds expensive', 'we've already tried that' and 'that'll never work', the 'yes, and …' rule triggered a much more forward-looking approach. By creating a space of temporary anonymity, the tool eliminated not just the hierarchy among the participants; more importantly, it eliminated, even if just for a short while, the barriers between ministerial silos. It became entirely natural to build positively on a suggestion that may have come from another ministry, the result being that an official from the Ministry of Climate Change found herself expanding on an idea from the Ministry of Economic and Business Affairs.

The December workshops were only the kick-off to a longer innovation process, involving a series of panel sessions with high-level stakeholders from business, institutions and academia, each session led by a minister, and additional workshop sessions, also held at MindLab, targeting key fields such as clean technologies and climate finance, and even a session where young design students enacted their personal visions of a CO_2-neutral future. Across these activities, solutions were developed jointly by public servants and the business community. Two years down the road, however, the majority of the overall policy proposals within the climate change strategy that were finally adopted were broadly in line with those that had been crafted during the early kick-off workshops. The strategy was presented at a seminar at the Bella Centre, site of the 2009 UN 'COP15' summit, and the then Minister of Business and Economic Affairs publicly launched the strategy with, amongst others, US author and *New York Times* editorial contributor Thomas Friedman. Notwithstanding the mixed international negotiation results of the 2009 Copenhagen Summit, Denmark had successfully crafted one of the world's first and most ambitious business strategies on climate change.

This example of how a public sector policy innovation process can take place is not in itself significant; it is significant because it illuminates a larger trend. It shows how the work of public servants can benefit from innovation *capacity* – resources and platforms such as facilitation experts, physical space and social technology. It illustrates how it is possible to *co-create* new solutions across the powerful organisational silos of central government, and with the people and businesses that new policies will impact. It illustrates how alternative types of knowledge and perspective, for instance by connecting with the arts or directly with the hands-on experience in the business community, can shape a common understanding of key challenges and opportunities. The multiple ways in which the Danish policymakers collaborated are all part of the trend of embedding innovation in government.

Highlights from a global movement

Public sector innovation – new ideas that create value for society – is not new (Mohr, 1969; Hartley, 2005; Mulgan, 2007). However, public leaders around the world are demonstrating how a significantly more *conscious* and *systematic* approach to creating innovative solutions can effectively address some of our most pressing societal challenges.

In the UK, the National Health Service's Institute for Innovation and Improvement is involving physicians, nurses and patients directly in radically improving new treatments and service processes. In the county of Kent, the Social Innovation Lab Kent (SILK) is reshaping social services through creative working methods, ethnographic research, service design and empowerment of citizens to take part in service delivery. In London, the Design Council has pioneered new models of pre-procurement conversations and design-led innovation processes that lead to new solutions in diverse fields like independent living and hospital hygiene, while powering business development and growth. In the Netherlands, the Department of Public Works and Water Management is using scenario planning, creative physical spaces, facilitated workshops and visual technology to engage civil servants across the organisation to collaborate more, empowering them to tackle the complex future challenges of living in a flat country in times of climate change.

Across the globe in Brazil, the CGEE, a government-run foresight unit, is working to provide long-term strategic insight to policymakers, using new web-enabled tools like a Future Timeline, visualising trends and generating a better basis for decision-making. And in Rio, Restorative Circles, a community-based justice movement supported by the Ministry of Justice, is helping reduce violent crime dramatically through new approaches to conflict resolution in crime-ridden neighbourhoods.

In the United States, the Transportation Security Administration is applying human-centred design to reinvent how citizens experience airport security. Through new insight into citizens' *service journeys*, the agency has developed new solutions to improve the efficiency and experience of airports, and enhance the level of security. To drive innovation efforts, the Obama administration has included public sector innovation in a new national innovation strategy. It is also opening up access to data through new online platforms, allowing citizens, businesses and social innovators to find new valuable uses for the information stored in public databases. And there is now a White House Office of Social Innovation, which invests in effective social ventures through a new innovation fund.

In Australia, the Commonwealth government has proposed a new strategy to foster a culture of innovation in government; the Victorian Public Service has launched an ambitious Innovation Action Plan to embed innovation and cross-cutting collaboration in the civil service; and in Adelaide, a new Centre for Social Innovation is running open 'innovation challenges', leveraging the potential of *crowdsourcing* to find the bold ideas that can create better lives. In France, Paris-based *La 27e Région* works as a social laboratory for the country's 26 regional councils, applying service design and other innovation approaches to tackle challenges in the fields of education, urban and city development, and social cohesion. For instance, they have helped involve local communities and students in co-creating the architectural blueprint for entirely redesigning a high school in the south of France.

And in Denmark, the government-run innovation lab MindLab is pioneering new methods of co-creation to power innovation from within the public sector. Much of the practical methodology in this book, and a number of case examples, draws from our work and research at MindLab.

This book argues that, in spite of significant barriers, it is possible to systematically apply the practices and tools of innovation that are embodied by these organisations to create radical new value. Real-world cases show that cost savings of between 20% and 60% are possible while *also* increasing citizen satisfaction and generating better outcomes. In order to make such 'paradigmatic' innovation much more likely, leaders in government must build an infrastructure of innovation – a public sector innovation ecosystem. The ecosystem is built through four simultaneous shifts in how the public sector creates new societal solutions:

- a shift from random innovation to a *conscious* and systematic approach to public sector renewal;
- a shift from managing human resources to building innovation *capacity* at all levels of government;
- a shift from running tasks and projects to orchestrating processes of *co-creation*, creating new solutions with people, not for them;
- and finally, a shift from administrating public organisations to *courageously* leading innovation across and beyond the public sector.

Executing these shifts within government is the essence of leading public sector innovation. It implies specific challenges and new tasks for public leaders at all levels – from the politician over the chief executive to mid-level managers and institution heads. It requires closing the gap between recognising that innovation is important, and doing something concrete about it. Most of all, it requires courage.

A brief history of public sector innovation

The growing momentum of public sector innovation has roughly evolved over four stages, which, although they overlap, represent distinctive steps forward. The stages roughly follow the overall trajectory of public management since the early 1970s, and which Benington and Hartley have characterised as 'traditional', 'new public management' and 'networked governance' (2001). Although all of these conceptions still thrive in government, significant elements of networked governance are seen in countries such as the UK, the US and Australia (Hartley, 2005; Goldsmith and Eggers, 2004; Dunleavy et al, 2006; Hess and Adams, 2007). The stages of the evolution of public sector innovation are:

- *Awareness.*
Looking back to the 1970s and 1980s, innovation in government was largely a study object of academics (Mohr, 1969; Gray, 1973). However, during the past two decades public managers have recognised that innovation is not only a possibility; it is an imperative. There has been a dawning awareness that government must also be able to 'reinvent' itself to adapt to new challenges and opportunities (Osborne and Gaebler, 1992). This stage is by no means over, but many public managers in today's fiscal environment no longer question the 'why' of innovation.

- *Cases and practice.*
The second stage had to do with not just recognising why innovation is important, but also *what it looks and feels like*. Public leaders may still not

characterise successful change initiatives as 'innovation', but they have a sense of how the concept applies to the public sector. For instance, novel uses of information technology and web 2.0 solutions vis-à-vis citizens are often dubbed 'innovative'. In addition, increasing academic interest has meant that there is now a significant platform of research-based analysis of the dynamics of public sector innovation (Libbey, 1994; Borins, 2000, 2001a; Osborne and Brown, 2005; Eggers and Singh, 2009). During the last two decades we have also seen a growing number of awards and recognitions that highlight the best examples of innovation in government, spanning from Harvard Kennedy School of Government's long-running *Innovations in American Government Award* to the *All-Africa Public Sector Innovation Awards* and the *European Public Sector Awards*.

• *Barriers.*

The third stage, which also characterises much of the conversation about public sector innovation today, has to do with the inherent barriers and dilemmas that face public innovators (Wilson, 1989; Mulgan, 2007). The list of reasons why innovation in the public sector is hard is disturbingly long and disheartening. And it isn't new. The workings of public bureaucracy and its negative implications for innovation have been addressed from numerous angles stretching back to Graham Allison's *Essence of Decision* on the Cuban Missile Crisis, in which he stated that government bureaucracy is 'indeed the least understood source of unhappy outcomes produced by the US government' (1971, p 266). However, as James Wilson stated in the classic *Bureaucracy* (1989), we ought not to be surprised that organisations resist innovation, since they are supposed to resist it. His argument was that the fundamental role of organisation is to reduce uncertainty and introduce stability of routine. In other words, the very DNA of bureaucratic organisations is resistant to innovation. I will share my own summary of barriers later in this chapter.

• *Practice.*

Beyond creating awareness and understanding barriers, some organisations are now explicitly increasing the ability of public organisations to make innovation happen. Government leaders around the world, from Finland and Denmark to Australia and the US, are recognising that it is not enough to wait and hope for random flashes of inspiration. For the very reasons that barriers to innovation abound, public organisations must *consciously* try to tear them down. As Bill Eggers of Deloitte, a consultancy, and John O'Leary of Harvard

Kennedy School point out in *If We Can Put a Man on the Moon ... Getting Big Things Done in Government*, there is still a long way to go. In one telling comment, a US government senior federal executive says, 'policy design at the federal level is pathetic' (Eggers and O'Leary, 2009, p 66).

Innovation, like budgeting or human resource management, must become a natural discipline in government. This implies the need to reassess the public institutions that may have served us well throughout much of the 20th century, but that may no longer be fit for purpose in a global and networked knowledge society. Public leaders must find better ways to institutionalise innovation, setting up the structures and processes and building the *capacity* that effectively embed innovation as a core activity in the organisations they run. At the cutting edge of this new paradigm is a different practice of leading innovation in government: *co-creation*.

Co-creating for a better society

Co-creation, a term first used by management thinkers Prahalad and Ramaswamy (2004), is used in this book to characterise a creation process where new solutions are designed *with* people, not *for* them (Sanders, 2006; Sanders and Stappers, 2008; Halse et al, 2010). This challenges how public managers think about their roles in policy development, going far beyond committee meetings, traditional stakeholder hearings and customer research. Co-creation is strongly connected to notions of 'participatory design', 'co-design', 'design attitude' and 'design thinking' – approaches that in recent years have been emphasised as absolutely central to innovation (Boland and Collopy, 2004; Brown, 2009; Martin, 2009; Kimbell, 2010). As illustrated by the crafting of the Danish government's business strategy on climate change, co-creation brings a different creative process, a different involvement of people and a different mode of knowledge to the forefront of public sector innovation and decision making. Involving people inside and outside the organisation throughout the process of creation is the key: recognising that everyone can be creative, and engaging people from other public agencies and institutions, private actors, social innovators and, not least, end-users such as communities, families and individual citizens and businesses.

There are two key benefits of co-creation: divergence and execution. *Divergence* means that a greater variation of different ideas and suggestions are brought to the table, providing inspiration and giving public servants a wider palette of options to choose from before decision making and implementation. Divergence is increased by opening up the innovation process to new types of knowledge, such as qualitative, ethnographic research, graphic visualisations, audio-visual material and, not least, to seeing for oneself how citizens and businesses experience their reality. Bringing such knowledge into play amongst policymakers, their colleagues, citizens and businesses (for instance in collaborative workshops), triggers dialogues that can enable new common interpretations of problems, challenges and opportunities (Hartley, 2005; Hess and Adams, 2007; Scharmer, 2007, Bason et al, 2009).

Successful *execution* is the other benefit: co-creation anchors the creative process with the people it concerns, whether they are the IT developers in the neighbouring office (whose commitment might be crucial to getting a new programme operational on time), or the citizens who will ultimately use the new services (who can help us understand how the new solution would work in their everyday lives). Such anchoring greatly enhances the possibility of ultimate success (Attwood et al, 2003; Ackoff et al, 2006; Halse et al, 2010). The early ideation phase, where the first designs are imagined, should in fact be viewed as the beginning of the execution of the policy. Eggers and O'Leary, therefore, advise policymakers to 'involve implementers' (2009, p 75).

Connecting end-users and other stakeholders to the entire creation process – not just to final piloting or implementation – is a powerful key to driving public sector innovation. As a recent study of more than a hundred cases of change in public organisations shows, sharp productivity increases, enhanced service experiences for citizens and business, stronger outcomes and increased ownership are possible to achieve – *simultaneously* (Gillinson et al, 2010). Such *radical efficiency*, as the authors coin it, is mainly generated by leveraging new (outside) perspectives on how public organisations solve their tasks today, and by redefining the relationships between government institutions, communities and citizens. Co-creation can thus lead to radical solutions that overcome the silos, dogmas and groupthink that trap much of our current thinking, and can give us more and better outcomes at lower cost.

A century of wicked problems

Public sector organisations seek to achieve politically desirable goals. However, in a turbulent and changing world, governments are under pressure to increase their ability to deliver 'good', while increasingly lacking the resources to do it.

'Wicked' societal problems, which are complex and open for interpretation, characterised by competing or conflicting options for solutions, and which will most likely never be fully solved, abound (Rittel and Webber, 1973). Chronic health problems such as obesity and diabetes, an ageing population, climate change, inner-city social problems and crime, long-term unemployment, and faltering educational systems are among the most pressing challenges in modern economies. None of these problems are easily dealt with; all of them require fresh thinking and bold public leadership. Nineteenth- and 20th-century type organisational structures, processes and competencies will not be sufficient to tackle those challenges. Unfortunately, the more intractable the problem, the less likely government organisations are to run the risks associated with addressing them (Bhatta, 2003). As Charles Leadbeater, a British thinker, has said quite succinctly, 'We are scientific and technological revolutionaries, but political and institutional conservatives' (2000, p viii).

However, new opportunities for addressing key societal challenges and creating value arise from the forces of new technology, social media and new patterns of citizen engagement. What if governments saw each interaction with citizens as a potential to add more value and meaning to the relationship, to the benefit of both parties? Already we are seeing the early contours of a new public sector, much more in touch with the behaviour of citizens and business, and seeking out more intelligent intervention designs. Former Labour Secretary during the Clinton administration Robert B. Reich points out that while the financial crisis has propelled government into a new ascendancy, it will not apply the same tools as in earlier eras of government power. Instead of using 'hard' legislation to achieve social objectives, government will increasingly rely on 'soft' interventions that seek to alter behaviours among enterprises or citizens through more subtle tools. The call to businesses will be to engage with government, rather than try to shield themselves from reform, for instance in the case of health care (Reich, 2009). Similarly, in *Nudge: Improving Decisions About Health, Wealth, and Happiness* (2008), University of Chicago professors Thaler and Sunstein suggest that we need to build appropriate 'choice architectures' in order to give people a sense of freedom of choice, but within an environment that gently directs them towards desired behaviour and outcomes. 'Nudging', according to the authors, is to create the social architecture that alters people's behaviour in a predictable way that helps make people's lives better.

The approaches suggested by Reich and Thaler and Sunstein reflect a deeper current that is pervasive in all modern governments, but far from realised: the emphasis on behaviour and the search for smarter interventions that help governments truly embrace an outcome focus. From online tax services to social work, public organisations recognise that, ultimately, outcomes are what matter. However, outcome strategies require a significantly deeper understanding of the drivers of human behaviour and social change, and how to affect them, than most of our current tools, methods and thinking allow for. They require a consideration of how and when the efforts of government can be better aligned with the motivations, resources and efforts of citizens and business, and how mass production and consumption of public services can shift to a hybrid model: how can the division of labour in the delivery of services meaningfully shift from government to citizens and communities, to a mode of co-production? As a consequence, disciplines such as behavioural economics, psychology, sociology and anthropology are suddenly attracting the interest of public managers.

A double innovation challenge

Continuous organisational change has become the order of the day in many parts of the public sector, driven by shifting political agendas and desire for action. The global financial and economic crisis has accelerated the trend, spurring government into new, sometimes spectacular, attempts of reforming, restructuring and reorganising in the hope that these initiatives will bring about large-scale productivity gains.

It has been said that a crisis is like the tide – when it recedes, it makes everything visible. Whether the new visibility of government will really help transform the public sector to a higher level of performance (at lower cost) is not clear. Political, socio-economic, environmental and technological driving forces are becoming more violent and unpredictable. An obvious case in point is the scale of impact of the financial crisis that began to unfold in 2007–08. Within months, global trade virtually imploded, with falls in exports in many Western countries of 10% or more. Banks and other financial institutions needed varying degrees of government support and, in some instances, bail-outs. Now, governments themselves are in trouble. In Europe, from Greece to Ireland, from Spain to the UK, governments are scrambling to find ways of 'humanely' cutting state budgets and preparing for a period of austerity in the face of the budget crunch. The US is likely to face decades of federal budget deficits. No one seems very certain what will be the characteristics of the future global economic order. What does seem certain is that governments have become acutely aware that their actions are central to not only their countries' long-term competitiveness, but also the very cohesion and resilience of society. These and a number of other major driving forces are shaping the acute need for public sector innovation:

• *The productivity imperative.*
In spite of the ascendancy of government, citizens and businesses expect the public sector to increase its productivity and utilises taxpayers' resources as efficiently as possible. However, as management professor Peter Drucker pointed out more than 25 years ago, government is more attuned to maximising the use of inputs than to optimising its production model (Drucker, 1985). The challenge is perhaps best illustrated in the health sector: sharp productivity increases are becoming an imperative as governments around the world must serve an ageing population that lives longer and demands higher quality care – while technology costs are exploding. For instance, in Australia, the state of New South Wales is expecting health-related costs to soar to 55% of total state funds by 2032, up from just 26% today (*Sydney Morning Herald*, 2010). In the US, booming health costs were among the key motives for pushing through health care reform. How can government organisations radically increase their productivity in times of scarce resources? Could it be necessary to reinvent the entire system of care, of social support, of education?

• *Growing citizen expectations.*
Citizens increasingly become used to world-class services in private institutions ranging from hotels and retail, hospitals and schools, to cutting-edge online bank services (Stewart-Weeks, 2010). Many leading firms are not only inherently innovative and service-oriented; they are quick to adopt new technologies to systematically enhance customer experience (Cole and Parston, 2006). Many of them have leveraged clever new models for shaping closer and more personal, tailorised relationships with customers. It is only natural that citizens would expect similar service innovations when they interact with government. For instance, as senior citizens have become wealthier, they increasingly want to be in charge of how they are going to be cared for, and they certainly expect a higher standard than the generations before them. How can government meet the ever-increasing demands of a wealthier population for greater choice and quality in public services (Pollitt, 2003; Osborne and Brown, 2005; Cole and Parston, 2006; Parker and Heapy, 2006)?

- *Globalisation.*

A highly networked and interconnected world puts governments (and, in particular, welfare states and quasi-welfare states) under pressure (Hirst and Thompson, 1999; Pollitt, 2003; Osborne and Brown, 2005). Taxes and customs, education, research, environment, labour markets, not to speak of financial regulation, are just some of the fields of government responsibility that are being challenged by increased economic, cultural and social interdependence across the globe (Wolf, 2004; Friedman, 2005). As the spotlight falls on governments to leverage innovation policy as a source of national competitiveness, public organisations themselves must identify new approaches and solutions in the new global environment (Kao, 2007). How can government work to harvest the benefits of globalisation while minimising the risks and pitfalls?

- *Media.*

The news media cycle is becoming ever-more compressed and demanding not just for politicians, but also the staff who serve them. The rapid rise of electronic media, in addition to sharply increased competition amongst 'old media', has intensified competition. The media focus on single-issue themes and demand fast and accurate responses from government, 24/7 (Rosenberg and Feldman, 2008). So how can government effectively respond to the intensified media cycle?

- *Technology.*

Technological innovations are a major driving force for new public sector solutions in areas ranging from internal administration to e-government citizen services, new health care solutions and the transformation of learning. However, the new technologies are often also costly (not least in health care), and it can sometimes be a challenge to accurately assess the benefits of new public investments in advanced technology. Meanwhile, citizens expect government to be at the forefront of the uptake of new technology (Cole and Parston, 2006). How can the public sector best utilise new technologies, including web 2.0 solutions, to the benefit of society, without costs soaring?

- *Demographic change.*

An ageing and, in some cases, dwindling population is one of the driving forces that is most commonly mentioned by public sector managers when they talk about the need for change. First, the cost of serving a larger population share of senior citizens will be significant, putting government budgets under stress (as in the case of New South Wales). Second, government itself may be running out of talent. In the coming years, as the baby boomers leave the labour market, we will see a renewed 'war for talent' also in the public sector. By some estimates, 90% of senior US government officials are on the verge of retirement (Cabinet Office, 2009). In Denmark, every second public manager will retire within the next five to seven years. How can government be competitive vis-à-vis leading private sector organisations that may be able to offer higher pay, more flexible work arrangements and, not least, greater prestige?

- *Shocks.*

During the last few years, we have witnessed an almost unprecedented series of systemic shocks that require immediate and concerted attention from public sector organisations. From the SARS outbreak to the terror of 11 September 2001 to the devastating tsunami of South East Asia in 2004, Hurricane Katrina, the Danish cartoon crisis and the Haitian earthquake in 2010, sudden crises have challenged the ability of government agencies to respond rapidly and effectively. Such 'unthinkable events' upset the institutional surroundings and may redefine the rules of the game (Bessant, 2005). Not all instances during the last decade (although some) have demonstrated a high public sector innovation and response capability (Eggers and O'Leary, 2009; Kettl, 2009).

- *Climate change.*

Environmental sustainability has come to the forefront of the public agenda, casting the public sector into a key role in designing the strategies, programmes and (not least) regulation that can help societies achieve the ambitious goals of reducing CO_2 emissions, reducing the impact of global warming, while managing a growth and employment agenda at the same time (Friedman, 2008). Devising effective schemes that are politically, socially and economically feasible is yet another innovation challenge.

To sum up, these driving forces embody a double challenge between adaptations to (planned, internal) ongoing public sector reform on the one hand, and (emergent, external) turbulent socio-economic driving forces on the other. As Osborne and Brown (2005) have argued, it is particularly the second type of factors that call for more radical innovation in public organisations.

Not up to the job yet

Unfortunately, most public sector organisations today are ill-suited to develop the kinds of radical new solutions that are needed. The rate of change and the turbulent environment dramatically increase the risk that public organisations lose even more of their touch with the enterprises and citizens they are meant to serve. Research from the US, the UK and Denmark, amongst others, shows that most modern public organisations' innovation capabilities are focused on internal administrative processes, rather than on generating new services and improved results for society (Danish Ministry of Finance, 2005; Eggers and Singh, 2009; NAO, 2009). New ideas mainly arise from internal 'institutional' sources (mostly public managers themselves, and sometimes their employees), and to a much lesser degree via open collaboration with citizens, businesses or other external stakeholders. Innovation efforts are typically driven by a few isolated individuals, dependent on their personal initiative and willpower. At all levels, from the political and regulatory context over strategies, organisational models, management style, staff recruitment, involvement and incentives, to the relationship with end-users, the public sector is characterised by numerous barriers to innovation (Wilson, 1989; Mulgan and Albury, 2005; Bason, 2007; Mulgan, 2007; Eggers and O'Leary, 2009). Add to that a lack of awareness or knowledge of the innovation process, and lack of good and relevant data on how the organisation performs, and we have an almost perfect storm crashing down on any innovation effort. The result can at best be characterised as random innovation, rather than strategic or systematic. In particular, the following barriers to public sector innovation come to mind:

- *Paying a price for politics.*
First, the framework conditions in the public sector are rarely attuned to innovation. Politically governed organisations can be prone to keep and maintain power, rather than to share it. Politicians sometimes (some would say often) prefer short-term positive media exposure over what could be the most effective long-term solution. Incentives for sharing tasks and knowledge amongst public sector organisations are not very high, and internal politically motivated competition may overrule sensible collaboration. The requirement to respect citizens' rights and equality before the law implies that it may be difficult to conduct experiments that temporarily change the rights or benefits of certain groups of citizens. Regulation of detailed processes in local or deconcentrated government agencies may be needed to ensure service

quality and consistence, but such 'standard operating procedures' can also be a key barrier to creativity and innovation. Often, funding for new and risky public ventures is extremely limited (Borins, 2001a). A significant dose of creativity may be needed by public managers to secure funding in the first place (Bason, 2007).

- *Anti-innovation DNA.*

Second, public sector organisations are hardly fine-tuned innovation machines. In spite of the trumpeting of 'reinvention' and entrepreneurship (Osborne and Gaebler, 1992), many of them still embody the type of hierarchy and bureaucracy that private companies have been fighting to throw away since the 'downsizing' era of the mid-1980s. In most countries, the public sector is highly sectorialised – vertically between administrative levels (for instance in the US, federal government versus states, counties and municipalities), and horizontally between distinct policy domains. The possibilities, and perhaps the desire, to cooperate across these divisions are not always present, in spite of a growing demand for coherent and 'joined-up' government. Organisational silos, traditional roles and lack of cross-cutting coordination are still significant challenges (Pollitt, 2003; Eggers and Singh, 2009). New forms of collaboration such as project organisation, virtual organisations and dedicated innovation units are still in many countries considered exotic. A conscious strategic approach to innovation is rarely found in public sector organisations. In most countries there is no national strategy for innovation in the public sector. One would think, as Wilson (1989) also pointed out, that most public sector organisations were built to counter innovation, not to foster it. In fact, as Young Foundation director Geoff Mulgan points out in *The Art of Public Strategy* (2009), there may be some truth in that: to maintain stability in society, might we even want public sector organisations to be somewhat slow, bureaucratic but (at least) stable?

- *Fear of divergence.*

Third, in many areas of the public sector there is, luckily, a high level of professional identity. Patients in hospitals, parents of pre-schoolers, and senior citizens in nursing homes all value that. But strong professional identity can also imply a mono-professional culture that doesn't allow for the constructive clashes between different professions that is often a catalyst for radical new solutions. Public professionals may feel that due to their education and experience as a nurse, a teacher, a social worker or (perhaps especially) a policymaker, they know more about the citizen's needs than the citizen herself. Part of such a strong professional identity is also to avoid error (Bhatta, 2003). Avoiding failure is usually absolutely necessary in a hospital, but maybe not always in a government agency seeking to develop innovative new policy, or in a job centre that seeks to provide more effective employment services. Of course many public managers and employees do wish to create positive change. That's why many of them chose the job in the first place. But their ideas aren't always allowed to thrive. In Denmark, for instance, a study showed that one in three of the staff in central government did not feel that their talent and abilities were used fully in their work (Danish State Employer's Authority, 2006). To some extent they have themselves to blame. Part of the reason is that there is a significant discomfort: there is often a lack of willingness to really, *really* explore which new ideas and solutions could be possible. As co-founder of the design consultancy IDEO, Tim Brown, has pointed out, the major innovation barrier in most organisations is that leaders don't allow for innovation projects to diverge sufficiently (McKinsey Quarterly, 2008; Brown, 2009). They are afraid that the projects will never return to address the original objective. While that may be a problem in the private sector, it's an even greater issue in the public sector. Public managers and employees tend to shy away from the edge of something new, sometimes even before they know what it is. Some of it has to do with a lack of experience and competence in managing the innovation process. But most of it is cultural: most public organisations intuitively do not seek to be at the forefront of a change agenda. Risk-taking is typically not embraced, but discouraged. Individuals are left without resources, backing or incentives to develop, embrace and realise their good ideas (Bason, 2007).

- *Where's the citizen?*

Fourth, most public organisations have a long way to go before they honestly can claim that they are putting citizens' needs and their reality at the centre of their efforts. This point has been at the core of observations by the OECD, the European Commission and in several reviews of British public sector innovation (OECD, 2005; Parker and Heapy, 2006; NAO, 2006, 2009; Barosso, 2009). It is the case in the US, where a more citizen-oriented focus is highlighted in President Obama's new national innovation strategy. It is the case in Australia as well. As former Australian Prime Minister Kevin Rudd (2009) pointed out in a speech about the country's civil service, 'its challenge now is to become more strategic and forward-looking, more outward-looking, and more citizen-centred'. Achieving administrative efficiencies is somehow more natural to government than delivering high-quality services and outcomes. It seems that public sector organisations are pretty good at improving how to do things right (creating a smooth-running bureaucracy), but not necessarily at how to do the right thing (addressing the actual needs of the citizens they serve).

• *An orchestra without a conductor.*
Fifth, in many public sector organisations there are few or no formal processes for conducting the innovation process (Eggers and Singh, 2009). Managers focus on budgeting, operations and tasks, and employees may be highly skilled lawyers, economists, doctors, nurses and schoolteachers – but few of them have formal skills in creativity or innovation (Osborne and Brown, 2005). At best, public sector organisations operate with highly linear, 'stage-gate' project processes (if they even have a formal project organisation). However, innovation, particularly in its early 'front end' phases, needs to focus more on co-creation: open collaborative processes, iteration, active user involvement, visualisation, prototyping, test and experimentation (Kelley, 2001; Sanders and Stappers, 2008; Brown, 2009). Many public sector organisations simply have not put into place the formal systems, or built the capacity among leaders and employees, that enable such processes to take place. In particular, they have not put into place the types of practices that may generate more radical or 'discontinuous' innovations (Bessant, 2005).

• *Leading into a vacuum and the 80/20 rule.*
Sixth, while managers and employees in private companies ultimately have one clear bottom line (are we making money or not?), the 'bottom line' in most public sector organisations is a lot more complex (Wilson, 1989). From health to social work to education, the outcomes of public regulation and expenditure programmes are not as easy to assess as a profit statement. But without a clear and direct feedback mechanism on organisational performance, how do public sector organisations even know whether their innovations, to the extent that there are any, are successful? While there has been a growing culture of evaluation over the last two decades in most advanced economies, many public sector organisations are still essentially navigating blind when it comes to real-time, relevant management information on performance. Mainstream evaluation studies are usually heavily retrospective, and often arrive far too late to inform policy decisions in any meaningful way (Pollitt, 2003). Although there is much good to say about evaluation and evidence-based policymaking, evaluation has become such a prevalent tool in the public sector that it risks overshadowing the need for faster, more

experimental, forward-looking problem-solving. When it comes to their development efforts, public sector organisations seem to spend 80% of their energies on understanding the past and (at best) managing the present, and perhaps only 20% of their efforts on systematically exploring future directions for better policies and services.

- *The scaling problem.*

Finally, one of the most significant challenges to realising the potential of innovation in government is that of 'scaling'. Too many innovations stay locked in their location of origin, not spread, scaled or diffused – regionally, nationally or internationally. Traditional methods such as best practice publications, websites, toolkits, command and control efforts, networks and various forms of collaboratives have proven to be of limited effectiveness (Mulgan, 2007; Harris and Albury, 2009). Even when studies show that if only every local government, region, public agency or department adopted the most innovative practices of their peers, it would be transformational, it is extremely difficult to make 'scaling' happen in practice. In the absence of a market mechanism, which in the private sector generates significant demand for solutions that can lead to a profit, how might we create an army of 'willing adopters'? (Mulgan, 2009). What are the tools, approaches and means that can scale public sector innovations from one domain to all the domains they might benefit?

Towards an innovation ecosystem

In spite of these barriers, public sector innovation obviously does take place – every day. The string of examples that introduced this chapter are cases in point. However, at this moment, 'random incrementalism' is still the rule rather than the exception. New thinking often happens by chance and against the odds, and the potential of a more conscious, strategic and systematic approach to innovation across public organisations and sectors is not realised. The objective of this book is not to say that there is only one way of leading innovation in the public sector. However, just as great pianists master the entire scale on a piano to create truly great music, public managers and staff must master a much broader range of ways to conduct their efforts to craft better public policies and services, and increase productivity. At one end of the spectrum are the more incremental, internally focused change processes that we often see today. At the other end is a significantly more explorative, open and collaborative process of co-creation that can deliver more radical change. Government needs both.

Unlike much of the work to date on public sector innovation, this book is prescriptive. My ambition is not only to share an understanding of the field, but to propose concrete ways forward for leaders and employees – 'to dos' that significantly expand the approaches and tools that are typically used today.

The book is shaped around the framework of an innovation ecosystem, encompassing the four Cs of *consciousness, capacity, co-creation* and *courage*. The ecosystem is introduced in detail in Chapter 1.

I then explore how the level of *consciousness* of innovation as a distinct, professional discipline could be raised among politicians, public managers and staff, emphasising key concepts and definitions of innovation. This section is covered in Chapter 2.

Second, how might the innovation *capability* of public sector organisations be increased? What are the fundamental barriers and the potentials that allow for creative processes to take place, and that make innovation more or less likely to happen? What are the key elements needed to make innovation part of the organisational fabric? Capabilities are addressed in Chapters 3–6.

Third, what does it entail to create new ideas and concepts through a process of *co-creation,* designing solutions *with* people, not *for* them, thus expanding the scale of available innovation approaches? What can design thinking bring to government? What are the approaches to the systematic involvement of citizens, businesses and the third sector through ethnographic research and collaborative workshops? How can the process of co-creation be orchestrated in practice? And how can a continuous feedback loop of learning and performance improvement be tied to the innovation process? These are the topics of Chapters 7–10.

Fourth, what kind of *courageous* leadership is needed at all levels? What are the key roles of innovation leadership in the public sector? This is the theme of Chapter 11.

The four Cs of the ecosystem are highly interdependent, but do not necessarily have to be read chronologically. The book may be read selectively, depending on whether the reader's interest is in the *what* of innovation (consciousness), the *where* (capacity), the *how* (co-creation) or the *who* (courage). Taken as a whole, however, the four Cs represent what I believe is needed to finally bring government up to par with the daunting challenges of the 21st century.

1

The innovation ecosystem

'Governments cannot be complacent about their ability to innovate.' (Willam B. Eggers and Shalabh Kumar Singh, 2009, p 12)

Melbourne, the capital of Australia's state of Victoria, and a city of nearly four million people, is often touted as the city of festivals. Indeed, a recent US visitor to the city wrote on her travel blog that just during the week of her visit there were five simultaneous festivals taking place: film, fashion, food, flowers and comedy.

It should be no surprise, then, that the state's public service chose to launch its ambitious new Innovation Action Plan by running an Innovation Festival. In late February 2010, the Department of Premier and Cabinet and the Victorian Public Service (VPS) brought together hundreds of public servants from across the state administration for four days of presentations, seminars and workshops. According to Maria Katsonis, a senior official and one of the key officers charged with the plan's implementation, the Action Plan was the first document she was aware of that had been signed by every chief executive of the VPS. Aiming at bringing the public service's innovation efforts to a new level, the Action Plan addresses four interrelated themes: creating stronger networks between people, ideas and opportunities (through new collaboration software and by creating an Advisory Group to steer the implementation of the plan); building innovation capability (through recruitment, skills development and making innovation tools available); enhanced reward of best practice (through challenge and awards programmes); and, finally, opening up and sharing information and data across the state government. The ambition of the plan is clear: 'Making innovation an integral part of how we approach our day-to-day work will result in better policies, better services and better value for the community' (VPS, 2010).

As they gathered for the festivities in late February 2010, the public officials were exposed not only to the new plan itself, but to a substantial series of events that were designed to help them see what innovation could mean to them in practice. From the dilemmas of using new social media in government to how to involve citizens in the innovation process, the festival became a starting point for what will in all likelihood be a challenging but exciting journey.

The jury is still out on what kind of lasting impact the VPS Action Plan will have. It is early days. However, with the Action Plan, the VPS is doing something that more and more governments around the world are realising is necessary – laying the first foundations of an innovation ecosystem: an explicit, systematic approach to strengthening the awareness, competencies and ways of working that can power innovation within the public service.

This chapter introduces the framework of such an ecosystem and addresses the following questions:

- What is the relevance of the concept of an ecosystem of innovation?
- What are its key dimensions?
- What are the main *barriers* to and *potentials* for public sector innovation that characterise each of the dimensions of the ecosystem?

An ecosystem for public sector innovation

To lead public sector innovation, public managers and staff must develop and master four interrelated dimensions, which reinforce each other and together form an integrated approach. Just like ecosystems in our natural environment, the different components in social ecosystems are mutually dependent and cannot flourish without each other. I therefore suggest we characterise the four dimensions as an ecosystem of innovation in the public sector.

The innovation ecosystem proposes an integrated way of looking at public organisations' innovation efforts that includes the key mutually dependent structures, processes and leadership roles that can drive or impede change within and beyond the public sector. Also, just like Victoria's Innovation Action Plan, it is a blueprint for action.

There are two sides to the innovation ecosystem: barriers and potentials. For instance, a barrier to innovation that was identified in Victoria was that public servants weren't always collaborating sufficiently across agencies. The potential that was identified in the Innovation Action Plan was to build online networks that could underpin more cross-cutting exchanges of ideas and possibly more focused joint projects. This friction between the inertia of bureaucracy and the promise of new ideas in government, as was also discussed in the introduction, is classic, to the point where public sector innovation is often characterised as an oxymoron. The dilemma has perhaps been best captured by Eggers and O'Leary (2009) who pose the question, if we can put a man on the moon, why can't we necessarily get big things done in government?

Figure 1.1: The public sector innovation ecosystem

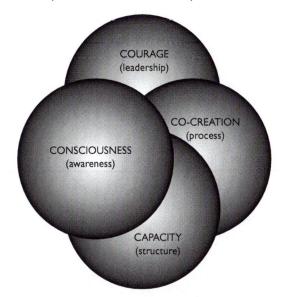

Public sector innovation thus happens in an ongoing tension between constraining and enabling factors. The tables connected to each section below provide an overview of the key barriers and potentials across the four Cs of the innovation ecosystem: consciousness (awareness), capacity (structure), co-creation (processes) and courage (leadership). Public leaders must address *all four dimensions* of the innovation ecosystem to not only ignite the power to innovate in the public sector, but to sustain it.

Consciousness: the innovation landscape

At roughly the same time as the government of Victoria pledged to build a toolbox for the state's public innovators, across the globe in Denmark, the Ministries of Economic and Business Affairs, Taxation, and Employment launched *www.innovationsguiden.dk*, a practical online portal designed to enable their more than 20,000 staff to practise innovation – adding another layer to their own innovation ecosystem. A year earlier, in the UK, the county of Kent's SILK innovation lab collaborated with the consultancy Engine Group to create a Methods Deck to share tools and approaches in public and social sector innovation. Similarly in the UK, the Revenue and Customs administration has developed a toolbox, called SIMPLE, in both hardcover and digital formats, about creative 'customer involvement'.

To embed innovation in a public sector organisation it is necessary to build, share and maintain a common language and create awareness of key innovative practices. Without shared concepts and notions about what it means to engage in innovation, common meaning is blurred, leadership cannot take hold and innovation efforts falter. Fostering a climate receptive to change and innovation is crucial (Osborne and Brown, 2005; Eggers and Singh, 2009). The Consciousness section of this book offers components, models and frameworks that can help embed a common understanding and awareness of what innovation means and why it is important. It explores the relevance of the language of innovation to the public sector and provides an overview of the innovation landscape: some of the key triggers of creativity and change in public organisations, and analytical perspectives of what innovation is and the types of value it can create.

Table 1.1: Consciousness

	Barriers >>	Key factors	<< Potential
CONSCIOUSNESS (Awareness)	No awareness of innovation as concept	**The innovation landscape**	Educate in innovation terminology
	No recognition of what innovation means in practice to the organisation		Communicate examples of own innovations and innovators
	No reflection over own practices		Establish dialogue and reflection about the value of own practices

Capacity: building innovation potential

Building innovation capacity increases the likelihood that the organisation can effectively generate and execute the ideas it needs to tackle tomorrow's problems. As Osborne and Brown (2005) have pointed out, innovative capacity in public organisations is a function not just of organisational characteristics, but also the internal culture, external environment and institutional framework. Capacity is thus concerned with the *structure* of the ecosystem, and how it can evolve or even be (re)designed. Capacity can be thought of as a pyramid structure – with the overall structural, institutional and political contextual conditions at the top, and the day-to-day practices within the organisation – people and culture – at the bottom. The innovation pyramid offers public managers a view of the external and internal factors that they must take into account in order to increase innovation capacity, and thereby the *potential* of the organisation to innovate.

Figure 1.2: Capacity: the innovation pyramid

The barriers to and potentials for enhancing innovation capacity lie at all four levels of the pyramid:

- *Political-structural context* is concerned with the framework conditions that public sector organisations, managers, staff and end-users act within. This addresses the degree to which fundamental democratic principles, administrative frameworks, regulation and financing hinders or promotes the public sector's innovation capacity.
- *Strategy* is the specific organisational arena where the need for innovation links with the objectives the public sector organisation is pursuing. This domain deals with how strategy can drive innovation. How can an innovation strategy be formulated, and what is the difference between internally and externally focused strategies for innovation?
- *Organisation* is also key. How can organisations approach innovation? What is the potential in open, systematic collaboration with external actors in the private and third sectors – approaches that are already increasingly embraced by leading enterprises (Chesbrough, 2006a)? How can a balance be struck between focused innovation activities and ongoing service delivery? Which methods and tools are available,

and what is the potential of innovation labs? What is the potential of digitisation, new social media and e-government?

* *People and culture* focuses on the people whose role it is – or could be – to make innovation happen. This domain considers the degree to which competencies, culture, incentives and so on support innovation. Without managers and staff who take responsibility for embracing new ideas, and who dare take a risk against the odds, innovation will not get off the ground (Behn, 1995; Borins, 2001a; Osborne and Brown, 2005; Hamel, 2007). The theme focuses on the individuals and groups that carry the innovation efforts. How is

Table 1.2: Capacity

	Barriers >>	Key factors	<< Potential
CAPACITY (Structure)	Inflexible regulation Lack of competition No risk capital Political climate	**Context**	Establish innovation legislation Create innovation incubators Make risk capital available Explore the innovation envelope
	Task-oriented; no overall strategy No strategy for what innovation means to the organisation Strategic planning	**Strategy**	Establish overall strategy for the organisation Innovation strategy Strategic innovation
	Organisational silos No place for innovation Random *e-gov* efforts Lack of network thinking	**Organisation**	Organise to power collaborative innovation Create innovation labs Build new digital business models
	Top management driven Zero-error culture Mono-professional skill profiles No strategic competence development Lack of incentives	**People and culture**	Active employee involvement Innovation culture Increased diversity Strategic competence development Innovation incentives

a culture of innovation promoted and anchored? What are the roles of diversity, talent management and incentives?

Co-creation: designing and learning

A third dimension of public sector innovation is to lead the co-creation process, building on principles of design thinking and citizen involvement, leveraging the potential of the organisation's innovation capacity to shape its future. The innovation process is often thought of as a black box. However, drawing on global best practice, including our experiences at MindLab, this book aims to show how it can be orchestrated as an explicit, systematic process. I will share the methods and approaches that we've found to be the most effective.

The first element of co-creation is an appreciation of *design thinking*. This term is currently undergoing significant exploration as an approach to innovation in business and in government (Boland and Collopy, 2004; Sanders and Stappers, 2008; Brown, 2009; Martin, 2009; Verganti, 2009; Kimbell, 2010). I highlight some key credos of design thinking and share examples of how they apply to the public sector.

Citizen involvement is also key. People – including citizens, business and third-sector actors – are not only at the receiving end of public regulations, interventions and services, but also stakeholders and innovators in public policy. People relate to the public sector as much more than clients, users or customers. People relate to government as citizens who have certain expectations, rights and powers, as well as benefits and obligations. Citizens are at the same time beneficiaries, paymasters and voters (Tempoe, 1994). However, there is a rapidly growing recognition that citizens might also be sources of inspiration and a driving force for public sector innovation. New technology and social media offer new platforms for civic engagement, opening up for potential mass collaboration in the innovation process, and for de facto co-production of service delivery. The chapter shares a range of approaches, methods and concrete tools, from ethnographic interview techniques to *personas,* which MindLab and other public innovators are using today to capture citizen insight.

Co-creation ties design thinking and citizen involvement tools together in a joint process. The chapter shows how public sector organisations can relate effectively to citizens and other end-users, and orchestrate the processes that involve them to create better solutions that will have the intended value in their lives and for the community. The seven steps of *framing, knowing, analysing, synthesising, creating, scaling* and *learning* provide a comprehensive and detailed process of co-creating public solutions with people, not for them.

Managers and staff must also put into place the processes that allow relevant data on performance to be collected and brought into play to drive organisational learning, renewal and accountability. How can measurement drive performance? How do we measure and learn from the value of innovation? This theme includes a further consideration of the four key bottom lines that express value in the public sector: productivity, service experience, results and democracy. Will the building of new performance management systems be killers of or catalysts for innovation and organisational renewal?

Table 1.3: Co-creation

	Barriers >>	Key factors	<< Potential
CO-CREATION (Process)	No recognition of design thinking as approach Lack of design skills	**Design thinking**	Educate in design thinking Institutionalise design principles Recruit and source design skills
	No involvement of citizens or businesses Few experiences and methods for involvement	**Citizen involvement**	Involving citizens and businesses in the innovation process New tools and methods for citizen-centred innovation
	No knowledge or tools Lack of platforms	**Orchestrating co-creation**	Methods and tools to drive innovation Innovation labs as platforms
	No overview of potential Lack of feedback from innovation processes No data on value creation Lack of learning from performance	**Measuring and learning**	Know your innovation metrics Continually improve innovation processes Measure four bottom lines Driving organisational performance

Courage: leading the public sector of tomorrow

Managers and staff must display the *courage to lead innovation* at all levels, against the odds and in spite of the daily constraints and pressures. The overall challenge to public leaders is to give up some of their power and control by involving people – thereby achieving more power to achieve the desired outcomes. This section addresses the various roles that public managers play in the context of innovation, ranging from the top executive to the head of a local institution, and addresses how to lead change across complex organisations and systems. The leadership roles are tied in different ways to the innovation ecosystem:

- *The visionary* is the political leader, who must formulate the vision and set the level of ambition, while overcoming the temptation to interfere with ongoing experimentation and development.
- *The enabler* is the top manager, who must be both protector and the number-one champion of the organisation's innovation ability.
- *The 360-degree innovator* is the mid-level manager; potentially the greatest barrier to fresh thinking and change inside government, but also, at best, a 360-degree facilitator of innovation.
- *The knowledge engineer* is head of institutions that deliver services and enforce regulation, and that ultimately determine how the public sector serves citizens and businesses – every day.

Table 1.4: Courage to lead

	Barriers >>	Key factors	<< Potential
COURAGE (Leadership)	Internal recruitment	**Inspiration and execution**	Visionary leadership
	Diffuse relationship with political level		Clarifying the innovation space
	No tolerance for divergence		Encouraging and managing divergence
			Four leadership roles

Generating resilience

It may seem a daunting task to consider and address all levels and processes of the innovation ecosystem at once. However, leveraging all the four Cs at the same time radically increases the likelihood that more and better ideas can materialise and create value. In other words, building an innovation ecosystem across all its dimensions greatly enhances its *resilience*: its capacity to tolerate the pressures and disturbances that will seek to diminish its stability and performance. For public organisations to become true 'serial innovators' in a turbulent external world coupled with strong internal bureaucratic, conservative forces, resilience is critical (Mulgan, 2009; Westley & Antadze, 2009; Stewart-Weeks, 2010). According to the Resilience Alliance, a multidisciplinary research organisation that explores the dynamics of social–ecological systems, resilience is important to ecosystems because it defines:

- the amount of change the system can undergo and still retain the same controls on function and structure;
- the degree to which the system is capable of self-organisation;
- the ability to build and increase the capacity for learning and adaptation.

These characteristics are greatly enhanced by organisations that strengthen all four of the dimensions of the innovation ecosystem. For instance, the bold business strategy for climate change that was co-created by the Danish government agencies could not have happened without establishing some fundamental understanding of what themes like 'an innovative climate strategy' or 'a high level of ambition' might mean, reflecting the significant environmental, economic and political pressures for change. The inspiration delivered by an artist helped the group establish those parameters. Further, without the innovation capacity and infrastructure of the MindLab facility and staff, it is likely it would have been more difficult to meet and collaborate in ways that effectively moved the policy process forward. And without the explicit orchestration of the co-creation process itself, involving end-users, stakeholders and other ministries in the process, the end result would have been very different. Finally, the political courage to put forward a bold vision of how to both generate growth and tackle the climate change challenge was indispensable.

Like conducting a symphony orchestra, the public sector organisation must activate multiple instruments, engaging them all at once. Innovation capacity is built at both the contextual level, at the strategic and organisational levels, and at the level of people and culture. Putting the right processes in place and enabling co-creation with citizens and powering continuous learning are central. And the courage to lead innovation is essential.

Part One
Consciousness

MAPPING THE
LANDSCAPE

2

Mapping the landscape

'Innovation is a terrible word. But there's nothing wrong with its content.' (MindLab, 2010)

Most people usually agree with the quote above, which is from our communication strategy at MindLab. Much like 'design', 'innovation' is so all-encompassing and open for interpretation that it risks losing its meaning (Stewart-Weeks, 2010). Perhaps that is why it is almost a given at innovation conferences and seminars that some participant eventually asks 'How do you define innovation?'

As discussed in the introduction, public sector innovation has evolved over a number of stages since the 1970s, the momentum picking up pace, the discourse changing from 'what' to 'how'. Today, most public leaders tend to agree that more positive change is needed in government, as societal challenges ranging from ageing to chronic illness to increasing productivity pressures are mounting. What is more difficult to articulate is what innovation is exactly, and in what way it is relevant and meaningful to the organisation.

So, we do have to start with definitions. Their number is of course massive. The amount of literature focusing on business management and entrepreneurship is huge and growing by the week. It arguably started with the Austrian-born economist Joseph Schumpeter, who famously characterised innovation as 'creative destruction'. He linked innovation to the rise of capitalism as the fundamental impulse that kept capitalist society in motion through the creation of new consumers, new goods, new methods of production, new markets and new forms of industrial organisation (1975, pp 82–5). Subsequent business thinkers like the late C.K. Prahalad, Clayton Christensen, Gary Hamel, Eric von Hippel, John Bessant and Henry Chesbrough have expanded significantly on the concept of innovation, adding new dimensions and layers onto the fundamental notion of 'newness'.

Uncovering how the insights of these thinkers, and others, might apply to the complexities of the public sector across sectors, levels and national cultures is no easy task. So why even try? Because, as should already be clear, innovation is critical to addressing how the public sector can better respond to the massive challenges facing our societies, just as it is critical to businesses seeking the next source of competitive advantage. Strategic, sustainable, ongoing innovation activity, as opposed to one-off hits or misses, requires *awareness*. As British professor Fiona Patterson, who studied everyday innovation practices across more than 800 companies, said, 'Our results showed that organisations that clearly articulate what is meant by "innovative working" are more likely to be successful in their attempt to encourage innovative behaviours' (Patterson et al, 2009, p 12). Without a vocabulary, it becomes impossible for managers to communicate with, support and empower staff to meaningfully undertake innovation activities. It doesn't mean innovation can't happen anyway. The efforts are just fewer and a lot less effective. According to the National Audit Office, which recently examined the innovation practices of the UK central government, confusion about the meaning and purpose of innovation among staff was among the key barriers to generating innovative ideas (NAO, 2009).

This chapter therefore addresses the following questions:

- What is innovation in the public sector?
- Where does innovation come from?
- What types of innovation are there?
- What kinds of value can public sector innovation generate?

Innovation: from idea to value

I define public sector innovation as the process of creating new ideas and turning them into value for society. It concerns how politicians, public leaders and employees make their visions of a desired new state of the world into reality. The concept of innovation therefore places a laser-sharp focus on whether the organisation is able to generate and select the best possible ideas, implement them effectively and ensure they create value.

Government organisations can take various roles in the innovation process – placing the emphasis, respectively, on the generation of creative new ideas, on the implementation of them and on the continuous delivery of value. The challenge for the organisation, and thereby for

Figure 2.1: Innovation defined

public leaders, is to *consciously* navigate between these different roles. In spite of the mounting pressure to embrace innovation, public sector organisations are usually much more comfortable with the right-hand side of the figure – delivering the same type of value over and over again. Public bureaucracies are relatively good at maintaining stable models of production; not so good at inventing new ones.

As Roger Martin, Dean of Toronto's Rotman School and author of *The Design of Business* (2009), has argued, this is also the case for private enterprises. Most large organisations are effective at delivering products and services according to *algorithms* – stable and precise specifications of how to carry out a certain process of production with high reliability. Mass production of public services, exploiting the high returns to scale of standardised, low-variance, high-volume delivery, has been one of the great successes of post-war Western societies. From managing welfare payments to school systems and hospitals, standardisation has been the order of the day. But when the world changes, are our organisations ready to adapt? Are they able, where necessary, to embrace the more flexible 'hybrid' modes of production with the higher degree of individualisation required in a complex, networked knowledge society? Can they identify and define the new solutions needed to battle spiralling welfare costs, failures in our educational systems and the cries for more individualised treatment of hospital patients?

Martin points out that most organisations are much less capable of exploring the 'mystery' of what *might* be, and discovering new approaches to creating value, than they are of executing the algorithm of 20th-century-style mass production. But the exploration of mystery is the starting point of innovation; a fact that many public organisations today are forced to acknowledge. The challenge is how to grapple with the early phases of the innovation process, which are also referred to as the 'fuzzy front-end', the innovation process looking more like a half-rolled-up ball of yarn than a smooth 'innovation funnel' (Koen et al, 2001; Sanders and Stappers, 2008). Defining innovation as the ability to create new ideas and turn them into value for society thus offers several important considerations for public leaders.

First, great ideas do not come from nothing. Of course, people and organisations get lucky and a bright idea will surface from time to time. As a panel participant said at an innovation conference during the 2009 Swedish EU presidency: 'Any idiot who has ever taken a shower has also had an idea'. But just like the fruits of Thomas Edison's inventions were the results of many years of focused and collaborative team efforts in his workshop, public sector innovation is not about luck (Leadbeater, 2009a). It is a conscious effort. It is hard work. It is a profession in itself. Innovation theories and tools offers public leaders a way to think and a way to build institutional capacity to systematically increase the probability that mysteries will be explored and great ideas will be developed, surfaced, assessed and selected, and to ensure that there will be a minimum of barriers in their path as they are moved through the organisation. How can such a capacity be built?

Second, the ability to carry through with the most promising ideas is critical. Without successfully executing the ideas with the highest potential, there is no chance of innovation happening. As Bill Eggers and John O'Leary have said, 'The requirements for achieving great things are two simple but far from easy steps – wisely choosing which policies to pursue and then executing those policies. The difference between success and failure is execution' (2009, p xi). Similarly, Martin argues that organisations must be able to transform the exploration of mysteries into *heuristics*: building a causal understanding of what sequence or combination of actions *might* generate the desired outcome (2009). Public sector organisations that embrace innovation as a way of thinking also recognise that no innovation occurs until an idea has been realised and made a positive difference. The ability to quickly and efficiently leverage resources behind new desirable efforts is not something all public sector organisations can claim. But the most innovative ones can. They systematically, rapidly and purposefully move ideas forward, ensuring ownership, execution and scaling in the process. Ultimately, they move along a 'knowledge funnel' from *mystery* to *heuristic* to a new *algorithm* of how to deliver the new policy or service efficiently to scale. The move from idea to implementation to value.

Third, the emphasis on 'value' in innovation is key. Many public sector organisations are not sufficiently aware of whether or not they actually produce the good in the world they think they do. Once the 'algorithm'

Figure 2.2: The knowledge funnel

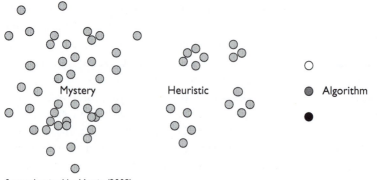

Source: Inspired by Martin (2009)

of service production has been identified and is executed, how do we know it continues to work? Lack of relevant performance measurement and management approaches mean that public organisations have great difficulty learning systematically from their innovation efforts. Ultimately, value for society has to do with the four 'bottom lines' *productivity, service experience, results* and *democracy*, which I present in this chapter and in Chapter 10.

To put the spotlight on innovation in any public organisation, then, is to ask just a few questions: how do we create more and better ideas? How do we select the best ideas? How do we make sure they are implemented and create the intended value? Public sector innovation concerns governments' ability to manage all aspects of this process, from start to end; and – not least – back to the start again. As Martin (2009) argues, the innovative organisation, or, in his terminology, the design thinking organisation, is able to move consciously along the knowledge funnel, diving into the exploration of mystery, and then moving to the exploitation of new ideas.

Where does innovation come from?

There are many ways of describing 'where innovation comes from'. Overall, there seems to be evidence that innovation is more likely to happen in environments that are turbulent and undergoing significant change. The sources of such change may be very different, including both external and internal conditions (Mohr, 1969; Osborne and Brown, 2005; Mulgan, 2009). But what are the specific 'triggers' of new ideas? Across the classic innovation literature, the following triggers of innovation are often highlighted:

• *Research and development.*
Academia and dedicated R&D efforts provide an innovation trigger by creating new knowledge and insights. For instance, the Brazilian government runs a Centre for Strategic Studies and Management Science, Technology and Innovation (CGEE), which amongst other roles advises public agencies across sectors on long-term strategic forecasting and trends. Such organisations help the government enhance its 'peripheral vision', spotting new trends and emerging economic and social patterns that may require a strategic response (Day and Schoemaker, 2006). Research and development for the public sector can thus take place in universities and other academic institutions, in think tanks or in dedicated R&D units. In Denmark, there is now a public programme for 'industrial PhDs in the public sector', where government organisations are supported

to hire PhD students to conduct research in close collaboration with one or more academic institutions. Similar models for joint public–academic applied research exist in other countries. However, the degree to which there is a strong tie and relevant dialogue between public sector institutions and academia varies quite significantly across countries. As a public manager, one must ask: am I aware of domestic or international academic research that could serve as a driver of innovation for my organisation? Should I fund some? How might we collaborate?

• *New technology.*
New technology is a powerful driver of public sector innovation. Improving productivity through internal administrative IT systems is one aspect, but more citizen-oriented uses of web technology are the real challenge. Effective e-tax filing is an example found in many countries with Singapore, Canada and Denmark as some of the pioneers. Traffic payments is another area for digitisation, where a country like New Zealand runs smooth online payment services for its Auckland motorway toll. In a recent review of world-class public services, the UK Cabinet Office sums up several ways that information technology can drive public sector innovation, connecting government efforts closer to citizens' needs: provide outcome-based data online to citizens so they can make informed choices about the quality of public services; open up information for use and reuse, mobilising citizens to find innovative ways of using public data; and harness the power of networks through new interactive 'web 2.0' technologies, for instance to facilitate more dialogue between citizens and professionals (Cabinet Office, 2009). The potential certainly seems to be there. But since there is often an absence of a market mechanism in many public sectors, in particular in welfare states, what should be the incentive to search out and quickly apply relevant new technology? Often 'risky' IT projects are avoided (or, alternatively, they are implemented with huge cost and time overruns) and public managers, staff and ultimately citizens miss the opportunities for efficiency and service gains offered by new technical solutions (Bhatta, 2003).

• *Efficiency demands.*
Efficiency demands are a significant trigger of innovation, for instance when a Treasury or Ministry of Finance carries through cuts in expenditure, and innovations are needed to find fast efficiency gains. In Denmark, massive efficiency requirements are the primary driving force behind the innovation efforts at the Ministry of Taxation: the ministry has invested in advanced e-government tax solutions, reorganisation into virtual centres of competence and central call centres to attempt

to meet efficiency gains of around 25% over a few years. Longer-term and more systemic demands for increased productivity are also strong innovation drivers; as I mentioned in the introduction, the Australian state of New South Wales is expected to see its health bill double over the next 20 years. How will the state avoid budgetary disaster without very significant changes in the operation of the health sector?

• *Employee-driven innovation*
Employee-driven innovation is when the public institution activates and leverages the experience and ideas of 'ordinary' staff across all levels and areas of the organisation. Also dubbed, perhaps more appropriately, 'everyday innovation' (Patterson et al, 2009), this is of utmost importance to any modern work organisation. Rather than deposit the innovation efforts with the experts in the R&D department, everyone must be involved in the creative process. As Robert D. Behn (1995) and Sanford Borins (2001b) have documented, new ideas can arise from anywhere in a public organisation. They do not only originate from top management or from dedicated 'innovators'. Some government administrations are already responding to the consequences of this insight. For instance, in the Netherlands, the Ministry of Public Works and Waterways has established a facilitated physical environment, LEF, which is used by all employees and all parts of the organisation as an incubator for innovation, bringing out creative ideas and insights. In the United States, the Transportation Security Administration has launched Idea Factory, an internal secure website that allows employees to submit innovative ideas (Eggers and Singh, 2009). Studies show that such a broad involvement of employees increases productivity and growth in private sector companies (LO, 2006; Patterson et al, 2009). In public bureaucracies, where there isn't always a tradition of employee involvement across organisational hierarchies, boundaries and professions, employee-driven innovation holds major potential. Usually it takes an organised (leadership) effort to get off the ground, such as when the Victorian Public Service created online collaboration platforms as part of its Innovation Action Plan. Employee-driven innovation is considered further in Chapter 6.

• *Citizen-centred innovation*
Citizen-centred innovation is when organisations systematically involve citizens, businesses and other end-users in the creation of new solutions (Bason et al, 2009). This approach combines harvesting in-depth qualitative insights about people's lives, for instance through ethnographic research, combined with various methods for involvement through workshops, town hall meetings, social media, 'crowdsourcing'

tools and so on. It can also involve seeking out 'lead users' who are themselves innovators, and from whom we can learn lessons that can be adopted in new product or service offerings. This type of innovation process has many different flavours and implications, such as user-driven innovation, demand-driven innovation, customer-driven innovation, human-centred design, co-design and interaction design, to name but a few (Kelley, 2001, 2005; Ulwick, 2005; von Hippel, 2005; Sanders and Stappers, 2008). Citizen-centred innovation is taking hold in the public sector. In a number of countries, ranging from *La 27e Région* innovation unit in France to Kent county's Social Innovation Lab (SILK) in the UK and MindLab in Denmark, ethnographic research and design approaches are being combined to explore interactions between citizens and public services, and to identify how social outcomes can be created more effectively. Citizen-centred innovation is treated in Chapter 8.

These triggers of innovation are by no means complete, nor are they mutually exclusive. An employee can find a great idea for how to meet new efficiency demands; a new internet-based service can be prototyped and tested with citizens, to explore how it might be most valuable in practice and so forth. However, the innovation triggers listed here can help public managers think more broadly about how they drive innovation. Are we aware of new technological solutions that could be valuable in our policy area? Might we increase our ability to obtain insights into citizens' experiences, and make that a driver of innovation? And, more fundamentally, have we involved those closest to the problem, who have a real stake in the changes necessary through implementation to the creation of value?

What types of innovation are there?

While everyone can agree that innovation is about creating something new, there is often quite a bit of confusion as to what this 'newness' is. Two key questions are: how new is it? And in what way is it new?

The distinction between incremental and radical innovation is usually helpful. *Incremental innovation* is a gradual improvement of existing processes or products, while *radical innovation* is characterised by entirely new processes or products. Radical innovation typically is associated with higher degrees of uncertainty and risk, and might happen through more discontinuous 'jumps' or breaks from the current state, rather than steady development (Christensen, 1997; Boyett, 1996). Some scholars, including Osborne and Brown (2005), have argued that 'ordinary' change should be seen as something entirely different from 'disruptive' innovation. However, like Professor John Bessant, Director of Research at the University of Exeter Business School and a leading authority on innovation, I believe that innovation is better seen as a continuum. *Change* is, in this view, a result of innovation. Table 2.1 below adds a distinction between the system level and component level, and also gives increased granularity to the spectrum between incremental and radical with the category 'new for us', which is likely to be where quite a few innovations belong. As, among others, Sanger and Levin (1992) have pointed out, many innovations in public organisations are better characterised as 'evolutionary tinkering', where existing resources and solutions are combined and implemented in new ways.

Table 2.1: From incremental to radical innovation

	Incremental ('Do what we do better')	('New for us')	**Radical** ('New in the world')
System level	New editions of existing services (for instance an updated version of an online tax service)	New generations of products and services (for instance digital patient journals in health care)	E-government Nuclear power
Com-ponent level	Improving product components Improving single work processes (for instance improved human resource tools)	New components or processes in existing systems (for instance the introduction of *lean management* in public administration)	For instance entirely new forms of collaboration between schools, social workers and police

Source: Adapted from Tidd et al (2005)

In what way might an innovation be new? Many attempts have been made to categorise types of innovation. The challenge, of course, is to strike a balance between detail and complexity – and to use categories that make sense in a public sector context. Hartley (2005) distinguishes between seven innovation types in government. Tidd et al (2005) propose four types of innovation, which together make up the innovation space, and which in my experience constitute a helpful way to think about innovation, also in the public sector. The first two are:

- *Process innovation* focuses on the inner life of the organisation. How are structures, work processes and routines organised, and how does changing these factors increase the value of the organisation's outputs? When public sector organisations use lean thinking to streamline case management and optimise workflow, it is process innovation.

• *Product innovation* has to do with changes in what is delivered to individuals and entities outside the organisation. 'Product' is the final output of an organisation's efforts and so in public sector organisations this could be services or policy. When a school develops and implements effective new learning methods, when financial authorities change their way of regulating banks or when a foreign ministry rethinks a key policy area, it is essentially product innovation.

In the public sector, both process and product innovation take place under different conditions than in private sector organisations, and to some degree public sector innovation should therefore be considered as unique (Koch and Hauknes, 2005). The complexity of the institutional surroundings and the political context can make a fundamental difference (Bhatta, 2003; Pollitt, 2003; Hartley, 2005). For instance, processes can be governed by national law, and so it is beyond the scope of the individual organisation to change them, even if it would make sense to do so. And the service an organisation should deliver is typically also regulated to some extent; in addition a wide range of stakeholders may have strong opinions about what the services should be. For a retirement home, this may include not only the seniors who use its services, but also their relatives, staff unions, politicians and the public at large. The political context is thus a key component of the innovation ecosystem that I discuss in Chapter 3.

In service organisations, it can sometimes be difficult to draw a line between what is process and what is product or service. A new treatment in a hospital can be both an expression of a new process and a new service. Building a new bridge is a product as well as a service. However, one way of distinguishing the two is that the process perspective takes its departure internally in the organisation. Managers and staff must ask themselves: 'How do we do things optimally?'. Or, in other words, '*How do we do things right?*'. Service delivery, however, takes its departure externally. We must ask: 'How do citizens, businesses and others experience what we do?. How does it impact their lives?'. Or, in other words, '*Are we doing the right thing?*'. Tidd et al (2005) add another two categories to process and product innovation:

• *Positional innovation* is when a product or service is placed in a new context, and therefore gains new significance for users, or targets new user groups. For instance, the town Horsens in the Jutland peninsula of Denmark was for decades known as a prison town. When the prison was shut down, however, the city reinvented itself throughout the 1990s as a centre for popular art and culture. Through a series of mega-concerts with artists like Madonna, R.E.M. and Bruce Springsteen, the city repositioned itself and became attractive to new groups of citizens, including upper-middle-class families. Suddenly it was cool to live in Horsens.

• *Paradigm innovation* is when the organisation's existing mental model is changed completely. In a number of countries, public organisations that used to see themselves as controllers are currently in the middle of a significant paradigm shift to see themselves as service organisations. In the UK, Her Majesty's Revenue and Customs authority (HMRC) has built a significant customer unit to help facilitate the shift from control to service. Their mantra is: 'If you think it's expensive to do customer research, what do you think it costs not to understand our customers?'

These four Ps, combined with the spectrum from incremental to radical, constitute the innovation space. The innovation space gives us a coherent model for thinking about what is the 'newness' of a given change and about in what way something is new.

Figure 2.3: The innovation space

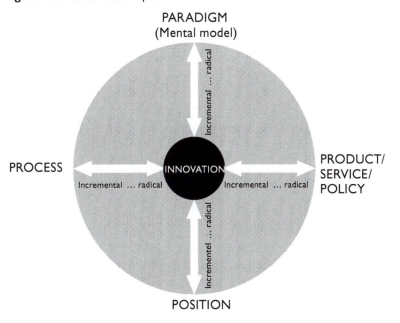

Source: Adapted from Tidd et al (2005)

Using the innovation space as a frame of reference is useful in several respects. It offers a way to consider the organisation's strategic ambitions: what do we want to change? How much? And what kind of change should we engage in? For example, in a Danish government agency, a project manager was preparing to run a major strategy project stretching to 2020. However, in spite of the long-term horizon, the project was to a high degree building on the organisation's existing thinking, systems and services. A colleague familiar with the 4P model asked the project manager to take a look at the innovation space. Was there anything even incrementally paradigmatic about it? Or positional? The project manager acknowledged that perhaps the scope should be reconsidered.

Most public sector organisations are rather good at process innovation – often of the more incremental sort. Some are even pretty adept at improving service delivery. But while there are plenty of calls for it, how many public sector organisations have really embraced the idea of radical, paradigmatic innovation? Opening up the innovation space can help us consider a wider range of options and start a dialogue about what could be the possibilities beyond process and product innovation.

The innovation space is also a well-suited tool to map current innovation practices. At MindLab, we carried out such an exercise by interviewing a dozen mid-level managers in three national ministries and their agencies. We asked: 'Tell us about something you helped change, and how it happened'. Building on the detailed stories of these managers, our team then mapped the results using the 4P innovation space as the framework. The survey was used for a strategic discussion in MindLab's board about the three ministries' innovation capability: how are our efforts distributed in the innovation space? Are we satisfied with the type and shape of current innovation activities, as relayed to us by the managers? What might be the potential in a shift from process and product innovation to paradigm or positional innovation? Do we need more radical innovation? How could such a shift be realised?

The value of public sector innovation

One of the strongest arguments for raising the level of consciousness about innovation in the public sector is its emphasis on value creation (Cole and Parston, 2006). Even though the types of value that most public organisations exist to create are very different than their private sector counterparts, value is nonetheless intimately linked to the rationale of public sector innovation (Moore, 1995, 2005). What is the value of spending taxpayers' money on government activities? How do we know that an innovative new activity represents an improvement over the past?

Raising the consciousness of innovation in government is to a large extent about making the case that innovation will help us get more of what we want. Innovation is what can bridge the gap between the 'stretch' strategic objectives that are increasingly required of public organisations, and the achievement of the results that document that we have reached them. The cycle from strategy to innovation to organisational performance and value creation is two-way. First, strategy tells us where we want to go. Innovation is the process of identifying and implementing the solutions that we believe will help us get there. The contribution (value) of those solutions can be measured in order to document whether we are in fact getting closer to realising our strategy. Second, with that documentation we can learn whether our innovation efforts worked, and we can (if needed) reassess the strategy.

This chain of causality is of course simplified; however, to raise the consciousness about innovation in the public sector, it is essential to remind ourselves that innovation is just a way of articulating what we do when we try something new in order to achieve the success we want. Chapter 4 considers the role of strategy in more detail.

In the private sector, success is ultimately measured in terms of increased revenue, increased profits, increased shareholder value or some combination of the three. What, then, does success, or value, look like in the public sector? Cole and Parston (2006) have pioneered the concept of *public value*, emphasising the dual 'bottom lines' of cost-efficiency and outcomes. However, I believe more nuance is needed to capture all the key dimensions of value in the public sector. Inspired by work by the London School of Economics and Political Science and the UK National Audit Office (NAO, 2006), I propose the following model for viewing the value of innovation in the public sector. Its foundation is a classical input–output–outcome model of public sector production. What it highlights (the circles) is where different types of value of public sector innovation might be generated.

The four types of value are:

- *Productivity*, which is an expression of the ability to achieve a more favourable relationship between the inputs and outputs of public service production, such as when smarter work processes allow an organisation to cut its costs, all other types of value being equal.
- *Service experience*, which can be measured by how well citizens or businesses rate their subjective experience of public service delivery, such as how patients would rate their experience of a hospital stay.

- *Results*, which are an expression of the degree to which the outputs of public sector efforts (such as the number of individuals placed in job training) in fact lead to desirable outcomes (such as jobs). Results are ultimately what public organisations are put into the world to deliver.
- *Democracy*, which is an overarching expression for the different types of value generated by innovations that might lead to increases in factors such as citizen participation and empowerment, transparency, accountability and equality, such as when online tax services give citizens insight and control over their personal financial data. While perhaps more difficult to capture, these types of societal value are nonetheless important.

Figure 2.4: Four 'bottom lines' – types of value of public sector innovation

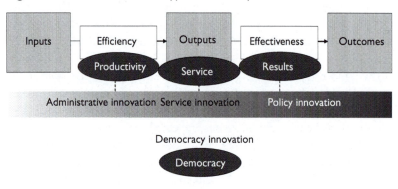

Source: Inspired by National Audit Office (NAO, 2006)

Creating value on just one or two of these bottom lines is often not difficult for public organisations. Creating value on some bottom lines without destroying value on another (such as increasing productivity without diminishing the service experience) is more difficult. As Cole and Parston (2006) discuss in *Unlocking Public Value*, public service organisations must view their production of value in terms of a 'balanced scorecard': the challenge is achieving positive value on all bottom lines simultaneously. That is difficult, but far from impossible. We are today witnessing an increasing number of public organisations that are able to create better outcomes at lower cost while improving the service experience (Gillinson et al, 2010).

The benefit of the 'bottom line' model for public innovators is that it provides a coherent framework for thinking about the kinds of challenges that innovation should address, how they fit into the strategic model (or 'theory of change') of the organisation and how they might be measured. I consider measurement and learning from innovation activities in more detail in Chapter 10.

Viewing the landscape

We have now seen three dimensions of the public sector innovation landscape.

Table 2.2: The three dimensions of the innovation landscape

What triggers innovation?	How new is it, and in what way?	What is the value?
Research	*Incremental versus radical ...*	Productivity
Technology	Process	Service
Efficiency demands	Product (service/policy)	Results
Employees	Paradigm	Democracy
Citizens	Position	

It would be wonderful if any given public sector innovation could be placed neatly in this landscape. However, the 'real world' rarely corresponds to our conceptual models, and this case is no exception.

Innovation is never triggered by one source only. Employees, citizens and other stakeholders should be part of the creative process – in one way or another. Cutting-edge research and new technology should always be taken into consideration, and often plays a key role in the types of solutions that are created.

Placing a given change very precisely in the innovation space can also be tricky. New products or services almost always require a new process of delivery. Paradigmatic shifts may fundamentally alter not just services but also the position of the organisation vis-à-vis end-users or other stakeholders. Generating new value on the 'results' bottom line may be closely related to improving the service experience. Radically improving services may have less favourable implications for productivity.

How to do it

Raising consciousness about the concept of innovation and its implications for the public sector is not a very easy task. That is why it is a responsibility for public leaders. To many people within and, for that matter, outside the public sector, innovation *is* a terrible word. Civil servants don't consider themselves innovators. Innovation is still considered to be something that takes place in laboratories deep within large R&D-driven multinationals, or that happens when engineering students mess around in their dads' garages, building the foundations for the next Apple, Microsoft or Google. Lack of reflection on what innovation means to the individual public servant and to the organisation leads to a lack of learning and improvement of performance. Given the formidable challenges the public sector faces, there is a need to formulate a concrete vision of what innovation is and how it can help. Taking the lead in shaping that vision will require public sector managers and staff to increase their awareness of the key triggers, dimensions and the value of innovation. The following efforts could be a beginning.

Educate in innovation terminology

A first step to raise awareness could be to make public sector innovation as integral a part of bachelor's, master's and executive programmes in law, political science, public administration and economics as it is in today's business and MBA programmes. A second step could be to introduce the language of innovation in internal educational programmes, such as project management courses. For instance, at MindLab we deliver a comprehensive training course in public sector innovation as an integrated part of a cross-ministerial project management education. The course focuses partly on terminology, partly on real case examples from people's own experience and partly on 'learning by doing' through hands-on field research and creative processes like ideation and concept development. Meanwhile, because innovation is still often a foreign word in a public sector context, public managers must ask:

- *What is an appropriate way to talk about innovation in our organisation?*
- *How do we identify, create and maintain the opportunities for staff at all levels to acquire a basic language of innovation?*

Communicate what innovation means to us

Public leaders must help shape the images and language used about innovation in the public organisation. An extremely powerful way to do so (and also a simple one) is to communicate which practices and people are considered innovative, and why. Building a shared understanding of what was done, how it was successful and what kind of value it has given the organisation is key. So as a manager, one has to ask:

- *What are our own successful cases and stories that exemplify what we mean by innovation?*
- *What are the types of efforts and behaviours we want more of – who are our role models?*

Reflect jointly on practice

One of the key barriers to innovation in today's public sector is that there is often a very diffuse understanding of the value the organisation is trying to create. If one asks front-line service workers they may answer 'follow regulations' or 'deliver quality', as seen from their professional perspective. If you ask managers, they may say 'deliver on process metrics'. If you ask top executives, they will be concerned as much with the political and legislative process as with actual policy outcomes. And, not least, and understandably, they will be occupied with how their political leader performs in the media that very day. What is needed is a common language across *all* these organisational levels about what value the organisation should create, and how we know it has been created. It is a leadership role to:

- *Create the opportunities for staff at all levels to reflect on how they innovate, and what the positive results are.*
- *Measure innovation activities and results to drive learning and performance.*
- *Identify, together with staff at all levels, how they can strengthen their efforts in practice.*

It is one thing to create a basic understanding of innovation amongst public leaders and staff; but quite another to build public sector organisations that are highly likely to generate valuable new ideas: organisations that have a high capacity to innovate. That is the topic of the next section.

Part Two
Capacity

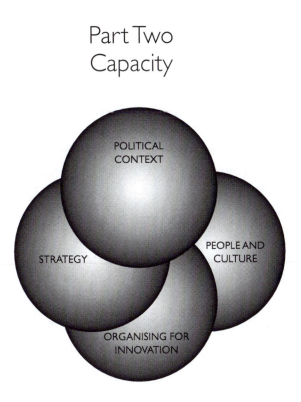

3

Political context

'High-level government executives are pre-occupied with maintaining their agencies in a complex, conflict-ridden, and unpredictable political environment.' (Professor James Q. Wilson, 1989, p 31)

Some years ago, the UK Department of Education set up an internal unit to foster new thinking and new practices in education, *The Innovation Unit*. Part of the legislation that set up the Unit included a clause called 'The Power to Innovate'. This enabled the Secretary of State for Education to set aside regulations or legislation if schools could show they constrained their freedom to innovate – if the schools could show that the changes they had planned would be likely to lead to the improvement of standards. The role of the Unit was to advise schools on how to go about this; and also to advise the Secretary of State on the course of action to take. The ambition, then, was that 'The Power to Innovate' could help eradicate central government barriers to innovation. Over the course of the programme, the Unit helped approve applications to innovate in everything from free school meals to internationally qualified degrees. However, in most cases 'The Power to Innovate' was not needed. The vast majority of proposals were in fact capable of going forward without any changes to the statutory or regulatory framework – but teachers assumed this was not the case.

In the case of UK schools, then, the legal and administrative constraints on public institutions were more imagined than real. However, not all policy areas and legislative regimes are necessarily as conducive to innovation as it seems was the case in the UK. Rather, public managers often experience that their ability to design new solutions are hindered to some degree by the conditions established by the existing political, regulatory and budgetary environment (Bhatta, 2003; Moore, 2005). That means that – in contrast to many innovators in the private sector – public organisations must relate more actively to the political and legal context in which they operate.

This chapter concerns the overall framework conditions for the public organisation. Context is at the top of the 'innovation pyramid' that I introduced in Chapter 1, and which includes the different organisational dimensions that together characterise a public organisation's innovation capacity. This chapter discusses key questions such as:

- What does the normative, political context mean for public sector organisations' ability to generate new and better ideas?
- How do citizens' expectations determine the public sector innovation challenge?
- What is the impact of competition as a barrier or driver of innovation?
- What is the role of risk finance?

These factors determine the political-structural context for innovation in the public sector, across policy domains and across levels of governance; these are also the factors that may constrain public managers, and which in significant ways distinguish the public sector from the private sector.

Normative context

A number of fundamental framework conditions are important to keep in mind. First, public sector organisations are (usually) democratically governed. Their institutional, organisational and strategic contexts are normative. Decisions and relationships are negotiated, and surroundings as well as tasks have different characteristics and a different dynamic than in the private sector. As author and *New York Times* columnist David Brooks pointed out in a commentary on the US presidency, 'It is only by coaxing, prodding and compromise that presidents actually get anything done' (*New York Times*, 2009). That goes for both the political and administrative levels. Public organisations need to respond and interact with their environment at least as much as they try to shape them. The innovation bottom line I've dubbed *democracy* is not only a potential value of the public sector innovation process, it is also a fundamental framework condition (Bhatta, 2003; Mulgan and Albury, 2003; Pollitt, 2003). Public leaders will tend to focus more on publicly authorised needs and legal accountability (van Wart, 2008). Values, ethics and intrinsic motivations all play a larger role inside government than in private firms. The implications for the possibility of a coherent, long-term public sector strategy and innovation are significant.

Second, expectations are high and complex (Osborne and Brown, 2005; Eggers and Singh, 2009). Most public organisations are not simply service organisations, they are also authorities with responsibilities, obligations and formal competencies that relate to citizens and the public at large. Service delivery and productivity – the first two bottom lines – are therefore determined by both possibilities and limitations. Service options may be severely limited by budgetary constraints and lack of resources. The mode of service delivery is easily politicised. In Scandinavia, for-profit firms are often not considered 'suitable' to handle certain 'sensitive' welfare tasks in areas like health care or schooling. The opposite logic seems to be at play in the United States, where the spectre of near-universal, government-run health care energised voters during the now infamous town hall meetings in the summer of 2009.

The third condition, competition, is also controversial. In much of the public sector innovation literature, it is highlighted that a major barrier to public sector innovation is a lack of incentives to innovate, due to the absence of competition. While, as discussed earlier, competitive pressure is among the absolute key drivers of innovation in the private sector, since the threat of failure and bankruptcy is omnipresent in the marketplace, what is the incentive for government? As I will address later in this chapter, many public sector organisations perceive themselves as being in some degree of competition (Hartley, 2005). Some are truly operating in a market, or pseudo-market. Others simply compete for influence, resources and power. And finally others are measured and benchmarked to a degree where they are under severe pressure to perform on the established metrics. So, many public organisations compete, but often under different terms than private firms (Moore, 1995). And public sector competition may not play out so directly in the favour of innovation. Sometimes to the contrary.

These framework conditions have implications for how government is run and the ability of public managers and staff to innovate. Public organisations find themselves in a constant balancing act between enhancing their services and efforts vis-à-vis citizens and businesses, and taking into account political, institutional and overall public concerns. At the same time, public organisations must defend their raison d'être in a semi-competitive environment. In the private sector, the innovation challenge is largely about *opportunities*: how to identify them and leverage them for competitive advantage (Martin, 2007). In the public sector, the innovation challenge is much more about *problems*: how to define them, what to do about them and how to know whether they are being fixed or not, taking into account that many of society's wicked problems will never, by definition, be entirely 'fixed'. The public sector innovation context can perhaps, then, better be described as a set of dilemmas that managers and staff face, often in each of their day-to-day decisions and service activities, and which are not necessarily resolvable. The consequences of these quite different operating environments for public managers and staff are significant. They have to maintain their institutions or agencies in a complex, unpredictable and conflict-ridden political context, trying to accumulate needed resources and perform under numerous constraints (Wilson, 1989). Two parameters seem particularly difficult to manage in public organisations: institutional surroundings and objectives.

Institutional surroundings

Nigel Tyrell, environmental manager at the London borough of Lewisham, was the key driving force behind 'Love Lewisham', a successful social media website. The innovative site encourages citizens to report trash, graffiti and broken public infrastructure with their mobile phones so the local government quickly can identify and fix what needs to be repaired (Prendiville, 2009). However, Nigel Tyrell had to do a lot of convincing of his own colleagues in the central IT and communication's offices to get the site up and running. First, it was against policy to establish a separate external website beyond the existing website structure. Second, because citizens (as the key stakeholders) were invited to take MMS photos of graffiti and trash, and upload the pictures themselves, the site would by definition conflict with the borough's formal communication standards. The institutional surroundings – stakeholders like other public organisations, interest organisations, media, citizens and business – take up more space in public sector organisations' environment, and require more active responses. The external stakeholders have shifting and more complex interests and needs. Further, the linkages and concrete contacts between the public sector organisation and its surroundings take place at many levels, not just at central level. In Lewisham, the initiative to establish the Love Lewisham social website was not a top management decision, but started at a lower management level. It illustrates how it is often next to impossible to control stakeholder relations. For some politically governed organisations this can lead to institutional schizophrenia, and ongoing efforts to limit and control who are the most important stakeholders. How do we innovate in such an environment?

One the one hand, many public organisations attempt to control and manage their institutional surroundings. A reduction of their importance can provide more stability and continuity, and increase resilience. One way to do so could be through a tightly run external communication effort, and highly managed top-level relations and negotiations. Such efforts may, however, be innovation killers. And they will certainly not be helpful in putting citizens and other of the most important stakeholders at the centre of the organisation's efforts, as we saw in the Lewisham example earlier. Therefore, the innovative public manager will need to take an active stand and be aware of how the institutional context promotes or hinders innovation. Or else managers will be governed more through internal limitations to stakeholder engagement than through the overall objectives of the organisation.

The challenge is to learn to deal with the dilemmas and ambivalence that is generated by the context. Complex institutional surroundings can also be a source of inspiration and lead to new innovations, for instance when private firms or social entrepreneurs develop new valuable solutions that can then be adapted or scaled up by government. Such open innovation can, in principle at least, be embraced more thoroughly by public organisations, who are generally not as limited by concerns of intellectual property rights and competitive differentiation as private firms (Chesbrough, 2006a). As I discussed in the introduction, and as we will see in later chapters, processes of co-creation might be the most effective way of capturing the multitude of interests through a conscious process of creating new common ideas and concepts that can be implemented by the public organisation, or through partnerships and networks.

Objectives

Objectives and tasks, understood as the concrete strategic goals, services or activities that the organisation must deliver, are often somewhat more narrowly and deeply prescribed in the public sector. Private firms can in principle choose to pursue a new business opportunity from one day to the other (even if it is not considered a core competence). Public organisations are usually formally bound by agreements and regulations that determine their activities. The complexity of the tasks themselves can imply that the objectives and results are also further complicated (Moore, 2005). Adding to the confusion is the fact that because objectives are essentially negotiated, it can be quite unclear, for large parts of the organisations, how they are shaped and decided upon (Mulgan, 2009). And even though they may be formulated narrowly, their nature can be ambiguous. This lack of transparency of how strategy is determined might lead to confusion and disillusionment. What are the implications for innovation? For one thing, some public organisations deliberately seek to expand their objectives. That could imply an increase in the scope and quality of citizen-focused services, or the adoption of entirely new objectives that didn't exist before, or were previously managed by other public (or private) organisations.

For instance, the Danish Ministry of Taxation has adopted a strategy of becoming the entire public sector's 'digital service provider', developing new services for other ministries and agencies. Public managers will be prone to fight for their autonomy.

A number of dilemmas arise, however, as soon as the public organisation moves beyond its formally defined objectives and environment. It risks initiating turf wars with other institutions (public, private or third sector). Further, if an organisation doesn't have the resources to actually take on a new and perhaps innovative objective, it might not have anywhere to go with it, as other institutions are as limited in the formal purposes as itself. Of course, an option could then be to identify new partnerships or business models that might deliver. An example of this is the Climate Consortium established by the Danish Ministry of Economic and Business Affairs – one of the results of the business strategy on climate change that I discussed in the book's introduction. Within the ministry's rather wide remit of facilitating growth and promoting a greener economy, an alliance was established between industry associations, large businesses and government to promote climate-friendly investments in Denmark. The partnership was essentially a tool to expand the ministry's policy scope, and an implementation mechanism at the same time. Some public organisations also partner across national or state boundaries. For instance, British Columbia, Canada has partnered with the US states of Alaska, Washington, Oregon and California to foster innovative solutions to environmental problems (Eggers and Singh, 2009).

Could the respect for determined tasks and objectives be a barrier to innovation? Considering for a moment the 4P model of innovation that I introduced in Chapter 2, there isn't a lot of *positional innovation* going on in the public sector. Roles and tasks aren't shifted just because a good idea arises, even if the organisation might be competent at solving it. There may however be a potential for cross-governmental collaboration, if the courage is in place to work together to bring the solution into reality.

Expectations

One of the most significant drivers of, but also barriers to, innovation in government is how external expectations influence everything from interactions with citizens to organisational culture to top-level decision-making.

Citizens' rights and responsibilities

Government cannot merely think of the population as 'clients', 'users' or 'customers' (Tempoe, 1994). The notion of the citizen is tightly connected with expectations of the obligations and responsibilities of government agencies. Citizens in similar situations, for instance families in need of assistance for a child with special needs, expect they will have access to the same government services, irrespective of where they live or what their income is. Close regulation of government procedures and processes may be needed to ensure equality before the law.

From an innovation perspective, however, a high degree of administrative regulation can inhibit not just potential productivity increases, but also the more fundamental possibility of conducting experiments and pilots (Bason, 2007). The challenge is not just how to deliver equal services to people in similar situations, but also to enforce the law in ways that go beyond 'one size fits all'. Could we treat citizens in similar situations differently, according to need and perhaps even according to the likelihood that interventions will lead to desired outcomes? As Attwood et al (2003) have pointed out, the categories of 'customer' (which for instance entails that we can tailor services to the individual) and 'citizen' (which entails everyone should have the right to the same services) are not mutually exclusive – but there is a friction or dynamic between them.

This touches on the dilemma between political 'democratic' imperatives on the one hand, and public sector productivity, service and results on the other. One of the most costly, but also difficult, areas of service and regulation is the control and oversight of enterprises. In fields such as the work environment, food safety, tax and financial regulation most governments carry out regular controls. Now, should all businesses be controlled at equal intervals, or is it acceptable to put in place a risk-based approach where only industries or companies that are considered highly likely to not comply are controlled regularly? As I discussed in Chapter 2, legal regulations and citizens' rights are not just a potential innovation barrier. Innovations can lead to increased transparency, public participation, empowerment and government accountability, delivering value on the 'democracy' bottom line.

Avoiding error and failure

The expectation of public organisations is often that they avoid any kind of error. This often translates almost directly into an internal expectation and part of the organisational culture: 'To operate, manage, and innovate

---

59

in this environment then is rather difficult, which invariably, it could be argued, leads to an attitude of aversion to risk' (Bhatta, 2003). Avoiding failure diligently in areas such as hospitals, policing, taxation and the justice system and in other areas that affect people's physical and economic well-being is usually a good idea. However, public sector organisations often take a very narrow view of risk and failure, which in turn limits their innovation capacity. Meanwhile, the consequences of error may be harsher in the public sector than in the private. Part of this is the public sector's own doing, for instance when public managers won't stand up to criticism and instead try to pass the buck. Sometimes political conditions mean that a sacrifice has to be made. As Marcel Veenswijk (2006) has argued, entrepreneurial initiative and the hunt for better solutions for individuals must be balanced against the common interest and issues of accountability and legitimacy. I take a closer look at key notions of risk and failure, and innovation culture, in Chapter 6.

The glass bowl

Usually by law, public sector organisations are 'glass bowls' that media, citizens and other stakeholders can look into and inadvertently find fault in (Mulgan and Albury, 2003). Public access to government documents and internal communication is in most democratic countries very far-reaching – and it is not diminishing with the rise of the internet, new social media and the *blogosphere*. The public scrutiny goes beyond questioning the wisdom of decisions and strategies, to how the organisation operates. So whenever a novel activity is undertaken, and risk is taken on, there is a possibility that someone outside the organisation will want a closer look. Are public managers courageous enough, and sufficiently confident of their practices, to let the public in? An organisation like the borough of Lewisham had the courage to open their process of identifying and fixing streets in disrepair to the public – in return for the public's help in identifying the problems in need of fixing. But most managers are only content to share the process when the activities or methods are business as usual, tried and tested or there is 'evidence' that they work. Many are uncomfortable with the unfamiliar terrain of innovation, where some of the methods are new and where the results are often, by definition, unknown.

Could the 'glass bowl' be used proactively as an innovation driver? Some public organisations, such as the NHS in the UK and their Institute for Innovation and Improvement, and the Danish municipality of Fredericia, which has kicked off a major Radical Innovation project, already brand themselves through innovative practices, organisational initiatives and strategies. They invite the public to see how they work and try to come up with better solutions. They also involve citizens, businesses and other external stakeholders actively in the innovation process through co-creation. It is, in other words, not evident that being an open, inclusive and transparent public organisation is necessarily an innovation killer.

Competition

'A key driver of Victoria's ability to compete against other Australian states and international competitors will be the degree to which the Victorian government is itself innovative.' Thus begins a paper written to inform the Australian state of Victoria's innovation strategy, clearly indicating that competition is not the domain of private business alone (Staley, 2008, p 1).

Why is competition interesting? Because public organisations' ability to leverage competition as a positive driver of performance increases innovation capacity; whilst the entire absence of competition, and certainly the presence of negative and destructive competition, stifles innovation. While in the private sector competition and the efficiency of markets is generally regarded as the main source of innovative pressure, the picture gets a bit more muddled in the public sector (Røste, 2008). Often, the lack of competition is mentioned as *the* key reason why government appears to be less capable of innovating than private businesses. However, there are clearly varying degrees of competition in the public sector, ranging from rather clear monopolies to near-free market conditions. So while some public organisations strictly speaking feel no competitive pressure, others experience market dynamics as fully as private firms. In the case of the state of Victoria, competition seems to be regarded as desirable, and public sector innovation is seen as an important source of competitive differentiation.

Internal competition

In the early autumn of 2009, just two months before the 'COP15' UN Summit on Climate Change in Copenhagen, Denmark, the chief negotiator of the Danish Ministry of Climate and Energy stepped down, officially because of administrative irregularities, such as too large an expenses and entertainment bill (the negotiator had up to 200 travel days annually to woo other nations as part of the negotiation process). Quickly, however, the media speculated that he had been sacrificed in a power battle between the Ministry of State and the Ministry of

Climate and Energy over which ministry would lead and, ultimately, take credit for the negotiations in Copenhagen. Climate change apparently lost that battle.

Even in instances of public monopolies, such as the relative power monopolies of the Ministry of State and the Ministry of Climate Change, the situation is usually not entirely free of competitive pressure. Many public managers would admit that there is a significant (informal) competition over tasks and resources. To some extent the competition is political and about power, to some extent it is also about core competencies. Both might have been the case in the example above. Competition internally in the public sector is often driven by very human desires such as the desire to do interesting things, to be at the heart of important public agendas, to gather resources to be able to do more interesting stuff, and to receive public recognition and respect (Pollitt, 2003). This can bring out the best in people, but perhaps sometimes the worst. It might lead to new innovative solutions and more efficient allocation of resources. When the US space agency, NASA, in the early 1960s sought the best method for achieving President Kennedy's vision of landing a man on the moon and returning him safely to earth, three internal groups offered competing approaches. At the time, NASA's philosophy was to encourage dissent up until the final decision, according to NASA's own records, because 'competition, most people concluded, made for a more precise and viable space exploration effort' (NASA, 2004).

Citizen-driven competition

For some years now, travellers have had the benefit of the user-generated hotel ratings of TripAdvisor when deciding where to stay on their next vacation. Increasing numbers of public service organisations are similarly rated, either online by users, or by other agencies or international bodies. In recent years, international surveys and benchmarks, such as the OECD's *PISA Reports* on national educational performance at different grade levels, have added to the transparency of performance. In some countries citizens are encouraged to 'vote with their feet' and choose the public services that best match their needs. Hospitals, day care institutions, care homes, schools and universities are to varying degrees and under different governance mechanisms parts of such markets, where their budgets may be allocated according to usage ('taxi meter' funding principles), or citizens given vouchers to spend on the services they prefer. Even if there are no formal structures in place for user-based resource allocation, other mechanisms might apply. Citizen satisfaction ratings, benchmarking of performance and other tools, often made available for public scrutiny online, introduce a degree of competition by increasing transparency of performance. In the city of Stockholm, Sweden, for instance, parents can visit a government-run website to compare staff-to-pupil ratios, staff qualifications and user satisfaction of childcare providers (Cabinet Office, 2009). This type of transparency puts the pressure to innovate on institutions, to brand themselves and to deliver services and results that can help them rise up the league tables. Sometimes this is highly controversial. For instance, in New Zealand there was significant resistance when the Minister of Education in 2009 wanted to post school performance cards online so that parents could compare results.

Geographic competition

We have already seen that the state of Victoria considers itself in competition with, amongst others, other Australian states and territories. Likewise, deep in Silicon Valley, a number of nations are competing to attract the attention of venture capitalists and major technology corporations. Countries such as Finland, Norway, Denmark and Sweden have established outposts – often termed Innovation Centres or the like – in order to support the establishment of national enterprises locally, and to attract foreign investment back to their home country. And in Denmark, as mentioned earlier, the city of Horsens has rebranded and repositioned itself from being the country's number-one prison city, to being an attractive city of culture and entertainment. A provincial city of around 40,000 inhabitants, Horsens has since the mid-1990s attracted world-class artists such as Madonna, R.E.M. and the Rolling Stones, forming an image that has attracted young families and businesses to the region. The city has even transformed the now former prison into an experience park, *World of Crime*.

Local government, regional states and even nations compete over attracting investments, people and resources across geographical divisions. All of this activity spurs innovation. In Silicon Valley, it is about how to effectively address foreign investors and support them with all the services needed for a smooth and non-bureaucratic location in a Scandinavian country. In Victoria, it is about attracting tourism, talent and investment. And in Horsens, it is about becoming an attractive city for tax-paying working families via more than a decade of transformation.

Competition within the public sector does not only lead to pressure for innovation; it might also spur conflict and power-games. But in many instances, competition does seem to have an innovation pay-off. The challenge is to be aware of how a given mode of competition impacts the incentives to innovate – and design the type of competitive environment that fosters fresh and constructive thinking. As long as certain public tasks are open for interpretation and not clearly defined, there will be room to manoeuvre for internal competition. Public leadership may be the only final determinant of whether that competition will be used to positively drive innovation in the interest of citizens and society, or to waste scarce resources on internal power plays and killing trust, openness and collaboration. In government, the power of leadership trumps the power of the market.

Risk finance and the innovator's dilemma

A final political-structural barrier to innovation capacity in the public sector is the relative absence of risk capital. Living off year-on-year budgets, usually with no possibilities for major longer-term investments, public managers and staff are forced into short-term thinking. Often, even seed money for small experiments and ventures is hard to come by (Moore, 2005).

What is worse, innovations that have documented their value and hold a potential for radical improvements of productivity, service delivery or outcomes, but are not entirely novel any more, often find it difficult to find funding to upscale. Harvard professor Clayton Christensen has described this as the innovator's dilemma: just when a business has become really good at producing some innovative technology at scale, and achieved market dominance, it will usually be upset by some disruptive new innovation, and market entrants will take over (Christensen, 1997). And given that the organisation has fine-tuned its core competence and core product towards its core customers, it will miss the opportunity and be more or less competed out of the market. It simply misses the gap between the present and the future.

A related problem goes for societal innovations, whether they are created by public, private or third-sector organisations. An example is the London, UK-based dance company, Dance United, which has found a novel methodology to engage marginalised youth, including young convicts straight out of prison, in contemporary dance classes six hours a day, five days a week, for 12 weeks of intensive contemporary dance training and performance. This 'Academy' model for young convicts, which is conducted at the company's branch in Bradford, helps the young people gain self-esteem and build new relationships that help them fulfil their potential. The results are remarkable, with recidivism nearly 40 percentage points lower for participants than non-participants (Dance United, 2009). The social and economic return on the relatively small investment of around £6,000 per participant per course is substantial. However, the initiative in Bradford struggles to cover its front-line costs and is therefore difficult to sustain at the required quality. Part of the problem is that the innovation is no longer so new as to attract attention from investors for that reason alone. At the same time it has not built such a major evidence base that it can approach potential government sponsors with what they would regard as a sufficiently solid academic record. In the words of executive director Andrew Coggins at a 2009 seminar: 'It is easier to start something up on the back of an envelope than it is to scale up something that works'. Dance United is caught in a public sector version of the innovator's dilemma.

The political-structural dimension of venture finance for public sector innovation is a truly considerable challenge. As Moore (2005) has argued from the experience of a major innovation project with the US Rockefeller Foundation, sometimes philanthropic organisations can play a constructive role in strengthening public sector innovation simply by providing risk capital to fund activities with risk profiles that wouldn't be politically acceptable in the wider public. In a recent development, the US Obama administration has set up a social innovation fund that is designed to support and expand innovative ideas that are transforming communities, thus acting as an innovation catalyst; the first round of funding was committed through a major competition in the spring of 2010.

The discussion of funding for innovative ventures also addresses the question of funding of (long-term) preventative measures. It touches at the heart of what British innovation guru and author Charles Leadbeater calls 'smoke alarms and fire engines': in a number of domains of our societies, we would rather purchase more fire engines to put out fires, than we would make the social, organisational and (much smaller) financial investment to help people put smoke alarms in their apartments (*The Guardian*, 2009). We are somehow avoiding, at a systemic level, investing in the preventative solutions that could radically improve the lives of our children, older people and the environment. An example of an organisation that has addressed such a preventative challenge is Slack and Slum Dwellers International (SDI), an umbrella organisation for national federations representing the urban poor. SDI was originally built on the foundation of member organisations from Asia and South Africa but now essentially spans the globe. SDI has responded to the problem that people who live in shacks and slums are often evicted and that their main challenge is not education or health, but to have a safe place to live. SDI therefore tackled the root of the problem, helping dwellers meet their immediate housing needs. The way SDI did this was to support local communities to negotiate better relationships with local and national governments, build their own confidence and capacity to undertake negotiations themselves (and even to build their own homes), and finally to connect with other communities they could gain support and learn from (Gillinson et al, 2010).

Where is the public leadership that addresses such problems, and identifies and channels resources into not just innovative new approaches, but into system-wide scaling and adoption?

Out of the mental iron cage

This chapter was introduced with the case of the UK education department that extended licences to schools to innovate even though, in most cases, the barriers to innovation were in fact non-existent. We've seen that on a number of counts, the context of public organisations ought to almost totally inhibit innovation. And yet, public sector innovation still occurs, all the time. Might the political and structural context of the public sector be more of a mental iron cage than a true barrier to innovation? Are many of the perceived limits in our own heads as public administrators and civil servants?

Or perhaps most public sector innovation is just not very radical, and it is through incrementalism over a sustained period of time that real public sector transformation occurs (Bessant, 2005; Moore, 2005). Stone is placed on stone, and some day, looking back, we are able to acknowledge real achievements. Some public sector reforms undoubtedly can be judged that way; just as the emergence of e-government has not heralded revolutionary new services overnight, but rather slow, sometimes even clumsy, improvements to the access of public services, until we one day realise that we have witnessed a decade-long revolution, the same is often the case in the private sector (Kanter, 2006).

In fact, in the UK Department of Education case that introduced this chapter, schools were highly conservative in terms of the proposals they put forward: believing perhaps that those that really would challenge the government's (then) prescriptive approach would simply not be approved. Whether UK schools were in fact deliberately limiting their own creativity to increase the likelihood of approval will of course never be known. But such an incremental pace of change may harmonise better with the mechanisms of governance (including the budgetary processes), and perhaps with the nature of politics and government as a social stabiliser (Mulgan, 2009).

What is certain, however, is that the external drivers of change that I considered in the introduction call for more radical innovation – and a permanent state of alertness to new solutions. Long-term future challenges in areas such as ageing, health and the environment are sufficiently serious as to call for more disruptive, systemic changes in our approaches to prevention (Bessant, 2005). This entails that politicians and top government administrators must acknowledge and act on their responsibility to tune the political-structural context more in favour of innovation. There just may not be time to wait for incrementalism anymore.

How to do it

This chapter has emphasised that the context of public organisations plays a key role in setting the scene for innovation, and can work as barriers or driving forces for innovation capacity, depending on how the system is structured. Some of the potential barriers include inflexible regulation, lack of (or negative, zero-sum) competition, absence of long-term risk capital and a political climate that is increasingly focused on the short term and is adverse to risk. However, public organisations can play a proactive role in shaping their external environment in order to enhance their capacity to innovate. From the discussion in this chapter we can pull away at least three concrete initiatives that might help increase the innovation capacity of the public sector.

Establish innovation legislation

There is a need to create more freedom to innovate, cutting away legislation, administrative regulation and operating procedures that are in the way of smarter solutions. To the extent that this is not always possible, politically feasible or entirely desirable, opportunities to formally dispense with existing legislative limitations should be created. Innovative organisations should be able to apply for political approval in order to test new methods, processes and services. There are already examples of such flexible arrangements in the Netherlands and the UK (Bhatta, 2003). If it turns out that such dispensation is unnecessary in the first place, all the better. As a public innovation leader, one might ask:

- *Which political or contextual framework conditions (legislation, regulation, formal procedures) inhibit or further our organisation's ability to innovate?*

- *Which of these contextual factors might we get entirely rid of?*
- *If we could dispense with certain legislation or administrative regulation and procedures, what would have the greatest positive impact on our ability to create and implement new solutions?*

Create public innovation incubators

Earmarked venture funding for innovation – within selected sectors – can help give a last, important push to realise the good ideas that grow among public managers, employees and private and social entrepreneurs. Government agencies might establish separate funds of risk capital; or private and philanthropic organisations may partner with government to help fund projects that may not be politically acceptable in the wider public due to their risk profile. Public innovation incubators could be established, perhaps as joint ventures with enterprises, research institutions and the third sector – supported in part by risk-friendly co-funding. One might ask:

- *Are there critical areas that we believe should be addressed, but where we cannot identify public funding sources, for instance due to their risk profile?*
- *What might be the opportunities to collaborate with external actors to set up 'innovation incubators' that could embrace innovation in such a higher risk environment?*

Explore the innovation space

Politicians and top public executives must agree to pursue innovation, in spite of the barriers posed by the context and nature of politics. Given the 24/7 media cycle, the political culture in many countries is becoming less and less attuned to long-term and perhaps risky innovation processes. But innovation sometimes demands radical new solutions. It may also demand a long-term, continuous effort, lasting several years, including idea generation, experiments, prototypes, tests and focused implementation before new solutions are finally realised and generate the intended value. Whether it be increased risk-taking or longer-term efforts, it requires mutual loyalty from the political and administrative leadership, and a true strategic perspective. Visionary politicians and top-level managers must be prepared to commit to innovation. Either they must mutually agree on the 'innovation space' – what is the available arena to try and experiment with new solutions? Alternatively, the top administrator must proactively *define* that space, by exploring its boundaries. The key questions for public leaders are:

- *Which specific challenges or opportunities should we address through long-term strategic innovation efforts?*
- *How might we create a common political-administrative platform to actively address these challenges?*
- *What is the commitment to innovation at the political level – what kind of conversation are we having about the organisation's innovation space?*
- *What is the top administrator's role in trying new solutions without necessarily waiting for a formal political mandate, thus exploring the boundaries of the innovation space?*

Political-structural context is the setting against which organisations formulate their objectives, strategies and means of implementing them. How does strategy relate to innovation? That is the topic of the next chapter.

4

Strategy

'Public strategy is the systematic use of public resources and powers, by public agencies, to achieve public goals.' (Geoff Mulgan, Director, Young Foundation, 2009, p 19)

In the mid-2000s, the leadership of the Danish Ministry of Taxation decided to fundamentally transform the organisation's relationship with citizens and business. Inspired by international discussions and experiences on the future of tax administration, not least within the OECD, the top executives asked: what if we believed that the vast majority of our users want to pay their taxes correctly and on time, but don't always know how? What if only a very small percentage of them really want to avoid compliance?

Adopting such a perspective would entail a fundamental shift in how the Ministry conducted its business, and how the organisation viewed success. If success depended on *helping* people comply with the tax code, rather than on *catching* people not complying, that would have fundamental consequences for all aspects of the organisation's activities. From running an organisation focusing mainly on control (and on process), the leadership would have to build an organisation focusing mainly on creating results and outcomes. It would have to shift from seeing all users as the same, to seeing users as very different segments that required very different types of engagement: a 'light touch' based on information and guidance for the majority of tax-abiding Danes, focusing on behaviour change, and a 'heavy hand' for the minority of non-compliers, focusing on punishment.

The tax ministry's top management chose to take a leap of faith, and embrace the new approach. At the heart of this transformation was a new compliance strategy, which today has reached such importance that the organisation characterises it as a 'fundamental philosophy'. Leveraging that strategy to increase productivity, service experience and outcomes, to date, the ministry has reached a productivity increase of nearly 25%, increased accessibility, service and transparency for citizens and business, and built a world-class compliance effort that delivers better outcomes. The result would not have been possible without a long-term strategic effort, and the technology innovations and organisational and cultural change necessary to underpin it. Leading tax and customs authorities across the world have to various degrees taken similar approaches, spanning from New Zealand and Australia to the UK and Canada. Interestingly, some of the most progressive public organisations in the world are tax services.

Strategy is the tool that defines the organisation's objectives and the means to reach them, giving managers and staff direction in their work. Strategy is the next level in the innovation pyramid, because it plays a key role in bridging the top-level political and contextual circumstances with the specific objectives and means to achieve them in the organisation. This chapter discusses the following questions:

- What are the key strategy concepts?
- Why are strategies for innovation important?
- What is an *innovation strategy*, and how does it help organisations approach their innovation efforts?
- What is *strategic innovation*? How can public organisations build innovation portfolios and manage the process of determining the challenges and opportunities on which they need to innovate the most?

Key strategy concepts

When it comes to innovation, the role of strategy often gets confused. What is the link between strategic objectives and 'strategic' innovation efforts?

First and foremost, we have to make the distinction between the organisation's overall strategic objectives and the strategies that explicitly deal with innovation. Overall strategic objectives should state the core business and the positive change that the organisation wants to make in the world. So, for instance, the Danish Ministry of Taxation has a strategy of collecting the amount of revenue that is mandated by law, in order to fund the Danish welfare state – no more, no less. This is a core objective of the organisation; really its main reason to exist. It is also a measurable objective: the ministry collects data about the gap between the amount of Danish *kroner* it should be collecting, and the amount it is actually collecting. The strategic goal, obviously, is to narrow that gap until it is next to zero.

Second, we must recognise that there are two ways of looking at innovation and strategy together – one more internally focused, the other externally focused:

- *Innovation strategy* is similar to an HR- or IT-strategy since it concerns the *how* of innovation, choosing approaches and building skills and capacity internally in the organisation. For instance, the Danish tax ministry today runs an internal Department of Innovation and Knowledge Management, which amongst other things operates an idea portal, an organisation-wide hub connecting employees with new solutions to the managers who can help implement them. Establishing that department is a way of building innovation capacity.
- *Strategic innovation* is an effort that addresses the *what*: it concerns identifying and making actionable concrete challenges that need to be addressed with innovative solutions that will ultimately create the desired value. As discussed also in Chapter 2, innovation is what we call those activities that are intended to bridge the gap between our strategic ambitions and the realisation of value.

Figure 4.1: Bridging strategy and value

Strategy
Where do we want to go?

Innovation
Which new solutions might
help us get there?

Value
Are we getting there?

For instance, during the last five years of massive strategic transformation, the Danish tax administration has run a large number of key projects that sought to identify and create new solutions that could make its compliance strategy a success. An example could be a new method of segmenting taxpayers between compliers and non-compliers, thus driving the day-to-day actions. Another example could be a major PhD project that the organisation runs jointly with MindLab, which seeks to answer the question: how is tax compliance (desired behaviour) created in small and medium-sized companies, and how might the tax authorities act in smarter ways to help more businesses comply? A third example is the development of a new and improved, easy-to-use web interface, which makes filling out tax forms much faster and smoother.

Why are strategies for innovation important?

To consider working strategically with innovation, organisations must have a strategy that describes in some degree of detail what they want to achieve, and how (Mulgan, 2009). A sound strategy should also state the organisation's *theory of change*: how are the selected means supposed to help achieve the stated objectives – what is the causal link between activities and outcomes? Such clear strategies are far from always the case, however, and, if not, formulating an overall strategy is the place to start.

Even if they do have a clear public strategy, very few public sector organisations today have an explicit strategy for *how to address innovation*. Governments around the world, however, are beginning to look at innovation strategies at different levels, and with different scope. A string of new national strategies include public sector innovation as an objective.

In September 2009, US President Barack Obama launched a national innovation strategy, which states that 'Innovation must occur within all levels of society, including the government itself', and goes on to say that the Obama administration will use innovation to improve government programmes (Executive Office of the President, 2009). In Finland, the 2008 national innovation strategy takes a 'broad-based approach' in the recognition that government has so far not been sufficiently innovative, and proposes that 'An implementation process for extensive and innovative public sector cooperation programmes' is undertaken (Finland Ministry of Employment and the Economy, 2008). In Norway, the Design Pilot programme, launched in 2009, a government-funded initiative executed by the Norwegian Design Council, focuses on how design approaches can lead to innovation in both public and private organisations. The UK government's *Innovation Nation* White Paper, also from 2008, outlines how the strategic investment in people and skills, science and technology, including government regulation and procurement, can help the country become the best place in the world to run an innovative business or public service (UK Government, 2008). In Australia, as discussed earlier, the state of Victoria has adopted a wide-ranging Innovation Action Plan. Additionally, under the heading *Empowering Change*, in mid-2010, the Commonwealth of Australia launched a nationwide set of proposals on how to foster innovation across the country's public service (Australian Government, 2010). In Denmark, the government's *Globalisation Strategy* from 2006 stated the objective of creating the most innovative public sector in the world.

Although many of these broad national strategies sound very good, the picture in most countries is not so rosy at department and organisational levels. As the NAO notes in its detailed 2009 account of UK public sector innovation, 'Few central government organisations have considered strategically where they need innovation or how to encourage and support it.' In Denmark, some central departments have started building strategies from their own initiative – not because of the national strategy. The Danish Ministry of Integration, which serves refugees, asylum seekers and other foreign residents, was the first in central government to pick up that challenge, and build an innovation strategy at department level. Now the Ministry of Employment is following suit, integrating an overarching public strategy with a strategy for building innovation capacity. And as mentioned, the Ministry of Taxation is seeking to embed its innovation efforts through a dedicated department.

The ambition of these different efforts is to do away with some of the randomness that has characterised public sector innovation, replacing it with a significantly more conscious and systematic approach. Strategies thus link with innovation in at least two ways: as the *how* of innovation (approach), and as guidance to the *what* (content).

Approach: innovation strategy

An innovation strategy is essentially a strategy for *how* an organisation wants to work with innovation. Implementing an innovation strategy could be part of the organisation's human resources strategy, as it is today in the Danish Ministry of Taxation and in the Ministry of Integration. Or it could be a strategy of its own, as it is now becoming in the Danish Ministry of Employment. It addresses a number of the elements of innovation capacity that are treated in this and the following chapters of the book, and can include answers to questions such as: how do we deal with our external environment, and collaborate with non-governmental actors to innovate and deliver services? What kind of organisation will help us increase the likelihood of getting more and better ideas, and how does the recruitment, development and assessment of our staff help foster innovation? Which specific competencies, skills and tools do we need, and how can they be made accessible to those that need them? How do we want to systematically engage with end-users to power our innovation process, what are our tools and how do we measure the level and value of innovation? What kind of talent and leadership do we need?

For instance, the US government has stated that it will emphasise open and social innovation as part of its strategy. The Finnish government wants, amongst other approaches, to adopt 'demand-led' innovation, which translates to user involvement. In Finland they also propose to link their innovation efforts closely with performance management programmes already in place.

Which alternative approaches to strategic innovation are available? In *The Public Innovator's Playbook*, Eggers and Singh (2009) propose five different strategies for driving innovation, ranging from highly internally oriented approaches to very externally oriented ones. The type of orientation is dependent on the primary source of innovation. According to Eggers and Singh, the five options that public organisations can choose are Cultivate, Replicate, Partner, Network and Open Source. The authors argue that the latter two are rarely (as yet) seen in practice in government.

Another suggestion for addressing innovation strategy originates with Lars Fuglsang, an academic at the University of Roskilde in Denmark, who has suggested a model that combines some of the sources of innovation we've explored in Chapter 2 with how the organisation leverages the sources for innovation. Like Eggers and Singh, Fuglsang (2006) distinguishes between sources that are external to the organisation, and sources that are internal. However, his approach treats the leverage, or 'power to innovate', separately. The two dimensions are:

- *Sources of innovation:* External (R&D, technology, efficiency pressures, citizens and other stakeholders) versus internal (the organisation's own managers and staff).
- *Power to innovate:* Individuals/individual organisations versus collectives, groups or alliances of organisations.

These two dimensions result in four different types of approaches or procedures for how an organisation can address innovation (Fuglsang, 2006).

Table 4.1: Strategic approaches to public sector innovation

'Power to innovate'	'Sources of innovation'	
	Internal (management and staff)	*External (R&D, technology, other organisations, citizens, etc)*
Collective	**Institutional innovation**	**Strategic-reflexive innovation**
Individual	**Entrepreneurial innovation**	**Open innovation**

Source: Adapted from Fuglsang (2006)

The four approaches should not be viewed as fixed roles but rather as expressions of strategic motivations that an organisation can choose flexibly:

- *Entrepreneurial innovation* is closely related to Joseph Schumpeter's innovation perspective: focus is on the dynamic individual or company that seeks to create something entirely new or to identify errors that can be corrected. In the societal domain, such individuals and organisations are often known as social or societal entrepreneurs or innovators. In the public domain, the 'entrepreneurial spirit' was a key perspective in the classic work on reinvention of government by Osborne and Gaebler (1992). As a point of departure the entrepreneurship is individual and internal, since the power for innovation is the individual's curiosity and engagement.
- *Institutional innovation* concerns organisations that seek to innovate from their own internal sources. Even though many public sector organisations are under significant pressure, and while society becomes increasingly complex, they are also often characterised by high degrees of path-dependency and inertia (Pollitt, 2003; Mulgan, 2009). Not least, public sector organisations will often be prone to leverage their innovative efforts internally, through their own staff's experience and tradition. The result might not be more than incremental improvements – but innovation nonetheless (Bessant, 2005).
- *Open innovation* builds on Henry Chesbrough's writings on that topic, as well as user-led innovation (von Hippel, 2005). In Chesbrough's view, modern organisations increasingly have to engage in interaction with shifting actors and stakeholders (2006a, 2006b). At the same time the innovative resources in today's global knowledge society are much more distributed, including (as discussed earlier) amongst academics, citizens, private enterprises, consultancies and think tanks, third-sector organisations, and at the political level. Open innovation could be considered a natural approach in politically governed organisations in democratic societies. However, in many countries the public sector is only open to certain types of input. In Northern Europe and Scandinavia, for instance, labour unions and industrial associations have typically been very close to government, taking formal roles in a variety of decision-making processes, while linkages to end-users and to academia have been weaker. As Eggers and Singh (2009) point out, 'network' and 'open source' approaches to innovation in government are still rare.

- *Strategic-reflexive innovation* is, according to Fuglsang, both open and collective, and seeks to combine a systemic approach to the external environment with a more reflexive perception of one's own organisation. In this view, the ability to consciously reflect on innovation efforts is an important sign of a more mature and potentially effective approach to innovation and change (Senge, 2006; Scharmer, 2007). The point of departure in the strategic-reflexive mode is external relations and sources of change, coupled with a collective (organised or structured) approach to innovation. The approach thus encompasses both formulation of externally directed strategy and internal resources and competencies. Meanwhile, strategic-reflexive innovation also depends on more temporary and fragile social structures that are more fluent and determined by circumstances. Strategic-reflexive innovation as a mode for organisations to address transformation and change is particularly interesting in a public sector context because:
  - it is critical towards internal organisational norms, traditions and procedures while opening up to the external environment;
  - it focuses on long-term stability and order through active utilisation of external inspiration;
  - it suggests that end-users (citizens) and other external stakeholders should be committed to take part in the innovation process, in a mode of co-creation.

As I emphasised in the introduction to the book, there is not one 'best' approach to public sector innovation. However, as the 4P 'innovation space' model illustrated in Chapter 2, and Fuglsang's (2006) categories here, show, there is a range of options available when it comes to approaches to innovation. Public organisations need to know that there is a broader scope of approaches than what is usually thought today, where most of the innovation efforts seem to be entrepreneurial or, at best, institutional.

It is one thing to have a strategy on a piece of paper; but it is quite another to make it a living part of the organisation, embedding its ambitions in daily practice. How might that be done? A number of tools can be helpful in implementing an innovation strategy. As discussed in detail in Chapter 1, the government of Victoria, Australia, launched an ambitious new innovation strategy – the VPS Innovation Action Plan – through, amongst other things, an innovation festival. At the Danish Ministry of Integration, which established its strategy in 2008, the starting point was a comprehensive analysis, or audit, of the innovation activities already taking place. With the backing of the permanent secretary, and with staff dedicated to the job, consultants assisted with a series of interviews and studies. This was quickly followed up with workshops that involved a broad cross-section of managers and staff to discover innovative ways of working in practice. The process concluded with a major innovation camp, which involved everyone in the department, to try out new modes of collaborating and working together. The camp was documented thoroughly with photos and a detailed narrative of the process, which helped create a lasting buzz in the organisation. The strategy was built at the same time as it was implemented.

Content: strategic innovation

Strategic innovation has to do with *what* the organisation chooses to do in pursuit of its objectives. It is a question of prioritising where innovative solutions are most needed, and channelling appropriate resources in that direction (Hamel, 2000). When the municipality of Fredericia in the region of Jutland in Denmark launched the project 'Radical Innovation in Local Government' in the summer of 2009, its leadership went all the way. First, they declared that they wanted to select the five most pressing and wicked problems the city faced, addressing themes ranging from preventative health care to primary school education to climate change. Second, they would dedicate the city's entire central development budget to tackling those problems and allow a year and a half for the process. Third, at the end of that period, they expected to see at least 10 radical suggestions for how to tackle those challenges. They then decided to essentially short-cut the political framework conditions and, for a time at least, take politics out of the public sector innovation equation. They agreed that politicians and union representatives would stay entirely clear of the process, to allow maximum freedom for divergent and possibly controversial ideas. They then set out on a journey to involve managers, employees and citizens intensively in the process, with the assistance of a host of external advisors to facilitate the work. The administrators would then invite the politicians back into the process, to decide on which of the radical solutions should be implemented.

It is still early to assess whether Fredericia's efforts will deliver. However, some promising first examples have already emerged – such as a radically different way of addressing home care for older people. Through the project, the municipality realised that older persons really didn't wish for government-paid home care; they would rather care for themselves if only they could. In response, the social services administration shifted resources from home cleaning to physical training for older citizens. Through the training, significantly more people were able to do their own cleaning, and the municipality could accomplish significant savings (initially of Danish *kroner* 8 million) on home services while the citizens were more satisfied with their lifestyle (*Monday Morning*, 2010). Fredericia's approach is a clear-cut example of strategic innovation – implying a conscious, systematic and focused approach that at the same time is open, exploratory and (let's admit it) a bit risky.

Managing strategic innovation

The strategic *management* challenge to public leaders is to shape a process that couples the overall strategic cycle of the organisation and with all other relevant cycles, including the measurement and (not least) budgetary cycle. We already saw how strategy, innovation and value are connected in Figure 4.1; Figure 4.2 also includes the budgeting process – arguably the best managed and understood process in most public sector organisations.

Figure 4.2: Coordinating the strategy and innovation processes

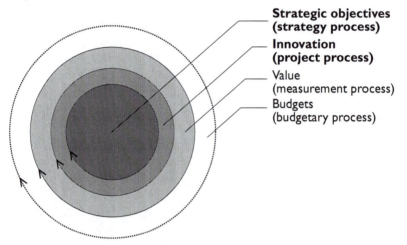

Strategic objectives (strategy process)

Innovation (project process)

Value (measurement process)

Budgets (budgetary process)

Public organisations that actively design and manage their processes like this are widespread; however, most organisations with some type of project organisation in place have good possibilities for moving further in this direction. The order in which organisations mature to this model seems to be as depicted in Figure 4.3.

Figure 4.3: Maturation of innovation strategy

Budgetary process (which all public organisations have in place to some degree)

⋯➔   **Strategy process** (which almost always exists in some form, at least as the setting of objectives)

       ⋯➔   **Innovation (or project) process** (existing in some of the more advanced organisations)

            ⋯➔   **Learning process** (basic metrics in most organisations, outcome-based metrics and learning dialogue in a few)

Identifying innovation priorities

How do we deliberately pick the strategic priorities that need to be addressed with all the force of innovation available to the organisation? A process in three simple steps might be helpful:

- *Diagnosis.* What are our main strategic challenges, and on what time frame? This may require scenario exercises, back-casting or other strategy tools. What are the 'weak signals' that may turn into real challenges? As Wharton School Professors Day and Schoemaker (2006) have pointed out, an organisation's *peripheral vision*, its ability to capture fast-moving change at its very outer boundaries, is critical to building effective strategic responses to new challenges. This is amongst others the role of the CGEE, the strategic forecasting unit of the government of Brazil. Other strategic challenges may be of a more internal character.
- *Gap analysis.* The second step concerns *matching*. The gap analysis matches strategic challenges against current innovation efforts. Do we have explicit, concerted activities in place to prepare for, or actively address, the strategic challenges that have been identified? If not, how might we allocate the people and resources to kick off new initiatives or enhance existing efforts to start dealing more effectively with the challenges? Such a gap analysis could be made using a grid like the one in Figure 4.4. At point A we are confident that we are tackling the challenge with the necessary creative efforts. At point B we could probably divert the efforts to a more appropriate focus, while point C is not of particular interest. Point D, however, is where our alarms go off: we need to build a portfolio of innovation efforts to tackle the challenge, and fast.
- *Build an innovation portfolio.* Strategic innovation is the ability of the organisation to build a portfolio of innovation efforts that addresses the identified gaps (Hamel, 2000; Bason, 2007). As the

city government of Fredericia, Denmark, has done, it is a question of coupling big problems with big and concerted efforts. Few organisations take on everything at the same time. Strategy-driven public organisations have a relatively clear view of what they are engaged in (typically in the form of projects), what their estimated time frame is and they may also have a sense of the degree of certainty that they will identify new solutions. This sort of overview could take the form of an ongoing innovation-management process, where various types of innovation projects with various timescales and degrees of (outcome) uncertainty are maintained.

Figure 4.4: Gap analysis

Strategic challenge

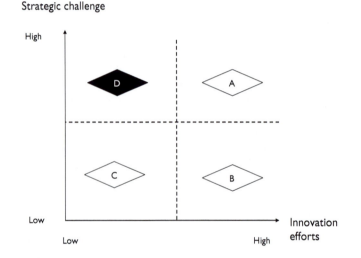

Source: Bason (2007)

As I discussed in Chapter 2, the distinction between 'innovation efforts' and 'traditional development projects' may not be very clear. Some change initiatives are rather incremental improvements, some are 'new to us', while yet others are radical or 'disruptive' (Christensen, 1997; Bessant, 2005). Their place on the dimensions in the 4P model I have described can be hard, if not impossible, to know in advance. When we speak of strategic efforts to innovate more radically, the efforts typically display the following characteristics, which I will examine further in the co-creation section of this book:

- Not just addressing solutions, but challenging underlying assumptions, problems, strategies, approaches, resources and relationships.
- Pulling together all relevant stakeholders in an open conversation about problems, insight, opportunities and 'innovation vectors' or 'directions', allowing for a large degree of divergence in the process.
- The outcome of the process is new ideas and concepts, which may then be prototyped, refined, matured and decided for implementation.

These efforts are sometimes called 'mysteries', 'the front end of innovation', 'double diamond' models or 'pre-jects' because they take place before more traditional stage-gate project development and implementation is put into place.

Figure 4.5: Innovation effort portfolio

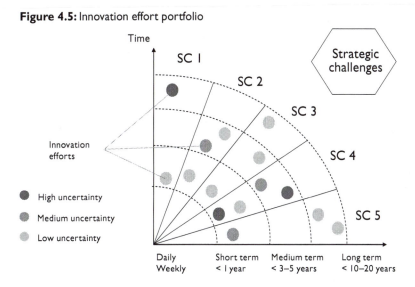

Ongoing (tactical) activities should usually not be part of the portfolio. Some efforts are relatively short term (typically in central departments), others are medium term (this often characterises activities in agencies), and others might be quite long term (and might be dealt with in special commissions, government-sponsored think tanks, foresight and innovation units and so on).

Some organisations in the private sector have created this kind of innovation or 'business development' portfolio in a pocket format, and distributed it to all employees. This gives everyone the opportunity to see and understand what the company is doing to actively develop new business opportunities and products. The purpose is to raise awareness and organisational alignment around innovation efforts, and help employees see where they might contribute. Public organisations could do the same.

Planning innovation?

The way in which I have addressed innovation and strategy in this chapter is, at face value, highly rational. However, public sector organisations need to embrace divergence, and with that comes a degree of uncertainty and risk. Everything cannot be planned and analysed up front. Taking strategic innovation seriously may very well also entail letting a more *interpretive,* ambiguous mode of work flourish. MIT Professors Richard Lester and Michael Piore define interpretive as the opposite to analytical: 'Interpretive managers seek not to eliminate ambiguity but rather to work with it and through it, using it as a resource out of which new discoveries and insight emerge' (2006, p 97). Interpretation is, in their eyes, the missing link of innovation. Certainly, the mode of interpretation, while existent in many organisations, is hardly recognised or captured in today's operating mode (Martin, 2007, 2009). Interpretation is also related to co-creation, which is essentially a process for how to orchestrate *both* analytical and more interpretive modes of knowing and decision-making that I will describe in much more detail in the next section of the book.

Table 4.2: Planning versus innovation

Strategic planning	Strategic innovation
Analytic	Creative
Focused on performance indicators	Focused on new insight
Internally focused ('inside-out')	Externally focused ('outside-in')
Logical-linear	Iterative and heuristic
Strategy for today *forecasted* to tomorrow	Strategy for tomorrow *back-casted* to today
Expand existing business model	Alternative business models
Create more value for existing users	Create value for new users
Assumes that the future looks like the present	Assumes that the future is dynamic
Follows rules and traditions	Breaks rules

Anders Drejer, a business professor at the Aarhus School of Business's Strategy-Lab has distinguished between strategic planning and strategic innovation (Drejer et al, 2005).

What may be most striking about the contrasting elements in Drejer's model is how accurately its left-hand side matches the current operating mode of most government organisations. The great management thinker Henry Mintzberg has even pointed out that 'strategic planning' is an oxymoron (Mintzberg, 2009).

How to do it

This chapter has considered the role of strategy and innovation. The barriers are significant: many public organisations are highly task- and mission-oriented, with no clear overall strategy to drive their efforts. Only a few organisations have as yet established a strategy for what innovation means to them, much less established a formal innovation portfolio. 'Strategic planning', oxymoronic as it might be, is often the order of the day.

However, the flip side of this picture is that across the globe, some governments are now launching innovation strategies, many of which describe both the *what* and the *how* of their relationship to innovation. They are following some of these steps.

Create an innovation strategy

Top executives must choose *how* the organisation wants to approach innovation, selecting among different strategies and approaches. Cutting-edge organisations are moving towards more networked, open and strategic-reflexive approaches to innovation. Top management must be able to formulate and communicate the innovation strategy to staff, involving management and employees in the strategy process. Key questions are:

- *What are relevant ways for us to work with innovation?*
- *How might we increase our capability to innovate?*
- *What are the skills, tools and methods we want our employees to possess, in order to increase their ability to generate better ideas and implement them?*

Manage strategic innovation

First, determine which of the organisation's strategic challenges should be placed at the centre of the innovation efforts, for instance using the three-step approach suggested in this chapter. Second, put in place a coherent management process for identifying, maturing and deciding on which innovation efforts to put in motion. It is necessary to ask:

- *Do we have a comprehensive, updated overview of our innovation portfolio, balancing short-term projects versus long-term bets?*
- *Is the portfolio widely communicated, known and understood in the organisation?*
- *Do we have mechanisms in place to track progress and to support project managers?*
- *Are we aware that innovation is never entirely a planned process, and that we have to allow for an emergent, interpretive mode of operating?*

Strategy is nothing without consequence for the running of the organisation, and for its concrete actions. Organising for innovation is the topic of the next chapter.

5

Organising for innovation

'The most influential people in public policy and management reform in the future may not be experts or people in ostensible leadership roles, but rather those who create new spaces and places for more complex, interactive and inclusive policy conversations.' (Martin Stewart-Weeks, Senior Director Public Sector, Asia-Pacific, Cisco, 2010, p 12)

A few years ago, Anne Lind, the Director-General of the Danish Board of Industrial Injuries, appeared on Tuesday evening television news to face citizens whose cases had been managed by her agency. The gist of the news story was that the board, a state agency, was not sufficiently professional in assisting people in their injury settlement process, adding to their distress in an already vulnerable situation. The low point came when one of the citizens in the television studio pointed out that she had been required by the board to see her doctor concerning the exact same issue – twice. All Ms Lind could do, on live television, was apologise. On her return to the agency, Anne Lind immediately asked the responsible manager why they had sent a citizen to the doctor twice. Having checked the case, returning again to Ms Lind, the manager reported that in fact, the agency had not sent the citizen to the doctor more than once for the same treatment. The other time it had been the local municipality. Recounting this story to other public top executives, Anne Lind said: "That was the moment I realised that not only do we have to innovate, we have to do it through collaboration with other actors and levels of government".

Organisations are where resources are allocated and distributed, development work initiated, and innovation can achieve momentum. Public organisations can combine opportunity with the resources of managers and staff into concrete processes, into action and value. The organisation is also the locus for cross-governmental collaboration, and it is where new knowledge and learning can be managed and leveraged. Organisations constitute the third level of the innovation pyramid.

This chapter discusses some of the key organisational features that are closely related to the open and strategic-reflexive approaches to innovation that I presented in Chapter 4, and which offer a broader avenue for innovation in government. The focus is, therefore, to a rather high degree on cross-cutting organisational issues. The following questions are central:

- How can public sector organisations build the ability to effectively *collaborate* to innovate with other organisations across and beyond the boundaries of government?
- What role can the support of *innovation labs* play to enable and facilitate innovation?
- How can public organisations leverage *digitisation* as a powerful enabler of both specific public solutions and more open cross-sector collaboration in the context of innovation?

The case for innovation collaboration

When the Danish government set out to build its new strategy for how to reduce carbon emissions while at the same time generating new business opportunities and growth, the innovation process involved five different government departments. As described in detail in this book's introduction, the strategy had to be sufficiently ambitious to put Denmark on the map as serious and innovative in the field of combating climate change. However, the interests in this agenda in the Ministry of Economic and Business Affairs (business growth) were nearly directly opposite those of the Ministry of Climate Change (CO_2 reduction), which again were in potential conflict with the Ministry of Science and Innovation (more resources for research).

Today, hardly any of society's wicked problems can be solved through the isolated efforts of a single authority. It is becoming increasingly difficult to reach public objectives in a complex and turbulent world. So although strategies are implemented by organisations, the actual policy or service design must inevitably be the result of multiple departments, agencies and other actors working closely together in new ways, achieving their results with others, not only on their own.

As a consequence, the past couple of decades have seen a surge in interest in 'joined-up', 'collaborative' or 'networked' government as a way of responding to the need for increased coordination, and unity of policy development and service delivery (Pollitt, 2003; Eggers and Singh, 2009; Mulgan, 2009). Sticking to thinking and acting through isolated organisational silos has time and again been identified as one of the main barriers to innovation in the public sector (NAO, 2006, 2009; Eggers and O'Leary, 2009). Although the functional departmentalism of classic governmental bureaucracy has its advantages in terms of (relatively) clear responsibilities and accountability, it also holds a number of disadvantages. According to Geoff Mulgan, who as a speech writer for UK Prime Minister Tony Blair coined the term 'joined-up government', some of the key challenges of the traditional silo structure are that:

- It becomes difficult to see and address problems that don't neatly fall within organisational boundaries.
- Government efforts may be skewed away from activities like prevention, since the benefits may fall to other departments.
- At worst, it may incentivise public organisations to dump problems on each other.
- Over time, departmental silos will reinforce the tendency common to all bureaucracies of devoting more energy to protecting their turf than to serving the public (Mulgan, 2009).

Government's need to collaborate internally across agencies and departments is one thing. The degree to which the public sector can flexibly interact and make relevant and valuable arrangements in the interplay with private and other non-governmental actors is also a key component of the public sector's innovation capacity. The public sector is a powerful societal force: in terms of the scale of service delivery; as a source of funding private firms through public purchasing; as initiator of new systems, services and product development; and as a partner of social movements and enterprises that take on difficult societal problems. What kinds of collaboration does it take to fulfil the ambitions of more open and reflexive approaches to innovation?

Collaboration around creation and execution of government policies and services can thus take place across the public, private and third sectors – or in a combination of them all. Some, like Murray, Caulier-Rice and Mulgan (2009), argue that entire new business models are arising in the cross-section of the three sectors, essentially giving rise to a 'fourth sector'. For instance, the Danish business strategy on climate change involved innovation collaboration through a series of workshop sessions between the public (ministerial) bodies involved. That process was supplemented with systematic insight and participation from private firms, institutional investors and industry and environmental organisations. The strategy itself, which was adopted in the autumn of 2009, involved setting up a governance structure in partnership between government, business, academia and third-sector organisations, to fund and incentivise some of the strategy's key initiatives. This partnership, the *Climate Consortium*, has proven to be an effective joint platform for developing and marketing Danish responses to the climate challenge – perhaps an example of such a 'fourth-sector' business model (Climate Consortium, 2010).

Public–public collaboration

A number of avenues are being pursued to find new models for internal public sector collaboration on innovation – from more or less informal networks to project organisation to new organisational structures and virtual organisations driven by e-government solutions. All such initiatives are designed, in one way or another, to help overcome what Eggers and O'Leary (2009) have characterised as the *silo trap*: the inability of government bodies to share information and collaborate effectively across organisational boundaries. In some instances this becomes a matter of life and death, as in the instances of breakdown of crucial information flows within and between US intelligence agencies immediately before the 11 September 2001 terrorist attacks.

Project organisation

Even though many public organisations still have not embraced a formal project organisation, cross-cutting ad hoc project work is one key way of driving public–public innovation, leading to what one might term an *adhocracy* (Mintzberg, 2009). As discussed in Chapter 4, working professionally with strategic innovation also means identifying types of innovation activities (a portfolio) – and that portfolio typically consists of projects. But what about organising projects *across* government silos? Danish professor and project management expert Hans Mikkelsen (2005) calls such project organisation of innovation collaboration the *grey zone*, because it usually concerns activities that are not neatly placed in one organisational silo, but, on the other hand, are not entirely placed outside the silos. Grey-zone activities are characterised by strong mutual dependency between the units responsible for development; need for a common understanding of the interplay; multiple stakeholders, each with their own interests and motives; uncertainty about both objectives and means; and, finally, limited knowledge and experience with the problem. The challenge thus becomes to *orchestrate* innovation activities, much in the same way as a conductor leads a symphony orchestra. This is the process of harmonising 'the different activities of many stakeholders in a joint activity, which is continuously able to shift focus and actors' (Mikkelsen, 2005, my translation). The challenge of creating a project organisation (and in particular a cross-cutting one) in government, is that it will typically need to exist alongside the traditional hierarchical organisation or, in Mintzberg's (2009) terms, the 'machine bureaucracy'.

Sourcing ideas across public organisations

We saw earlier how the notion of open innovation and strategic-reflexive innovation characterises organisations that seek outside sources of ideas. Authors of *Wikinomics: How Mass Collaboration Changes Everything*, Tapscott and Williams (2006) have stressed the need to open up to outside sources of innovation. They point out that organisations that don't source a growing proportion of new product and service ideas from outside their walls will find themselves unable to sustain the necessary level of growth, agility, responsiveness, global savvy and creativity. Similarly, thinkers like Charles Leadbeater (2009a), Clay Shirky (2008) and Eggers and Singh (2009) highlight the potential of online platforms such as blogs, wikis, tags, prediction markets and peer-to-peer networking to help transform how organisations collaborate. As I will also discuss later in this chapter and particularly in Chapter 8, this applies to how government can open up to outside stakeholders such as citizens, businesses, academia and so on, but of course it also applies to how government collaborates internally. While it is still to be seen how much cross-cutting collaborative platforms might eventually break down the internal silos of government, there certainly seems to be a momentum. For instance, as we saw in Chapter 1, as part of their Innovation Action Plan the government of Victoria has set up online collaboration tools to allow for more public–public innovation processes to take off.

New technology aside, many public sector organisations participate in forums where they could potentially learn about new ideas and practices. Organisations such as the UN, the OECD, the G20, ASEAN and the European Union bring public organisations together regularly and systematically. In every significant policy field there are associations, networks, conferences and seminars, and knowledge is shared. Often, however, such conferences are mostly about 'downloading' information rather than exploring new solutions through dialogue, which means that not much new insight or innovation is likely to arise (Scharmer, 2007). Also, most of the formal international activity is clearly focused on negotiation and brokering, not innovation (some would say the opposite). Sometimes, however, international inspiration can lead to radical new thinking. For instance, as mentioned earlier, the Danish Ministry of Taxation was strongly influenced by OECD working groups on compliance strategies. Building on experience from countries like Canada and Australia, the Danes initiated a paradigm shift in their approach to compliance, moving away from an activity-based (control) paradigm to an outcome-based (compliance) paradigm. Today the Danish tax ministry is at the forefront of compliance strategies and is itself giving OECD presentations on best practice.

Executive forums

In some countries, top-level forums and activities have been put in place to soften the ground for increased innovation collaboration, fostering new networks, and generating the trust and willingness to explore ways of working together. In the US, the intelligence community's top managers meet regularly, powering networks and collaboration across the host of agencies that are responsible for the country's security, no doubt motivated to not let events such as those of 9/11 ever take place on US soil again (Eggers and Singh, 2009). In the UK, the top 200 central government officials hold two annual conferences, interspersed with a series of topical smaller-scale seminars. In Denmark, the Forum for Public Top Management collected around 300 executives from state, regional and local government to develop a joint 'code' of good public governance (Danish Ministry of Finance, 2006). According to the participants, the Forum was a strong mechanism for breaking down barriers between the country's vertical levels of government and enabling more collaboration.

Super-departments

Another approach for joining government has been to simply establish larger units that can address more comprehensively a broad policy field. In the UK, establishing the Department of Business, Innovation and Skills (BIS) might be viewed as an attempt to integrate further the areas of enterprise development and business regulation with universities and higher education, and with innovation policy for both the private and public sectors. Finland has experimented with merging the Ministry of Trade and Industry, the Ministry of Labour and parts of the regional department into a new Ministry of Employment and the Economy. In Denmark, a Ministry of Welfare was established for a period, integrating departments of social and home affairs to better manage the entire portfolio of efforts that are largely operated by local government. The Danish initiative was dissolved a few years later; the jury may still be out on BIS and the new Finnish ministry.

Joint units

Cross-cutting collaboration on innovation and development activities by setting up special joint units is another approach. As Mulgan (2009) points out, shifting UK governments have in various ways tried to establish structures or processes, such as the Social Exclusion Unit and the Climate Change Office, to address the challenges of executing government priorities across departments. In Finland, the government has experimented with organising key national challenges around a small number of cross-cutting strategic goals, with their own budgets and political authority, with a lead minister appointed to oversee the execution of each high-level goal. In Denmark, there are numerous examples, including the Ministry of Finance's Digital Task Force, staffed from several government departments and regional and local government, and the *Branding Task Force* and Virk.dk, which coordinate 'nation-branding' and enable business-to-government digitisation, respectively. MindLab, which helps run cross-ministerial innovation activities, is another example that I will consider later in this chapter in the context of innovation labs.

Public–private innovation

In some countries, the private sector is considered better at nearly everything – not least by the people employed there (Pollitt, 2003). In others, only government can for some reason be trusted to take care of older people or to run a hospital. Mostly, it's a question of tradition, culture and coincidence how the political-structural set-up in a country plays out in favour of or against close collaboration between the private and public sectors. However, it seems to be accepted that one dimension of public–private collaboration is that the public sector can fund other actors than government to provide innovative new services on its behalf (Osborne and Brown, 2005; Harris and Albury, 2009).

Public sector organisations are full of skilled and engaged people. But after all, the public sector's GDP share only makes up somewhere between a fourth and a half of most modern economies. Could there be competencies in other parts of the economy that might help the public sector with fresh thinking and relevant solutions? To strengthen the public sector's innovation capacity is also to expand that capacity with the relevant skill sets of other sectors, powering innovation through the combination of multiple disciplines. As Professor John Bessant of the University of Exeter has pointed out, 'there is a strong case for learning across the two sectors, not just in terms of transferring well-proven lessons (adaptive learning) but also for "generative learning", building on shared experimentation and comparison of experiences around discontinuous innovation' (2005, p 35).

The public sector is not new to procurement or to collaboration with the private and social sectors. For instance, organisations such as the US military and NASA have for decades utilised private suppliers to innovate on everything from the first Jeep to the Space Shuttle. What might be new, and increasingly necessary, is the focus on creating products or services in a way that generates new solutions to complex societal problems, and at the same time helps foster revenue, growth and jobs in the private sector. A label for this could be Public–Private Innovation, or 'PPI'.

Joint ideation: designing bugs out of hospitals

How could we eliminate health care-associated infections in British hospitals? This was the challenge that an alliance of the Department of Health, the National Health Service (NHS) and the Design Council, an independent industry organisation, threw at private companies. Based on design research, a conversation between patients, health managers and staff, designers, and businesses led to new insight into where bugs in hospitals come from, and how infections might be reduced dramatically. The answer, according to the Design Council, was almost 'ludicrously simple': to reduce bugs in hospitals, create, make and buy furniture that is easy to clean (Design Council, 2009b). Through a process that the Design Council calls Research, Define, Specify and Buy, furniture designers and manufacturers were brought into the mix and through a tendering process a number of designs were prototyped. They are now in production and finding their way to UK hospitals with the promise of a cleaner and safer hospital environment. One solution was a cool-looking and easy-to-clean patient bedside chair, designed by the people behind Virgin Atlantic's upper-class airline seats. Another solution was a mattress with a special fabric that turns blue when a crack occurs, enabling nurses and porters to quickly identify damaged (and therefore potentially dirty) mattresses and replace them. The innovative elements of this procurement process guided by the Design Council are several, and are more generally applicable as key dimensions of public–private innovation:

• Identifying and challenging the problem upfront, rather than moving straight to specifications.

- Carrying out a creative pre-procurement conversation with all stakeholders, including the highly concrete observations of staff and user behaviour and context.
- Bringing in business from the start, and managing the process of procurement under existing national and EU regulation.
- Handling intellectual property rights in a way that satisfies all partners in the process.
- Providing sufficient seed capital for fast prototyping and testing, keeping contenders in the process.
- Making business sufficiently comfortable that there is a market for the products or services they will ultimately innovate and produce.

Figure 5.1, which builds on my definition of innovation, illustrates some of the key elements in such a creative conversation about innovation throughout the public procurement process.

Figure 5.1: Public–private innovation

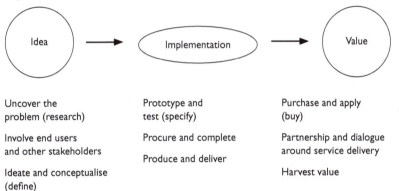

Uncover the problem (research)	Prototype and test (specify)	Purchase and apply (buy)
Involve end users and other stakeholders	Procure and complete	Partnership and dialogue around service delivery
	Produce and deliver	
Ideate and conceptualise (define)		Harvest value

The use of a commissioning process that specifies the required outcomes, but not the means used to achieve them, can be used to encourage more innovation from suppliers (UK Government, 2008; NAO, 2009).

Similar processes are being developed and tested by actors in Denmark, including the Innovation Centre Copenhagen (iCPH), which carries out public–private innovation schemes in care homes and schools in close collaboration between local governments in the Danish capital region, and MidtLab, a Danish regional innovation organisation that has helped build an innovation and procurement model around the future 'intelligent' hospital bed at Randers hospital.

Challenges to 'PPI'

Barriers, however, still remain. Finding a path through innovative procurement processes that can be managed by government agencies themselves, or orchestrating effective networks and partnerships, is a challenge. Whenever there is actual collaboration, it is often in much more classical forms, that is, traditional outsourcing. Even here, however, there are challenges in getting the traction that might bring in outside competencies to solve existing tasks more efficiently, at higher service levels and with better outcomes. There are a number of reasons why the outsourcing of public services is usually not very innovative, and they mostly have to do with context. First, principles of equality. There may be a tendency to believe that because citizens must be equal before the law, all service offerings must also look and feel the same in terms of organisation, process and delivery. More novel models offered by private suppliers may either be impossible within existing law, or they might not come close to winning public tenders because they unsettle the status quo. Lack of hard evidence of the effectiveness of new models can of course also be a barrier. Second, legal concerns. Public organisations must ultimately take responsibility for legality and consistency of delivery. Authoritative decisions cannot (usually) be left to private sector suppliers; public organisations must guarantee objective, independent decisions and assessments. Here there are clear limits to the innovation space. Third, politics. Procurement of new and smarter hospital furniture is relatively uncontroversial. Procurement of private services in care for older people, in public security or in hospitals is, at least in some countries, much more sensitive to the political culture and public mood. In some situations citizens and parts of the political spectrum can be fierce opponents of bringing in outside competencies with a (real or perceived) profit motive. The political nature of the public sector can quickly kill off public–private collaboration.

Public–third-sector innovation

The organisation of collaboration between the public sector and the third sector (non-governmental and voluntary organisations) is tightly linked with the notion of social innovation. Social innovation can be defined as innovation for the social and public good (Harris and Albury, 2009), or as new ideas (products, services and models) that simultaneously meet social needs and create new social relationships or collaborations (Murray et al, 2009). The field of social innovation and social entrepreneurship is, like public sector innovation, gaining momentum (Ellis, 2010). Countries like Canada, Singapore, New Zealand and Australia all boast Centres for Social Innovation, which in different ways seek to empower, involve or drive public, private and third-sector organisations to create more value for society. Some centres, like the Toronto, Canada, Centre for Social Innovation, are hubs providing physical infrastructure and creating network relations between a wide variety of social entrepreneurs and non-governmental organisations. Others, like the Centre for Social Innovation in New Zealand, or The Australian Centre for Social Innovation, employ a variety of methods to tackle specific challenges, including co-creation methods.

Increasingly, governments are recognising the key role of social innovation. For instance, the European Commission, the executive of the European Union, which for many years has focused on the role of civil society in social innovation, has increased its deliberations of how social innovation might be enhanced throughout Europe through, amongst other resources, the EU's structural funds. Social innovation was therefore a key part of proposals from a Business Panel to the Commission's future innovation strategy (European Commission, 2009). The US government has set up the White House Office for Social Innovation, and the Canadian government is currently deliberating on how it might most effectively further strengthen the interplay between public organisations and social innovators.

The case for social innovators

The rise of this interest within government is a sign of a recognition that non-governmental or 'third-sector' organisations play a key role in society. And rightly so. By some estimates, non-governmental organisations account for around 10% of national economies in developed countries (Münster & Münster, 2010). The voluntary and third sector takes on a number of key societal challenges, ranging from running programmes for the socially marginalised to fostering health through preventative programmes and sports. In the Catholic and Southern countries in Europe, third-sector organisations manage many social tasks that in other countries, not least in Northern Europe and Scandinavia, are considered a core business of government. Similarly, in the US and the UK, third-sector organisations are relied on, sometimes increasingly, to deliver value where government is not, by choice or tradition, active.

Governments collaborating effectively with social innovators in the third sector have in many ways the same incentives for collaborating with business – but also different ones in some respects. Because third-sector organisations are value-based and normative, rather than profit-maximising, they hold both additional potential and other types of barriers than firms.

First, to get the best ideas to tackle wicked social problems we need everyone to contribute – and savvy social entrepreneurs may come up with more radical ideas than might come from government bureaucrats as they have a wider scope of action, come from more diverse backgrounds and are motivated not only by values, but also by their competitive environment. In many instances, the mere fact that social innovators are not subject to the rules and mindsets of bureaucracy drastically increases the likelihood that they will come up with innovative ideas. Being entrepreneurs without the shackles of bureaucracy, they don't wait, they just do it. Of course the challenge is that they may, as we saw in the examples earlier, run into government rules anyway. Could there be a potential for government agencies to mimic the organisation, spirit and practices of social innovators? Second, social innovators are close to the citizens. One of the key challenges of many public organisations is how to get citizens and businesses involved directly in the innovation process. To most social innovators, a deep emphatic understanding of the underlying, implicit or explicit unmet needs of citizens is at the very heart of their work. For some, such as the social entrepreneur Thorkil Sonne, who founded *Specalisterne* [The Specialists], an organisation that employs people with autism in regular jobs to conduct highly technical software testing, the motivation is personal: Mr Sonne's own son was diagnosed with autism (Austin et al, 2008). For government to remain legitimate and relevant, it must also support those that make a difference in people's lives at the local level.

Third, a critical challenge for any innovator, whether in government or beyond, is not only to get the ideas, but to turn them into practice. Social innovators often possess the skills and dedication to get their visions implemented. Not only can government learn from that, but government can benefit from creating mutually positive alliances and partnerships with organisations whose ideas have already stood the hard test of meeting reality — but who may need the power and scale of government to make the solutions available to many more. Network-governance approaches that involve third-sector organisations as a natural part of the operational structure of government could be a way forward, as I will discuss later.

The social innovator's paradox

However, the links between third-sector organisations and public or private sources of funding and support are often weak (Harris and Albury, 2009; Westley and Antadze, 2009). These organisations find themselves in a vulnerable environment, having to compete for often short-term resources in the form of grants, contracts or from sales. While important social innovation may spring from these organisations, and while they may solve critical societal tasks, they are paradoxically without a safety net themselves. We saw in Chapter 3 on context, how the Dance United social enterprise was at risk of losing the funding it needed to sustain and scale up its efforts. In the context of the innovation capacity of the public sector, the key question becomes: how can government become sufficiently aware of the potential of the third sector as a source of innovation, and how might government much more effectively collaborate with third-sector organisations about innovation and governance, getting rid of regulation, collaborating on services and helping diffuse innovation? The UK in particular has in recent years experienced a substantial growth in awareness of the third sector's role in the economy. Organisations such as the National Endowment for Science, Technology and the Arts (Nesta), the Young Foundation, the Social Innovation eXchange (SIX), the Innovation Unit and the government-sponsored Innovation Exchange are playing key roles in facilitating and brokering social innovation through networks and support to third-sector organisations whilst also collaborating with government.

Giving innovation a home

On a beautiful autumn day in 2008, outside the city of Utrecht in the Netherlands, the Department of Public Works and Water Management proudly opened LEF, its new Future Centre. Hundreds of government officials, politicians, business people, innovation experts and international guests witnessed the inauguration. It was even relayed on national television. LEF, which means 'courage' in Dutch, is a major physical facility with a number of workshop spaces, open meeting areas, plenary rooms and a large exhibition space. As part of the ministry, LEF's ambition is to provide a creative platform for problem-solving, ideation processes and enabling breakthroughs for the more than 8,000 employees of the public body. Groups of civil servants can book the space and a team of facilitators to help them tackle their problems and generate new solutions (Rijkswaterstaat, 2009). LEF is just one example of the kind of innovation labs that have been set up by various public organisations over the last few years, ranging from the Netherlands to the UK and Denmark.

In Chapter 4 on strategy, we saw how building a portfolio of innovation activities is a way to give structure, content and direction to strategic innovation. A prerequisite, of course, is the ability of the organisation to work on projects, and the ability to manage them. So what about creating, building and sustaining the process skills needed to run the innovation efforts, bringing all relevant stakeholders into the mix? The competencies and mindsets needed for systematic innovation are not the same as those required for stable, daily operations and service delivery at the front line. They aren't even the same as needed for traditional, linear project design and 'stage-gate' implementation. We need approaches, skills, models and tools beyond what most trained civil servants usually possess. And we may even need to create dedicated 'safe' spaces and opportunities for collaboration on innovation across units, departments and sectors.

A demand for innovation labs?

In the view of US innovation guru John Kao, author and former Harvard Business School professor, innovation lives in places. It needs a home. He compares innovation labs with the atelier of an artist. Organisations, just like artists' homes, need a place where the creative process is at the centre. A place where the innovation process is a professional discipline and not a rare, singular event, and where people can meet, interact, experiment, ideate and prototype new solutions (Kao, 2002).

Innovation activities are vulnerable in public organisations, especially at department level where day-to-day managing of crises may take precedence over more strategic project work. At agency and institution levels, ongoing operations are often considered more important and critical than long-term strategic efforts. There seems to be an almost irresolvable dilemma between innovation and operations. Innovation activities may become a 'nice to do' rather than a 'need to do'. The creative processes are at risk of being caught in a stop–go process, teams fragmenting as key members are picked off for other pressing tasks. But as Rosabeth Moss Kanter, one of the world's premier thinkers on innovation, has emphasised, creative teams should stay consistent for the entire innovation process. That will often clash with the turbulent environment and the basic instincts of public organisations (Kanter, 2006).

Are there ways to create a competence environment with sufficient critical mass to be a laboratory for experimentation and the development of tools and methods, but at the same time function as a strategic resource for ensuring flow and progress in innovation activities? Six months before the opening of LEF, Danish innovation lab MindLab marked its first five years of existence by adopting a new citizen-centred strategy and adding two additional ministries to its circle of owners. At the opening reception, MindLab's chairman, the Ministry of Economic and Business Affairs' top executive Michael Dithmer, confirmed MindLab's mission by extending to MindLab's multidisciplinary staff a 'licence to be internal critics of the system'.

Across the English Channel, the Social Innovation Lab for Kent (SILK) was set up in 2007 with two ambitions. First, to provide a creative environment for a wide range of people across Kent to work together on some of the toughest challenges the county faces. Second, by drawing upon best practice from business, design, social science and community development, as well as local experiences in Kent, SILK set out to establish a way of working that would place people at the very centre of everything they did. SILK's main areas of work include supporting and running projects using a person-centred approach to inform strategic policymaking, building capacity across Kent to work in a person-centred way and connecting people to build networks across Kent.

From these labs in the Netherlands, Denmark and the UK, to Italy's *Laboratorio innovazione*, France's *La 27é Region*, the European Network of Living Labs, Finland's Aalto University *Design Factory* and neighbouring Sitra's *Helsinki Design Lab*, innovation labs are becoming a pervasive part of the social infrastructure of modern economies. What are they, how do they work and what is their contribution?

What is an innovation lab?

Innovation labs are entities that are established to assist people in one or more organisations in the process of creating new ideas. The European Commission has proposed that innovation labs are characterised by some common traits, including:

- involvement of users at all stages of development (co-creation);
- multiple partners from the private and public sectors;
- bringing together different disciplines and approaches from design, science, technology and business;

- a dedicated space (real or virtual) for experimentation and developing new ideas (Thenint, 2009).

Innovation labs can also be characterised as *creative platforms*. Danish academics Søren Hansen and Henning Sejer Jakobsen (2006) say that the creative process must be lifted away from the 'swamp' of everyday activities, which are often characterised by routine, fear of failure, prejudice, bureaucracy and rules. They point out, as does John Kao, that creativity needs its own place. It has to be lifted high above the swamp on the four pillars of *trust* (in each other, and in the creative process), *concentration* (ability to be present and aware), *motivation* (leveraging personal ambition to become selflessly and positively involved) and *knowledge* (allowing for a combination of perspectives and disciplines).

There are many labels for such labs: Future Centres, Innovation Units, Innovation Studios, Centres for Social Innovation, Innovation Gyms, Public Spaces, Living Labs, Social Innovation Labs, Dream Spaces, Creative Platforms and Concept Factories, to name but a few. And they can take many forms: physical or virtual; public, private or third sector; or cutting across organisations and sectors. They may be funded fully or partly by government, depend on a host of different sources of income or they may themselves have funds to disperse to innovation activities. For instance, Nesta's Public Services Lab in the UK invests in specific 'challenges' that are then addressed through competitive bids.

Innovation labs are, thus, instruments for focusing creative efforts and skills. Many innovation labs are both 'think tanks' and 'do-tanks'. At their best, they are platforms for co-creation and for identification of new opportunities. Innovation labs are also often places that embrace *design thinking*, where intuitive and interpretative styles of thinking may be practised more explicitly in balance with more logical and analytical styles (Thenint, 2009).

One role of innovation labs can be to help anchor innovation efforts more broadly in the organisation through networks that have the purpose of facilitating innovation and renewal across units of the organisation. In Norway, the local government of Arendal built an internal network of innovators, which accomplished a massive organisational change process, championing decentralisation, liberating managers and staff from rigid job descriptions, introducing value-based leadership and developing service quality through end-user involvement (FO, 2005). In Denmark, MindLab runs an Innovation Agent network of 50 project managers across three government departments, including 15 agencies. Likewise, in the private sector, Procter & Gamble (P&G) has worked to disseminate design thinking throughout the organisation by spreading design specialists across departments and units. Additionally, P&G runs its own physical and facilitated innovation space, *the Clay Street Project*. Innovation labs can thus play an important role in distributing innovative competencies across the organisation.

A key distinction concerning innovation labs is between pure 'creative platforms', which are physical spaces, with facilitation services, that mainly focus on group creativity, and 'strategic innovation units', which are more closely tied to top management and engage in longer-running innovation efforts, often carrying out their own research as part of the process (Hattori and Wycoff, 2002). Table 5.1 illustrates some of the key dimensions of these two types of labs.

Table 5.1: First- versus second-generation labs

First generation (Creative platform)	Second generation (Strategic innovation)
Physical creativity centre	Innovation resources part of business units
Focus on ideation	Focus on strategy and value-creation
Employee-oriented	User-centred
Training and facilitation	Team-oriented innovation culture
Individual and monetary rewards	Coaching and involvement of project teams
Individual/small group	Recognition of teams
Creativity tools	Tools scalable to entire organisation
Management passively supportive	Management actively involved

Source: Hattori and Wycoff (2002)

In practice, most innovation labs are of course a mix of the two generations, second-generation labs building on the practice and experience from the first generation. Some innovation labs may also be more classical R&D or research entities, without some of the dimensions of experimentation and creative working methods that characterise others.

Pitfalls

Establishing innovation labs is not without risk. In particular, they may quickly lose their feel with the organisation's core business and with operations, getting out of touch with key priorities and the core organisational culture. As US management professor Rosabeth Moss Kanter (2006) has pointedly said, there is the risk of creating a situation where one group of employees is perceived as being paid to have fun while another gets paid to do the real work. Harvard lecturer Robert

D. Behn (1995) has stated that in order to create a truly innovative organisation, *everyone* must be engaged in the innovation activities. Likewise, UK professor Fiona Patterson, who, as mentioned previously, co-authored a major study of 'everyday innovation' practices in British firms, states that 'The perception that there is a special "sub-group" of people who are "innovators" in organisations is a misinterpretation of the research evidence in this area. Labelling employees as innovators, or not, is precarious for many reasons' (Patterson et al, 2009, p 5).

A classic example of this challenge is Xerox's Palo Alto Research Center (PARC), which throughout the 1970s and 1980s became a hotbed for serial innovation of products and solutions. World-changing innovations such the graphical user interface, the mouse and the laser printer were all spin-offs but were never recognised as valuable by Xerox's East Coast headquarters.

It is important to underline that the mission of innovation labs usually is *not* to be the innovators themselves, but to help coach and facilitate their colleagues' ability to innovate. As such, it is their explicit mission, in fact, to help everyone become innovators. Still, the nature of their work makes innovation labs particularly sensitive to lack of backing not only from top management, but also from the wider organisation. The formal organisation of 'innovation support' is not yet regarded as highly as, say, the financial control unit or (even, some would say) the human resource department. There is some anecdotal evidence that innovation labs, whether in the public or private sector, often do not have a lifespan of more than three–five years. Swedish insurance giant Scandia, host of the world's first *Future Centre*, closed it again around 2003. Not long ago, major Danish health care product firm Coloplast shut down its *Nebula* (NEw BUsiness LAb) front-end innovation facility. Toy-maker Lego terminated its *VisionLab* after less than two years of existence as the company faced a serious crisis.

The problem is probably never lack of creativity, drive or will to innovate amongst the staff of the units. The problem, rather, is probably lack of connectivity with the rest of the organisation, lack of ability to continue to achieve top management backing and difficulty demonstrating the concrete value of the labs' efforts. A key challenge is to stay relevant by helping identify problems and showing genuine curiosity and interest in the central activities of the organisation, creating strong and valuable connections with the mid-level managers that are so crucial for sponsoring real organisational change. Given the drive for autonomy in many public organisations, particularly in independent agencies and institutions, it may not always be helpful that innovation labs are sponsored centrally by top management.

Who wants top management's 'innovation people' running around in one's own backyard? What kind of ideas might they come up with, or put into the heads of our staff, or relay back to the department head? Another challenge, which I will address later in Chapter 10, is the ability of innovation labs to document results. As former head of MIT Media Lab Europe, Simon Jones, has pointed out, innovation labs are by definition selling something 'uncertain, indistinct and hard to evaluate' (Jones, 2003).

The ambition for innovation labs is that they succeed in powering the innovation ecosystem. At their best, innovation labs are able to generate demand through strong internal networks and a proven track record, while they are at the same time *strategic opportunists* that place themselves exactly where there are concrete challenges to tackle in close interplay with their colleagues.

E-innovation in government

On the small island of Lyø, off the coast of Denmark, citizens were upset that they could not reach life saving emergency medicine on weekdays after 2pm, or on weekends. Without a resident doctor on the island, citizens would just have to wait, their lives on the line. But doctor Lars Kensmark came up with an idea: what if he established a medicine closet with an electronic lock that could be opened from a distance? What if patients could use their mobile phone to picture message (MMS) him to document how much medicine they took, he could manage the dosage online? The service, Medical Island Alert, is now in place and funded at state level; the regional authorities are spreading the solution to other small island communities with no resident doctor (Farmakonomen, 2006; Danish Ministry of Finance, 2010).

New information and communication technology is a powerful driver of public sector innovation – small scale and large scale. From the medical solution on the island of Lyø to the Dutch e-Citizen charter that establishes citizens' rights in the age of digital government to President Obama's drive to open government data to the people, the internet, mobile telephony and wireless services and social media are paving new avenues for public sector innovation.

'E-government' as such is no longer new. From the introduction of computers and basic communication networks in internal government administration of the 1980s, to putting citizen services online in the late 1990s and 2000s, e-government has become a pervasive part of the business of government, essentially expanding the toolbox available to policymakers (Hood and Margetts, 2007). However, the promise to citizens has not always been delivered. For instance, one study showed that only in 16% of cases did e-government projects lead to improved or faster service for citizens (NNIT and Computerworld, 2006).

What we are witnessing today is increasingly a systems-level transformation of how government works, including large-scale business-to-government payment systems, automatic 'intelligent' tax transactions with citizens and new digital mobile services (Stewart-Weeks and Johnston, 2007). Government is using new technologies to leverage its organisation and authority in new ways, often harvesting productivity gains as well as improving services (Dunleavy et al, 2006; Hood and Margetts, 2007; Gillinson et al, 2010). We are also seeing entirely new forms of citizen engagement, driven by social media platforms (Howe, 2008; Shirky, 2008; Leadbeater, 2009a). The promise is to finally shift from an internally focused 'institutional' digitisation to externally focused 'strategic-reflexive' models that serve citizens better. There are many visions and labels for the future of digital government. British public administration professor Patrick Dunleavy has labelled it 'Digital Era Governance' (Dunleavy et al, 2006), while the Australian government calls it 'Government 2.0' (Government 2.0 Taskforce, 2009). The United Nations speaks of 'Connected Governance', IBM proposes 'm-government' (as in Mobile) and broadband equipment giant Cisco proposes 'Government at the Edge'. Cisco, in this work, points to the power of using networks as a platform for harnessing distributed intelligence and empowerment, fuelling innovation, and connecting people, knowledge and services. Such a 'participative web' may become a central feature of the way government works – its organisational boundaries growing vastly more porous and thus enabling *edge centricity*: centralisation and decentralisation simultaneously (Stewart-Weeks, 2010).

Whatever the label, around the world public authorities are scrambling to harvest the promise of radical productivity and service gains, simultaneously enhancing transparency and democratic legitimacy through the new technological solutions (Dunleavy et al, 2006). Countries like Sweden, Denmark, Norway, the Netherlands, the US, the UK, Canada, Australia and South Korea are frequently ranked as the top countries on various measures of e-government maturity (United Nations, 2008). Some of the key features of the new face of e-government are social media, mobility and systems-wide integration.

In the following I will consider two different perspectives on 'e-innovation' in government. First, technology can be a core part of new solutions, such as when government uses a new technology to improve efficiency, service delivery or create better outcomes. New technology adds to the available possibilities for policy and service design. Second, new technology can be a tool for government to run more effective innovation processes, such as when government officials use a social media website to engage in mutual dialogue across geographic or organisational boundaries, or to interact with citizens to come up with new solutions.

New technology as part of the innovation

YouTube, *MySpace*, *Flickr*, *Facebook*, *LinkedIn*, *Twitter*, e-mail, texting, blogs, wikis – the list of new social media platforms is long and growing by the day. From Generation Y, or the Net Generation, those born between 1977 and 1997, to established knowledge workers and to senior citizens, digital connectivity is becoming part of life (Tapscott, 2009). It is also generating new social problems that pull government into new roles. As Clay Shirky powerfully demonstrates in his book *Here Comes Everybody: How Change Happens When People Come Together* (2008), social media can lead to new pressures on government. For instance, in a widely exposed case, pressure from citizens via social media pulled the NYPD to take action over a stolen mobile phone, squarely against normal New York City police procedures.

Government can also leverage social media as a platform for co-producing services with citizens. As we saw earlier, Lewisham in the UK has built the successful, widely recognised Love Lewisham site to enable citizens to help keep city streets clean, leveraging web media with mobile photo messaging. A similar non-governmental service, *Fix My Street*, relays citizens' photos and location information to city councils across the UK. As of 2009, more than 25,000 problems had been reported to the site (Eggers and Singh, 2009). In the south-west United States, the city of Albuquerque has created a similar service, enabling reporting and removal of graffiti to take place within 24 hours (IBM, 2010). A corresponding site in Australia is, of course, titled 'It's Buggered, Mate'.

At the University Hospital of Aarhus, Denmark, cancer doctor Jesper Stentoft has joined Facebook to become online friends with his young patients. According to Stentoft, the ability to follow his patients' activities up close on the social network enables him to much better plan the treatments in a way that interferes as little as possible with their lives: 'It allows me to not place the next blood check right on top of midterm exams' (*Kristeligt Dagblad*, 2009). In 2008, the Danish Consumer Policy Agency built a social media platform as a service to parents with online kids. On the site, parents could discuss what media behaviour is acceptable ('When should I allow my child to open a *Facebook* account?', 'What is an appropriate age to get a mobile phone?', 'How should I handle my kids' online shopping and gaming?'). Rather than letting public staff provide the service, citizens are empowered to provide the service to each other. Government provides a platform for citizens to co-produce the service.

Mobility

As in the case of the island of Lyø earlier, digital health services that cut down the problem of distance and access (*telemedicine*) is a field with massive innovation potential. Another case, also from Denmark, is a mobile platform for treating wounds linked to patients with diabetes. Untreated, the condition can lead to amputation. Between 3,000 and 6,000 Danes are affected each year, requiring home visits by doctors to assess what action is needed. By applying a mobile photo service, nurses can instead conduct visits (or patients can take photos themselves), and relay the information in real time to a doctor. Productivity increases, and service improvement and better outcomes (fewer amputations) are easy to foresee (Digital Health, 2010). In the Philippines, the country's 16 million mobile phone users can report smoke-belching buses and other vehicles via text message to a public environmental service. They can also report wrongdoing by police officers and seek emergency assistance via their mobile phone (Stewart-Weeks, 2010). In Australia, the New South Wales police department is active on *Twitter* as a platform for citizen communication, using the online tool to keep the public updated on emergency information, and to enable dialogue with citizens. (Incidentally, the *Twitter* account was first set up in the police department's name by a local ad agency, before it was discovered and the police took over control of the site.) Finally, the US state of Utah has moved to make government information and services available as iPhone applications via the *Utah.gov* site. Mobile services are bound to become even more pervasive as 3G networks expand and hand-held smartphones with internet access, until recently mainly a business device, spread to the general public.

Large-scale integrated services

Service Canada is an integrated, online service system for all of Canada's citizens, covering major government programmes within areas such as education and training, health and immigration. Some of the largest productivity increases seen in government have been driven by digitising large-scale systems in areas such as employment services, taxation and payments. In countries such as Australia, the US, Denmark and Canada, more than half of citizens file their tax returns online, at half or less the cost to government per e-filing (Dunleavy et al, 2006). The potential cost savings by digitising citizen-to-government interactions are huge, as they are for business-to-government services. In Denmark, the Agency for Government Management has harvested more than EUR150 million in savings alone by digitising all business payments to government. Collaborating with private partners to find the optimal technical solutions, the agency leveraged national legislation to make digital invoicing mandatory. The agency received the e-Europe award (today the European eGovernment award) for its achievements.

Opening up government

The potential of the internet to enhance transparency of public services is, by nature, massive. The US is paving the way in several fields. The Obama administration has already leveraged the web to show how public expenditure via its major economic stimulus package is channelled to citizens and neighbourhoods, all the way to street level. *SeeThroughNY* is similarly a site that accurately displays how New York residents' tax dollars are spent, down to individual payroll information for more than 1.5 million government employees. And the US government site *www.data.gov* provides machine-readable data for citizens, businesses and public institutions such as schools to use. One can only guess at what kinds of breakthrough innovations might arise from the creative efforts of thousands, if not millions, of people once they get hold of the relevant data. In the Netherlands, the e-citizen charter established 10 digital rights of citizens, at the heart of which are commitments to ensure that citizens' rights and duties are transparent and that government pledges to use citizen feedback to improve services. *Borger.dk* is a Danish site that integrates information about all public services in one joint portal, thus underpinning coherence and transparency. Through a personal login, citizens can view the government's information about them. A similar site, *Virk.dk*, is a unified portal for private business, providing links to all relevant government services, covering more than 1,300 types of reporting and also functioning as a platform for digital invoicing.

New technology as an enabler of government's innovation processes

There are at least three different approaches to leveraging new technology to power the process of innovation: collaborative platforms, idea boxes and *crowdsourcing*:

- *Collaborative platforms.*
Tweeting civil servants? Perhaps not surprisingly, at a conference in Melbourne, Australia, on the future of digital government, participating public servants were actively using social medium *Twitter* to comment on and discuss the proceedings as they took place. That is increasingly the experience when attending public sector seminars and conferences, at least in the most modern economies. The collaborative web has been embraced not only by the Net Geners but increasingly by civil servants too. *Twitter* is but one of the increasing range of options, ranging from internal blogs to *LinkedIn* groups that enable new forms of online communication. Communicating on entirely open, public platforms has the drawback that no one wants to discuss critical themes that the general public or the media might find of interest. Given the often confidential nature of governmental development processes, collaborative nets for public servants are, therefore, usually limited to a single department, or at least to the relevant set of public agencies. For instance, a key initiative in the Government of Victoria's Innovation Action Plan, in Australia, is the creation of the VPS Hub, an open technology platform providing the virtual space for collaboration, resources and cross-sector initiatives. At agency level, the Danish tax administration has established a site on the closed online platform *Yammer*, a tool for 'enterprise microblogging'. As an agency site, only tax authority employees can use it. Whether they should only enable intra-agency dialogue or, like the VPS Hub, also enable cross-sector processes, is one of the questions that public managers must address. Another is how to enable such platforms to be perceived as 'real work'. For instance, the *Yammer* user interface looks a lot like *Facebook*, making it seem familiar and easy to use. The potential drawback, however, is that employees misinterpret the site as more of a social network than a professional one. At the Danish tax ministry, one employee who was invited to log on immediately asked the administrator to revoke her licence once she saw the interface; she didn't want to be seen using social media at her workplace.

- *Idea boxes.*

Online platforms or 'inboxes' where employees and managers can submit their ideas are increasingly widespread in public departments and agencies. As mentioned in Chapter 2, in the US, the Transportation Security Administration (TSA) has launched a secure intranet site called *Idea Factory* that enables employees to submit their ideas online. Similarly, part of the Victorian Government's VPS Hub is an *Innovation Zone*, which enables staff to lodge problems and seek solutions from across the Victorian Public Service. The challenge with such platforms is of course not to get them up and running, or even to obtain ideas. For instance, according to Eggers and Singh (2009), by the end of January 2009 the TSA's Idea Factory had received nearly 8,000 ideas. The challenge is to make sure the ideas are selected, qualified and brought into play in a process where they can grab the attention of the relevant managers – and that employees receive prompt feedback about what happens to their suggestion. Of course, some ideas may be ripe for implementation right away, while others might be relevant in a much longer-term perspective – and be placed on 'standby' until the right opportunity arises. At the TSA, employees are invited to comment and to vote on ideas that are considered worthy of pursuing further. Without such explicit processes in place, and the resources to manage them, the promise of idea boxes cannot be harvested.

- *Crowdsourcing.*

As I will discuss in detail in Chapter 8, 'insourcing' ideas from people outside the organisation can be a powerful way of increasing divergence and tapping into the knowledge and insight of a much, much wider audience (Howe, 2008). Online platforms can invite citizens, businesses and other stakeholders to submit their ideas and suggestions, which can then be further developed. For instance, governments and organisations in Singapore and Australia are already successfully running 'innovation challenges' where they invite employees as well as the wider public to suggest their best ideas in areas such as enterprise policy (Government of Singapore), public policy, services and efficiencies (Victorian Public Service), and social innovation (The Australian Centre for Social Innovation). Another way to utilise the crowd in a smaller, focused way is to use mobile technology as 'probes', where selected users can be asked to respond quickly to questions about their activities and submit (for instance) mobile media messages (MMSs) to the researcher-innovator.

As the preceding paragraphs have demonstrated, the internet and social media are opening a plethora of avenues for creating more effective government that connect more directly to citizens' needs – and even brings them into the innovation process. The innovation challenge to public managers is to identify ways in which the new tools of technology can be drivers of renewal, producing productivity increases, enhancing access and citizen satisfaction, while helping drive better outcomes. Digital government is central not just in building innovation capacity; it is a cornerstone of crafting new solutions.

How to do it

This chapter has considered how government can build capacity by organising for innovation. There are obvious barriers to creating innovative public sector organisations: the persistence of functional, organisational silos, the lack of places – physical or virtual – where innovation can be nourished, and random application of digital government and new technology that can drive new solutions or enhance internal processes. We have, however, also seen that new cross-cutting collaboration models, supporting innovation through specialised labs and leveraging new digital solutions intelligently offer ways forward. The following to-dos can help get the innovative organisation off the ground:

Innovation partnerships

Orchestrating strategic partnerships between public authorities and private, third-sector or other public organisations holds a potential for tackling society's 'wicked problems' with much greater competence, power and focus than any one organisation is capable of. There seems to be a significant potential in public–private innovation at the very front end, orchestrating a design-driven conversation about problems and solutions, while running a 'classic' procurement process. The public leader should ask:

- *How capable are we of collaborating effectively across organisational boundaries within the public sector, both when it comes to generating new solutions and when it comes to implementing and producing them at scale?*
- *To what extent are we harvesting the potential value of innovative procurement processes, and of collaborating much more closely with social innovators?*

Innovation labs

Public organisations must identify the tools that match their needs for anchoring innovation. A basic project organisation is a first step. The establishment of dedicated innovation labs may be a future move. 'Second-generation' innovation units are closely integrated with the organisation's core mission, they are user-centred, team-based and focus on real value-creation. They directly work to enhance the innovation capacity of the organisation, and support or facilitate activities by engaging staff and external stakeholders in co-creating solutions. The questions to ask might be:

- *Are we sufficiently professional in organising and executing the innovation projects we need?*
- *If innovation is important to us, how do we invest in enhancing our capacity to achieve more of it?*
- *Might a dedicated unit help us leverage our innovative resources even better, and how could such a unit in practice fit with our organisation and deliver value?*

E-innovation in government

Utilising the tools of new technology is an extremely central opportunity for public sector innovation; however, public organisations have until now focused overly on using digitisation to generate efficiency gains, rather than radically improving services for citizens and businesses. In making such a shift towards more service-oriented solutions, public organisations must realise the potential in new mobile technology and communication forms such as texting, chat, mobile photo and video, social media platforms, GPS devices and so on. As a public leader the question becomes:

- *How does new technology enable us to create new and more effective solutions, and which technologies are most relevant to our specific challenges?*
- *Am I fully aware of how new technology, and in particular the internet and social media, can power our internal collaboration – and what have we done to start using them?*

6

People and culture

'An innovative organization engages everyone throughout the organization in the task of developing and implementing new ways to reach the organization's goals.' (Robert D. Behn, lecturer, Harvard University, 1995, p 221)

Over the course of more than three years, we at MindLab asked the project managers and staff we had assisted with innovation projects a number of questions about their experience of working with us. When assessing the projects they had taken part in, the vast majority said they would, to a high degree, apply our methodologies of co-creation and citizen involvement again in future innovation efforts. We took these responses as a powerful indication that a culture change was beginning to take hold.

Organisations don't innovate, people innovate. The organisation is the context in which people come to work every day, hoping to make a positive dent in the world. But people are, ultimately, carriers of the beliefs and practices that determine an organisation's culture – and which directly influence innovation capacity (Behn, 1995; Osborne and Brown, 2005).

Much public sector reform focuses on reorganisation. However, merely shifting the boxes of the public sector structure around, sometimes assembling larger boxes, other times splitting them up into smaller units, doesn't truly address how people run government. It doesn't necessarily affect the *process* of how solutions are developed, or how people interact. It is relatively easy to visualise and shift boxes around. It is not so easy to visualise complex processes or cultures, and devise ways to change them permanently. For all that organisational structures, open collaboration, dedicated innovation units and digitisation can do, not much permanent change will happen if the culture and everyday habits of those working in government do not change. Because innovation by definition entails something 'new', it also has the implication that it cannot be taken for granted (Mohr, 1969). Innovation must be everybody's job, and the challenge is to stimulate a culture and behaviour that enforces it (Behn, 1995; Borins, 2001a; FTF, 2007). The challenge for the public manager is, thus, to strike a balance between the seemingly opposite leadership styles of driving operational excellence and exploring the 'mystery' of entirely new paradigms and solutions (Osborne and Brown, 2005; Martin, 2009). And there is no lack of literature that points out the particular resistance of government organisations and their employees to change (Mulgan and Albury, 2003; Albury, 2005; Mulgan, 2007).

This chapter focuses on the people who are ultimately carriers of the innovation capacity in the public sector, constituting the fourth and final level of the innovation pyramid that I introduced in Chapter 1. The chapter addresses the following key questions:

- What is required of public employees in order for innovation to succeed?
- Is it really necessary to eliminate 'a culture of zero error', or can stable, high-quality delivery thrive alongside a strong drive to innovate?
- How can a culture of innovation encompass both security and risk?
- What role does diversity management and strategic competence and talent development play in strengthening innovation capacity?

The future of work

In the well-known children's films about Thomas the Tank Engine, the success criteria for the main characters, small trains on the imaginary island of Sodor, are quite clear. The trains are measured according to precision, efficiency, discipline and hard work. They are punished for making fun, arriving late or committing an error. The manager, Sir Topham Hat, dressed in his tie and jacket, oversees that everything is under control, and deals out praise when appropriate but often also ends up scolding the trains for being too playful and naughty. In the well-ordered and structured society of Sodor, as it is in industrial society, the manager always knows best. Enter the hyper-complex, conflict-ridden and turbulent society of the 2010s. Knowledge is deeply specialised, work processes are fast and complex and, as a rule, the employees know more about problems and potential solutions than the manager ever will. Meanwhile, the ability to 'manage' innovation becomes even more critical. In the view of some thinkers on innovation, this implies that we need less management. In *The Future of Management*, Gary Hamel argues that 'while the tools of management can compel people to be obedient and diligent, they can't make them creative and committed' (2007, p 60).

The way government operates is being transformed from the inside through the way public employees work. Empowered by technology, new approaches to human resource management and leadership, and driven by the values of the *Net Geners* and *Generation Y*, government employees are increasingly mirroring their private sector peers in taking on new work forms (Tapscott, 2009). Just as in globalised enterprises, some public organisations are leveraging virtual ways of working to enhance productivity and create additional flexibility. As Hamel argues, hierarchies are good at coordinating the work of many people, *aggregating* effort; but they are not very good at inspiring people, *mobilising* effort.

Continuous reform has become a staple of many public sector organisations. This implies that the work forms and processes must change as well, from a traditional mode of work to a more modern or 'flexible' configuration. This is not a new insight, although its application is as relevant as ever (Mohr, 1969; Bason et al, 2003).

Table 6.1: From traditional to flexible work arrangements

	Traditional	**Flexible**
Management type	Employees 'an attachment to the machine'	Employees a key resource
	Hierarchical structure	Flat structure
	Invisible HR	Professional HR
	Fixed work and employment terms	Flexible work and employment terms
	Management through rules and control	Management through objectives and values
Work organisation	Narrow jobs	Broad jobs
	Low degree of autonomy	High degree of autonomy
	Individual work	Teamwork
	Achieving formal qualifications	Competence development

Source: Bason et al (2003)

Workers in flexible work organisations are considered a resource and a source of innovation. Modern organisations are characterised with a (relatively speaking) flatter organisational structure, professional human resource management and flexible work arrangements (for instance in terms of time, place and tasks). Delegation, responsibility, teamwork and competence development are at the centre of work organisation. As Robert D. Behn has pointed out, innovative organisations are characterised by *broad*, as opposed to *narrow*, jobs, where workers are given better insight into the overall strategic direction of the organisation, and where the responsibility for thinking about how best to accomplish the organisation's mission is spread throughout the organisation (1995).

Innovation capacity is thus tightly linked to the ability to create, develop and maintain organisations that carry the traits associated with flexible work. The challenge is to counterbalance this against the tendency in public agencies to fight a turbulent external environment and create a degree of internal stability through bureaucracy and control (Wilson, 1989; Pollitt, 2003). This is the public leader's challenge.

Employee-driven innovation

One of the key concepts of the 'innovation landscape' that was introduced early in the book was the role of innovation triggers, and employee-driven or 'everyday' innovation (Patterson et al, 2009). The underlying thinking was that to build innovation capacity, organisations must leverage the collective insight, tacit knowledge and inherent creativity in *all* employees, not just certain managers, project teams, R&D staff or dedicated innovators.

How can employees in a wide sense be involved in the innovation process? One of the pioneers of the idea of employee-driven innovation is the Danish Confederation of Trade Unions, LO, who conducted a major survey of the topic in 2006, including private and public sector workplaces. The study showed that among the features that promoted innovation was deep engagement of employees in the innovation process, openness from management to take on new ideas from workers, room to experiment and fail, and ongoing competence development and lifelong learning (LO, 2006). According to Sandford Borins, as many as half of government innovations are initiated from 'ordinary' employees and middle managers (2001c). Other accounts are much less optimistic, with the British NAO mentioning a figure of only 8% of front-line workers playing a part in innovations (Eggers and Singh, 2009). Why is employee-driven innovation so valuable? There are at least three reasons:

* *Valuable knowledge.* First, employees (and in particular front-line employees) often hold detailed experience and first-hand knowledge about the processes, tasks and end-users they work with, which is essential to include in the innovation process. For instance, in the Danish Commerce and Companies Agency, an employee-driven process was put in place to enable multidisciplinary teams of administrative staff, systems developers and professionals to meet weekly, exchange ideas based on their experience and feedback

received from business and come up with new solutions. Their systematic collaboration led to new systems development and the improvement of work processes, which again increased user satisfaction and generated productivity gains. The staff now see their role just as much as problem-solvers as administrators (LO, 2006). In public organisations, the knowledge held by employees is often not only of internal relevance. As a consequence of growing complexity and the need for cross-governmental collaboration, staff often build relations with other authorities, and they obtain insight about problems and solutions in other organisations. They also harvest insight about what triggers complaints from citizens and businesses, not only as a consequence of their own actions, but often also as a consequence of actions and programmes run by other agencies (Behn, 1995). But how often does a public employee relay an idea for a novel new solution to *another* agency?

• *Ownership.* Second, employees' engagement in taking part in systemic change is obviously crucial. Involving them in the organisation's ideation process creates ownership for seeing change through (Behn, 1995; Eggers and O'Leary, 2009). In the Love Lewisham case, which I considered in depth in Chapter 3, it was clear that the environmental department's initiative to launch a new government service would have failed if it didn't have the communications and IT departments on board. Connecting with the colleagues who are instrumental in implementing potential solutions – upfront – is, however, often neglected. At MindLab, we therefore always insist on involving other key units in the internal organisation of our collaboration partners, even though they sometimes don't see the point. Why involve colleagues – they might run with our ideas?

• *Job satisfaction is an innovation engine.* Third, innovation is driven by meaning, creativity and positive relations, which thrive in environments where people feel trusted, respected, listened to and taken seriously. Such traits cannot be commanded (Hamel, 2007). An innovative work environment is also an environment with a high degree of job satisfaction. Still, many innovation efforts in government are markedly top-down. Although (as I will discuss in Chapter 11) top management must take responsibility for championing and enabling innovation, innovation is in practice essentially a bottom-up process.

Innovation culture, error and risk

When researchers at the Aarhus School of Business in Denmark examined innovation processes in local government, they interviewed a worker who exclaimed, 'There's innovation happening all the time. People are drowning in innovation. There's so much innovation going on that people hardly have time to do their real work' (quoted in Bason, 2007, p 198; my translation). Innovation culture is a culture where a group of people's shared values, customs and assumptions are conducive to new ideas and organisational change (Osborne and Brown, 2005; Eggers and Singh, 2009). One key challenge in building a culture of innovation is to recognise the equal validity of innovation and operational activities. Innovation can be perceived as a barrier to 'real work'. Conversely, 'real work' can be a barrier to innovation. The 2006 NAO analysis of innovation in British central government showed that the second-largest barrier to innovation was resistance to working in new ways and experimenting with new solutions (NAO, 2006). The same conclusion was reached in a similar study conducted for the Danish Ministry of Finance (2005).

Employees can find it difficult to think of operations and innovation processes within the same context; it must be a key role of leadership and communication efforts in the organisation to attract attention to both types of processes, and incentivise them (Behn, 1995). Co-creation approaches are, as we will see in the next section of the book, key to orchestrating a collaborative process that integrates the two views (Martin, 2009).

Misunderstanding failure

A central constituent of innovation culture in government is how error is perceived. As Cole and Parston (2006, p 138) point out, 'Traditionally, public service organisations have had little incentive to spend time and money on "experiments" that may fail, because that failure may affect people's lives'. Let's consider some of the common misunderstandings about the public sector as an error-free zone that pervades public perceptions and, in turn, internal organisational cultures.

'Minimising risk is a public sector specialty'

No. Although people often believe that public organisations are particularly sensible to risk, high consistency and a minimum of errors is important for many private firms too. Think of highly innovative organisations in fields such as biotechnology, aerospace, oil and gas, engineering and nuclear power plants. Across a variety of industries, there doesn't seem to be a contradiction between innovating and ensuring a low level of error.

'All failure is equal'

No. One can distinguish between many types of error, including the simple but central distinction between 'dumb' and 'smart' errors. Dumb errors happen when someone fails at a process that is well known and that they should be able to do without making mistakes. Smart errors happen when someone deliberately tries something new, and fails. Here, failure is part of the learning process, and essentially just a step towards success. But because public organisations often put into place process regulations and incentives designed to eliminate dumb errors, they inadvertently create an organisational culture and practice that also seeks to avoid smart errors. Setting up safe spaces and environments where experimentation and learning is encouraged, for instance through dedicated innovation labs, is one way of addressing this issue and getting more of the smart errors we need. As I will discuss also in Chapters 7 and 9, prototyping new solutions in order to 'fail early to succeed sooner' can power fast learning and innovation (Bason et al, 2009; Brown, 2009; Gillinson et al, 2010).

'Risk isn't a strategic issue'

To the contrary. Failure in virtually any social system is inevitable, it's just a question of how large an investment we're willing to make to avoid it. For instance, while US doctors and nurses surely do all they can to minimise failure, have access to more resources than any other health care system in the world and are readily punished by insurance claims and lawsuits, according to the US Institute of Medicine there are still up to 98,000 deaths annually due to preventable medical error in American hospitals. It is really not a question of whether to fail or not. It is a question of where in the organisation's processes it is OK to experiment and take a risk (and finding appropriate ways to do that) – and where it is not (and finding ways and means to, almost, eliminate failure). The acceptable failure rate is a strategic question of consequence to innovation capacity that public managers must be able to answer. Sometimes, accepting more failures can make sense. An example is the Danish Commerce and Companies Agency, which used customer surveys to determine what might be the acceptable level of failure in the forms registering newly formed companies. The agency used this input from business to bring the required proportion of correctly filled-out forms from almost 100% to just 95%, thereby harvesting a massive productivity improvement, reducing the time it took to register a new company from more than 20 days to just four days (Bason, 2007).

Reliable processes

There are two dimensions to this aspect of an innovation culture: first, building recognised and reliable approaches to the process of innovation itself; and second, optimising the key processes that (as discussed earlier) must be highly stable and, to the extent possible, error-free, for instance through methods of employee-led process optimisation. In other words, maximise smart errors and minimise dumb ones.

How do we make innovation a systematic and well-described process that is known and recognised widely in the organisation? Creating innovation labs to be stewards of the innovation process, building the discipline of innovation into formal educational and competence development activities, and providing practical tools and guides to support innovation projects are all means of professionalising innovation processes, paving the way for making them as much a part of the organisation's DNA as operations. Another powerful enabler is choosing a clear innovation framework and training all senior managers and project developers in that framework, and making the language and content of that framework an embedded part of the organisation's conversation. Over a number of years, the Danish Broadcasting Corporation (DR), inspired by the BBC, did just that. It not only established a Concept Factory as the in-house innovation lab, it sent all middle to senior executives to Silicon Valley to be trained in the *Needs Approach Benefits Competition* (NABC) innovation methodology by the Stanford Research Institute (SRI). At home, DR built its new media and programme development activities around the NABC methodology, for instance by making it mandatory to report and pitch all new ideas to management using NABC. Today, the methodology is embedded in the very fabric of how the organisation develops new business.

Conversely, organisations need to build robust processes for their core operations, and to work to ensure continuous learning and improvement. The value of this is twofold: first, it can provide the confidence and stability to focus also on the innovation process, taking a step back from the well-functioning machine of operations to think strategically about future opportunities and challenges. Second, it can deliver direct productivity and service gains. Over the years, many such tools and methods have been developed and implemented in both the private and public sectors, including *TQM, ISO 9000, lean management* and *Six Sigma.* These approaches or philosophies of increasing quality by eliminating waste and minimising variance are usually most relevant to agencies and institutions with high caseloads, reasonably coherent tasks and a potential to increase 'churn'. In Denmark, large agencies such as the Board of Industrial Injuries and the Immigration Service have achieved sustained productivity gains of at least 20% while shortening case-handling times markedly. In the UK, the Department for Work and Pensions has equally implemented lean management with success. Across the United States, and increasingly in Europe, hospitals are recognising the power of lean management to minimise unintended errors, enhancing patient safety and at the same time improving work conditions for (especially) nurses and porters.

Building the capacity to innovate and to operate efficiently at the same time is no easy feat, however. And certainly the tools needed are not the same. The process of innovation lives off *divergence*, the ability to take a longer route to ultimately arrive at the desired outcome with maximum impact (Brown, 2009). The process of standardised production lives off *convergence*, the ability to narrow the variance of outcomes to a minimum to ensure quality. The one focus may overpower the other. As famed and highly innovative US manufacturer 3M discovered when the company adopted the Six Sigma approach, the tight logic of operations can quickly take over and create a culture of incrementalism rather than of more radical innovation. Six Sigma nearly killed 3M's innovation machine before the company found a better balance between creativity and efficiency (*Business Week*, 2007). As Martin (2009) has proposed, and as I discussed in Chapter 2, design thinking represents an approach to balancing between managing divergence or, as he puts it, exploring 'mystery' in order to innovate (maximising validity) and exploiting the algorithm of convergent, efficient mass production (maximising reliability).

Delegation through value-based management

Trusting middle managers, institutional leaders and staff to do their work well, delegating responsibility and limiting formal control are, as discussed earlier, key traits of the modern work organisation. Not all public organisations can ascribe to these characteristics, but they are at the core of building a culture of innovation (Behn, 1995; Bason et al, 2009). Recognition of competence at the relevant level and providing mechanisms for feedback and learning on the basis not of simple control, but of conversations about results and outcomes, are key. Basing management on clear and recognised values, and acting transparently on them, is a tool for enabling delegation and enhancing responsibility. Value-based management may not (and probably should not) replace central control entirely, but leading the creation of common perceptions of right and wrong can be a powerful enabler of the freedom to think and to experiment within the framework of those values. The question then becomes, of course, what values to promote? An innovation culture must start from whatever core beliefs characterise the organisation, but also attempt to stretch them in directions such as continuous learning, experimentation and creativity (Senge, 2006; van Wart, 2008).

Formulating such new values can be a strong signal that innovation is considered important. For instance, a Danish municipality made one of their value statements 'We encourage risk'. Another related example is one of our values at MindLab, which is 'We experiment to achieve results'.

Diversity as driver of innovation

In *The Ten Faces of Innovation*, Tom Kelley, managing director of the design firm IDEO, shows how a wide variety of employee roles, ranging from 'the anthropologist' to 'the director' and 'the set designer' are crucial to innovation (Kelley, 2005). Innovation often takes place through a process of combining known elements into something new and more valuable. All other things being equal, the more diverse the perspectives that are brought to bear on a problem, the greater the variety of potential solutions. Diversity powers innovation.

Understanding diversity

When the Danish tax authorities hired a new project manager from a private insurance firm, they also hired an innovator. When he was charged with turning around customer service at a call centre, he could bring in an entire set of expertise and experience from running similar services, only in private business. Within a short time span, he and his team had helped reorganise work processes, train managers and introduce a learning organisation – resulting in better service, a radical drop in complaints and higher productivity. Introducing just that one person in a complex, difficult organisational environment was enough to trigger significant positive change. Wilson (1989, p 229) similarly points out that the very act of bringing in a manager with 'outside' experience can be enough to catalyse innovation.

Diversity can also happen on a larger organisational scale. After the 11 September terrorist attacks, the Danish police's secret service branch recruited a large number of professionals to increase the analytical capacity of the agency. Almost overnight, a professional culture dominated by vocationally trained police officers was mixed with the cultures of political scientists and social researchers. The expanded competence pool became a driver of innovation, opening the organisation up to external stakeholders and generating new methods of research, foresight and investigation (Bason, 2007).

Diversity is an expression of the variance in social and cultural identities between people in an organisation. Identity might be connected with gender, race, national origin, religion, age, profession and so on. One can distinguish between characteristics people are born with (gender, age, ethnic background, disabilities and so on), and characteristics that are more fluent and changeable over time, including education, religion, professional experience, language, personality, values, individual needs and so on. Diversity is therefore not only a question of visible differences, but also about a diverse group of people's relationship to notions of learning, innovation, creativity and value in an organisation (Brandi and Hildebrandt, 2003). There is no lack of research to confirm that organisations with a more diverse staff, including a diversity that reflects the surrounding society or marketplace, achieve better results than more homogeneous organisations. For instance, Harvard Business School's Thomas and Ely point out that 'organizations become effective in fulfilling their missions if employees are encouraged to tap their differences for creative ideas' (1996, p 122).

However, diversity may be hard to manage. And diversity may be hard to achieve in organisations that are very homogeneous, as many public sector organisations are, in terms of dimensions such as gender, age and profession. The homogeneous professional silos of government agencies may, on the one hand, be perceived as guarantees of legality and consistent case management – but, on the other hand, they may not be conducive to the divergence of ideas and solutions necessary for innovation (Mulgan, 2009).

A central feature of this book is the emphasis on design thinking and citizen involvement as enablers of co-creation and public sector innovation. To lead co-creation, competencies within 'classic' disciplines of public administration and professions must be combined with 'new' disciplines such as qualitative social research and design thinking (Kelley, 2005; Bason et al, 2009; Brown, 2009):

- *Public administration:* Understanding the dynamics and internal workings of politically governed organisations, possibly knowing the organisation(s) and internal stakeholders involved.
- *Design thinking:* The ability to leverage design thinking to orchestrate the key activities in the design process, and using applied design skills to visualise and prototype solutions.
- *Social research:* The skill set to conduct in-depth ethnographic research, applying the appropriate methods and tools to harvest insight in citizens' and other end-users' practices.
- *Profession:* Depending on the type of project, it might also be necessary to involve the relevant professionals (nurses, doctors, teachers, social workers) and possibly systems developers such as IT specialists, HR and communications in the core innovation team.

Figure 6.1: Public sector innovation competencies

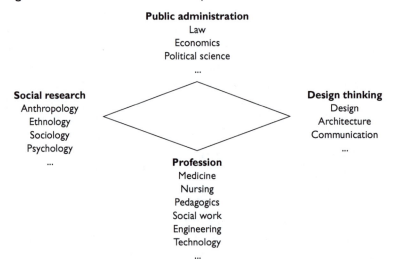

Public administration
Law
Economics
Political science
...

Social research
Anthropology
Ethnology
Sociology
Psychology
...

Design thinking
Design
Architecture
Communication
...

Profession
Medicine
Nursing
Pedagogics
Social work
Engineering
Technology
...

Source: Adapted from Bason et al (2009)

One can compare such transdisciplinary collaboration to a world-class football team, everyone possessing highly specialised and differentiated skills, moving at the same time, each doing their best (Kelley, 2005; Bannerjee, 2009). In this book's section on co-creation (Chapters 7–10) I will look closer into the features and processes that social researchers and designers can bring to the innovation process – and how that process might be orchestrated.

Strategic competence development

In the introduction to this book I touched on the changing demographics and the 'war for talent'. That war may have seemed far off during the depths of the financial and economic crisis, nearly freezing the outflow of staff from public sector organisations, and multiplying job applications to vacant public positions. However, in most modern economies, due to demographic change alone the public sector will be in dire need of new talent in the years to come; if the pace of economic growth increases again, the option of higher-paying jobs in the private sector will yet again become attractive. The public sector, therefore, faces a double challenge in leveraging talent to drive innovation: to increase its attractiveness to new talent in a competitive market with fewer young entrants, and to enhance the competence development of existing staff in the direction of more innovative ways of working.

The first challenge may be as much a question of branding as one of content. Public organisations offer meaningful jobs that often focus on making a substantial difference in people's lives. In fact, the kind of meaning and content that many private firms are desperate to convey to future staff in lavish employer branding schemes pretty much 'comes with the package' in the public sector. However, few public organisations are good at communicating it. And not least, the idea that welfare delivery and services also call for innovation is hardly a part of the communication. At MindLab, when we publicly advertised for new staff who would help 'Challenge the public sector from the inside', the ads generated hundreds of responses, many from private sector employees, a number of whom would state in interviews that the job description 'Simply spoke to me personally'. The energy and enthusiasm people can show for transforming public services when they are called to be part of such a mission is amazing.

The second question of how to strategically develop competencies for innovation within the public sector has to do with identifying which managers and staff are (or should be) in need of new tools and methods to orchestrate or take part in the innovation process. A coherent innovation strategy, which clarifies where innovation capacity needs to be enhanced, can be the platform against which competence development needs are assessed.

What could be the delivery modes for competence development? A powerful way of demonstrating what innovation and innovation competencies are about is, obviously, to be sure to involve the relevant internal stakeholders directly in the process of innovation and co-creation whenever relevant and possible. However, just 'show it, don't tell it' may not be enough. It can be difficult to drive a coherent innovation process while at the same time training the participants in all the theories, methodologies and tools involved. At MindLab, our experience is that civil servants who participate directly in innovation projects do come away with improved competencies – but not enough to be able to run the entire process themselves the next time around. More formal approaches, such as systematic training, may therefore be necessary. MindLab thus delivers a focused course on innovation and citizen involvement as an integrated part of three ministries' project management course, cutting across more than 15 departments and agencies, training in design thinking and ethnographic research methods. The course is supported by a permanent network of innovators and an online methods toolbox.

A similar approach is taken in Australia: as part of Victoria's VPS Innovation Action Plan (Victorian Public Service, 2010), the government is launching a host of initiatives to power competence development. The actions including *Innovation Transfer* (a secondment programme for VPS staff to the private and community sectors), *Innovation Skills* (an effort to embed innovation skills in recruitment, learning and development) and performance management. They are also creating an online *Innovation Toolbox* (a collection of innovation tools, resources and best practice guides), and finally the action plan establishes *Communities of Practice*, which are opportunities to form groups of mutual interest across the Victorian Public Service. In the UK, the Design Council has developed a mentoring and peer learning programme for public managers on design-led innovation, *Public Services by Design* (Design Council, 2009a). The Social Innovation Lab in the county of Kent (SILK) has pioneered a comprehensive set of tools (a 'methods deck') and an educational programme for public project managers. Other tools that can prove effective in supporting strategic competence development for innovation include ensuring a diversity of staff on innovation projects, leveraging e-learning and online tools, and organisation-wide talent development programmes.

Incentives

In Singapore, innovation incentives have been built into the performance management appraisal and reward scheme; it builds on a benchmarking system where the individual teacher can see his or her own performance against peers, and how to improve. For extraordinary performance, the monetary incentive is up to four months' salary. The evidence suggests that teachers' performance and innovative capability is enhanced through this incentive structure (Cabinet Office, 2009).

To many, the question of incentives is central to driving organisational change. For instance, the Finnish government declares in its innovation strategy that in support of public sector innovation activity, 'clear incentives linked to the Government's performance management' will be created (Finland Ministry of Employment and the Economy, 2008). And in their most recent review of innovation in the UK's central administration, the NAO points out that individual and organisational targets must create incentives that focus leaders and staff 'on continuous and radical improvement and which are outcome based (as opposed to prescribing how they do their jobs) so as to give flexibility in allowing for innovative responses' (2009).

Agreeing that incentives are probably important is, however, not the difficult part. The difficult part is to pinpoint what kinds of more extrinsic motivations might be created to help build innovation capacity. Not many countries have found the magic bullet, as Singapore's school administrators seem to have. What are the most powerful motivations in the public sector? Monetary rewards, or recognition and accelerated career development?

Dominating paradigms of what is considered 'good' can be powerful drivers of the kind of behaviour the organisation wants. For instance, if nurses are rewarded mainly for efficiency and not for providing care, no wonder policymakers find it difficult to provide a 'citizen-centred service'. By some measures, only a quarter of public institutions in Denmark have a clear incentive structure for employees to take part in innovation (Bason, 2007). That might imply that as many as three quarters of workplaces could have a *negative* incentive to innovate.

Some public organisations have successfully rewarded innovative staff with money. For instance, at the US General Services Administration, a handful of staff members were able to share a substantial cash award because they were instrumental in new solutions that generated savings of as much as $25 million (Eggers and Singh, 2009). However, such programmes would often not, for political reasons if nothing else, be possible in public sector organisations. They may also not be desirable, as support for public services, as well as public service cultures, are tightly connected with notions of neutrality, fairness and equity.

The problem is usually the opposite: that not only is the individual or organisation not rewarded for a substantial saving, but the typical response in the public sector would be for the funding authority to actually *take the entire saving* away as part of the regular procedure of the budgetary process. This leaves a negative incentive for innovation, as there is no sense in spending the time and energy achieving savings just to see it all disappear into the big black box of the Treasury.

Probably a balanced approach, where at least three key motivations are applied in concert, would be the most sensible:

- Building incentives for innovation into organisational, team and individual metrics and targets, thus embedding innovation as part of the regular performance review process alongside other relevant targets.
- Tying at least some part of salaries, reasonably sized bonuses and career development to the metrics, as many public organisations already do.
- Celebrating and valuing innovative thinking and results publicly, through awards and other forms of recognising departments, teams or individuals – awards such as Harvard's *Innovations in Government* and the *European Public Sector Awards* are good models.

A final incentive for innovation may be the simplest of all: there is nothing as demotivating as experiencing that your ideas are not recognised and taken seriously. True innovators are ultimately motivated by succeeding in taking on big challenges and tackling wicked problems. The ability of organisations and managers to not just support and invite new ideas, but to consistently pick them up and act on them, is perhaps the most powerful motivator of all.

How to do it

To many, the culture of public sector organisations is key to explaining why innovation in government is difficult. Barriers include a top management-driven approach to innovation and change, and a culture that punishes failure of all sorts. Large bureaucracies, whether they be central departments, agencies or institutions like hospitals, schools and care homes, are often characterised by homogeneous staff with strong professional identities, but perhaps a lack of exposure and openness to other perspectives. Competence development is rarely very strategic, and the incentives to contribute to innovation are sometimes meagre or even negative.

This chapter has addressed how modern work organisation is a powerful enabler of innovation, also in the public sector. We've seen a number of approaches to building innovation capacity through people and culture, dealing with risk and managing diversity, skills and incentives actively to promote innovative behaviour. Public managers must pay special attention to four sets of efforts.

Employee involvement and innovation culture

Employee-driven innovation is fostered by modern work organisations. From state agencies to day-care institutions, employees hold a massive potential for submitting new creative ideas and solutions – if only they are asked. It is the public manager's responsibility to systematically involve the staff in the strategic development of the organisation and to create a culture where inquiry and involvement is natural – also across professional boundaries and organisational silos. The public manager must ask questions such as:

- *To what extent is everyone aware that they too can contribute to innovation?*
- *Are we systematically harvesting ideas from across the organisation, and how do we ensure that they are taken seriously and transformed into real organisational change and value?*

Diversity

A diversity of educational backgrounds, age, gender and ethnicity are – if well managed – drivers of innovation in all types of organisations. Generally speaking, public sector organisations are not very diverse. They can most likely boost their innovation capacity significantly by taking a much more proactive approach to increasing diversity in a broad sense, reflecting more of the surrounding society in their staff make-up. In addition to the range of 'classic' diversity parameters, recruiting individuals with design and ethnographic skills can be strong innovation drivers. Key questions are:

- *Is the composition of our staff conducive to innovation? If no, which profiles and skills might we need?*
- *Are we actively seeking to benefit from diversity by inviting everyone to be part of the creative process?*

Strategic competence development

The effort to attract, retain and develop staff with the right skills and competencies in the face of a renewed 'war for talent' is crucial for the future ability of public sector organisations to become more innovative. Taking a more active and creative approach to their activities and making it visible might in itself make many public organisations more attractive to future talent:

- *Do we have an attractive brand, and are we able to recruit the employee profiles we need to become a high performing and innovative organisation?*

Innovation incentives

Most public employees haven't chosen their careers because of the fat salary. However, experience shows that employees in public organisations can be motivated by results-based salary and other benefits, provided that the incentive model is the right one and, probably, team-based. In the US, some public organisations provide cash rewards. In Denmark studies have shown positive results from using performance-related pay based on group outcomes among social workers. There is no excuse not to work actively to create positive incentives for generating ideas and making innovation happen. So we have to ask:

- *What are the positive incentives in our organisations to embrace a higher level of risk and help generate and drive through new ideas and solutions?*
- *Can we do more to make it attractive for employees and managers to contribute actively to foster innovation and positive change?*
- *How might we in concrete terms celebrate when employees have taken on big, audacious challenges and made a significant attempt at addressing them?*

Part Three
Co-creation

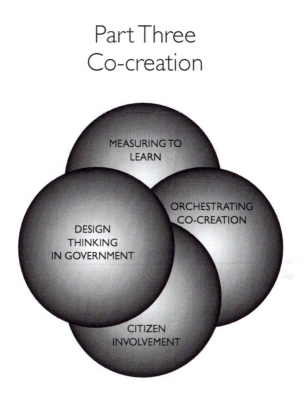

MEASURING TO
LEARN

ORCHESTRATING
CO-CREATION

DESIGN
THINKING
IN GOVERNMENT

CITIZEN
INVOLVEMENT

7

Design thinking in government

'Design thinking can remind public servants to ask the obvious: What's it like to check in to a hospital, call the police or collect the dole?' (Tim Brown, CEO and President, IDEO in Design Council, 2009a)

When the City Council of Sunderland, UK, engaged with LiveWork, a service design company to find new approaches to helping economically inactive people into work, they also engaged in an entirely different development process. Over the course of the project, the designers spent three months following 12 people to gain deep insight into their lives, and more than 280 people were involved in idea-development sessions. Building on design approaches such as ethnographic research, service journeys, fast experimentation and prototyping, LiveWork helped the city council identify a range of possible solutions that could get people more efficiently on a path back towards work. Their key solution became a platform that built on the resources within the existing local network of community organisations in fields such as mental health, drug rehabilitation and caring. LiveWork found that these community groups already had relationships with the citizens in need – relationships that could be leveraged not just at the beginning, but at every stage of citizens' path back to work. The organisations could function as an 'activity coalition', serving as mentors, providing resources and helping citizens along each step of their journey in collaboration with established Jobcentre Plus employment services and back into work (Livework, 2006; Gillinson et al, 2010).

The application of *design thinking* – the intellectual and practical foundation of the co-creation process – is expanding rapidly in the public sector. From the design of open learning environments in French schools to transforming staff–patient interaction and designing bugs out of UK hospitals to reshaping services for injured Danish workers, design thinking is a core driver of innovation in government. Scholars and practitioners alike have claimed that design is the 'midwife of innovation' (iLipinar et al, 2009, Design Council, 2009a).

This chapter introduces the co-creation section of this book, which consists of four interrelated themes: design thinking, citizen involvement, the co-creation process and learning through measurement. The present chapter considers how design and, more specifically, design thinking offers a new approach to leading innovation in the public sector. It asks:

- What is design, and what is its relevance to public sector innovation?
- What are the key characteristics of design thinking, and how does it relate to other perspectives on design?
- What might be the central credos of design thinking in government?
- Are there challenges in applying design thinking within the public sector, and, if so, what are they?

Design, innovation and the public sector

In October 2009, the *Wall Street Journal* did something rather unusual: it published a book review about design. Within a few months, three new management books on the potential of *design thinking* had hit the bookstores, apparently spurring the editors to think that this was something that the world of business needed to know about. Roberto Verganti's *Design-driven Innovation* (2009), Tim Brown's *Change by Design* (2009) and Hartmut Esslinger's *A Fine Line* (2009) all argue that applying the intellectual and practical tools of design is an efficient means of paving the way to innovation. These books, along with Rotman School's Roger Martin's *The Opposable Mind* (2007) and *The Design of Business* (2009), reflect a strong current in the business sector, where design thinking and design-led innovation is increasingly recognised as a key driver of competitiveness and value-creation.

Advocates of design even have the numbers to prove it. A study by the UK Design Council showed that design-aware companies outperformed the market by 200% over a 10-year period (Dubhthaigh and Barter, 2006). As mentioned in Chapter 6, the Design Council has applied its tried and tested design tools by acting as advisor to not just enterprises, but also to the public sector, proposing that *public services by design* are a new route to innovation in government (Design Council, 2009a; Fora, 2009). Likewise, Sitra, the Finnish Innovation Fund, has created the Helsinki Design Lab to help tackle real-world problems faced by government, by bringing designers together with public sector content experts.

To many public sector employees, design is still about the creation of 'stuff'. However, most would probably also agree that strategies, organisations and systems are designed; that services and policies are designed. This would be in the vein of Herbert Simon, who in his 1969 *The Sciences of the Artificial* proposed that 'design' is opposite to 'science' as it is concerned with the artificial, as opposed to the natural, world. Simon stated that 'everyone designs who devises courses of action aimed at changing existing situations into preferred ones' (quoted in Kimbell, 2010). Designs are, thus, attempts at solving problems – or, as the midwife metaphor suggests, at delivering something new into the world. A design might solve the problem of how to contain a liquid in a smart container, or it could tackle the challenge of getting reliable foetal heart-rate monitors to the developing world. Increasingly, designers find themselves creating fewer products and more social solutions.

In fact, a hand-charged foetal heart-rate monitor was a recent winner of the world's largest design prize, the INDEX Award by a Copenhagen-based organisation that leads the way towards the new shape of design. The motto of INDEX is 'design to improve life' (Index, 2009). In the same vein, industrial designer Emily Pilloton, founder and CEO of the US-based design firm Project H, encourages designers to shift their focus from consumerism to help create societal change, saying that designers 'need to stop talking big and start doing good; to put the problem-solving skills on which we pride ourselves to work on some of the biggest global issues; to design for health, poverty, homelessness, education, and more' (Pilloton, 2009).

As John Heskett, professor at the School of Design at Hong Kong Polytechnic University, says, design 'is the human capacity to shape and make our environments in ways that satisfy our needs and give meaning to our lives' (Heskett, 2002). Verganti (2009) condenses this definition even further, saying that 'Design is the creation of meaning'.

Liz Sanders and Pieter Stappers (2008) sum up this underlying shift in the role of design as a shift from 'traditional' design disciplines to 'emerging' design disciplines.

Given that the role of government in people's lives often is to create meaningful change, whether in the social services, education or health, this shift in the design industry offers us something important: the approaches and tools that can help us consciously create the meaning

Table 7.1: The new shape of design

Traditional design disciplines	Emerging design disciplines
Visual communication design	Design for experiencing
Interior space design	Design for emotion
Product design	Design for interacting
Information design	Design for sustainability
Architecture	Design for serving
Planning	Design for transforming

Source: Sanders and Stappers (2008)

and value we want citizens, businesses and other actors in society to experience.

Defining design thinking

As should be clear, design comes in many different shapes and sizes. How does design thinking fit into the picture? Bill Moggridge, co-founder of the design firm IDEO and now director of Cooper-Hewitt National Design Museum, suggests a hierarchy of design that distinguishes between the following levels (Moggridge, 2009):

- *General awareness of design*, which concerns how we as individuals relate to design in our own lives.
- *Specialist design skills*, which has to do with the design discipline and the methods of educated designers, such as graphic design.
- *Design thinking*, which is concerned with the design process and how it can guide collaboration across different disciplines.
- *Design research*, which is the academic subject of researching the world of design.

The emphasis in the following is mainly on design thinking. It addresses a number of the key tenets of the emerging design disciplines that Sanders and Stappers (2008) highlight. Although there is no uniformly accepted definition of design thinking, at least two interrelated approaches may be pinpointed (Kimbell, 2010).

First, design thinking can be characterised as the discipline of melding the sensibility and methods of a designer with what is technologically feasible to meet people's real-world needs (Brown, 2008; Design Council, 2009a). This definition highlights the tools and practices of forming teams, running specific design projects, powering organisations, and shaping innovative new products or services, much like LiveWork did for Sunderland City Council.

Second, design thinking can be viewed as an 'attitude' (Boland and Collopy, 2004) or a way of reasoning. As I discussed in Chapters 2 and 6, Martin (2009) characterises design thinking as the ability to manage and move between the opposing disciplines of *analysis*, involving rigour and 'algorithmic' exploitation on the one hand, and *synthesis*, involving interpretation and exploration of 'mysteries' on the other. At the heart of design thinking is, thus, the balancing, or bridging, of two cognitive styles: the analytical-logical mindset that characterises most large organisations and professional bureaucracies, and the more interpretative, intuitive mindset that characterises the arts and creative professions. As we saw in the introductory chapter to the book, where public servants interacted with artist Olafur Eliasson on climate change strategies, interesting things happen when these two mindsets enter into a conversation. In that context, Martin highlights the capacity for *abductive reasoning* – detecting and following a 'hunch' about a possible solution, bridging the gap between analysis and synthesis. In Martin's view, such 'integrative' thinking is the essential core of design thinking (Martin, 2007, 2009).

Although these two definitions taken at face value appear different, on further examination they mostly support each other. Behind the practical orchestration of 'design thinking projects' lies a set of principles and a style of thinking that Tim Brown also acknowledges explicitly, referring to Martin's *The Opposable Mind*: 'design thinking is neither art nor science nor religion. It is the capacity, ultimately, for *integrative* thinking' (Brown, 2009, p 85). Likewise, Martin takes Brown's view of design thinking to heart and applies it as a key definition (2009, p 62). The distinction between the two definitions, blending design practices with a cognitive style, is therefore quite blurred. I will treat them in this book as broadly in tune with each other; as expressions of complementary perspectives.

Table 7.2: Design thinking: Bridging the gap

Analysis (Splitting)	Synthesis (Putting together)
Rational	Emotional
Logical	Intuitive
Deductive	Inductive
Solutions	Paradigms, platforms
'Thinking it through'	Rapid prototyping (think through doing)
Single discipline	Multiple disciplines, T-shape
Elegance	Impact, value, diffusion

Sources: Inspired by Bannerjee (2009), Brown (2009) and Martin (2009)

Just as we saw the opposites of *strategic planning* and *strategic innovation* in the former section of this book, the opposite characteristics of analysis and synthesis are striking. It is also striking how clearly most public sector organisations do not allow for many of the elements in the right-hand column.

Introducing design thinking to the public sector is, thus, likely to be a challenge. Lawyers, economists and political scientists are expert analysts, but rarely comfortable with more interpretive thinking styles. Emotion and intuition is hardly recognised as a basis for decision-making. Nor should it perhaps be, in itself. But much decision-making – especially at the political level where it is fuelled by the dynamics of the media – is in fact often quite intuitive and emotional, even though we may not like to admit it. As management thinker Henry Mintzberg (2009) has pointedly argued, 'judgement' is, at the end of the day, what managers have to rely on. Second, the point with design thinking is not to throw analysis or logic away, but to consciously balance the two modes as part of the innovation process. As Roger Martin describes convincingly in *The Opposable Mind,* the test of a first-rate intelligence is, in Nobel Prize-winning author F. Scott Fitzgerald's words, 'the ability to hold two opposing ideas in the mind at the same time and still be able to function' (Martin, 2007). This is a competence and an approach that needs to be much better understood and practised by public managers at all levels.

A model of the design thinking process

What does the design thinking process look like? To design new solutions that reach the desired results, we need to deliberately orchestrate a process that captures the contributions of both mindsets of design thinking, and shifts from the present to the future. This implies an iterative process encompassing the following dimensions:

- *Knowing* the present in *concrete* terms through design research, often applying the tools of ethnographers, harvesting deep knowledge about people's lives.
- *Analysing* the present state of affairs by structuring our knowledge and generating the abstract analytical categories that help us see individual dimensions or parts.
- *Synthesising* from the different parts to potential new, holistic solutions, interpreting the findings and generating a divergence of ideas and concepts, shaping possible solutions that take account of complexities at an (abstract) systems level.
- *Creating* the prototypes of solutions that can be tested and assessed for their practical usage, and implemented.

For each overall dimension in such a process, there can be a number of discrete steps and methodologies. For instance, when LiveWork helped Sunderland City Council create new solutions to help people back to work, they started by taking an extremely concrete look at the everyday practices of the people in question – following 12 of them closely over a long period of time. Based on this process, LiveWork analysed the rich ethnographic data and other inputs, applying a more analytical mode, trying to reach a better understanding of the present state by understanding its individual parts. LiveWork then involved hundreds of people in interpreting, or synthesising, the information into distinct findings. Finally, new service solutions were created with people, leading not just to a new system design, but also to the discrete activities that could power the redesigned service journey in practice. I will describe this design-thinking process and its concrete methodology in detail in Chapter 9, characterising it as a process of co-creation.

Figure 7.1: The design thinking process

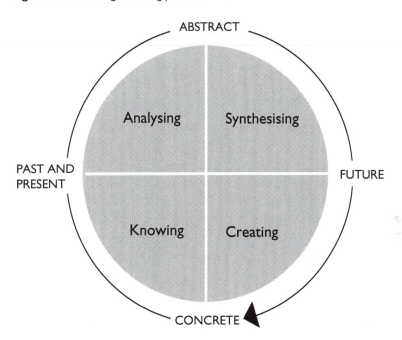

Since its application within the public sector is very recent, there is not yet much hard evidence of how the design-thinking process works. For instance, there seems to be no consensus on when and how to most appropriately bring end-users (citizens, businesses) into the mix. As Brown (2009) has pointed out, there is no precise road map. Instead, 'There are useful starting points and helpful landmarks along the way', and the process is 'best thought of as a system of overlapping spaces rather than a sequence of orderly steps' (Brown 2009, p 16). Likewise, the optimal configuration of transdisciplinary collaboration between various public professions, as part of the design process, is not very well understood.

However, there is a rapidly growing body of convincing case examples from public sector innovation labs and social innovators such as La 27e Région, the Innovation Unit, SILK, Helsinki Design Lab and MindLab, and from service design firms such as IDEO, ThinkPublic, Engine, LiveWork and Participle of the UK, and Designit, 1508 and Via Design of Denmark. There is increasingly a proven track record of design thinking adding real value, spanning from government agencies such as the UK National Health Service to the US Transportation Security Administration and even to the Danish Prison Service. International institutions such as the United Nations, the European Commission and the OECD are showing a rapidly growing awareness of the potential to both public and private organisations. Design thinking in government looks set to stay.

Four credos

How does the definition of design thinking and the design process translate into key principles and actions? In the spirit of the US designer and social innovator Emily Pilloton, founder and CEO of Project H Design, who is committed to creating 'impactful design that enables lives', I will highlight four *credos* of design thinking that help capture the essence of how the approach can help drive public sector innovation.

Credo 1: See everything as an experiment

What if government viewed any new intervention in the world as an experiment? In spite of the growth of evaluation practices and 'evidence-based policy', and in spite of elaborate implementation strategies, plans and systems, do we ever *really* know in advance whether a new public policy or service is going to work in a highly specific context? If we don't, we involuntarily end up experimenting with the entire population (Harris and Albury, 2009). Might we instead have to learn in smarter ways, reshaping stage-gate projects into iterative and more open-ended, reflexive learning processes (Senge, 2006)? 'Even if your ambition is big, make it small', said one noted design thinker at a seminar. Public organisations must become much better at embracing the notion of 'failing forward': practising and experimenting deliberately in small scale, making the 'smart errors' that feed learning. As Tim Brown says, 'fail early to succeed sooner' (Brown, 2009).

It is one thing to allow experimentation in the early innovation process, but quite another to view daily practice the way an experiment would be viewed. Google, the information search giant, almost always launches new products, such as its email software Gmail, in 'beta'. In tech language this means it is not yet the final version, and customer input is welcomed to help improve the final product. What might be the consequence of viewing all government programmes as 'beta' versions that should continually be refined, or even regularly redefined?

Clearly, as discussed in Chapter 3, in a political environment it can be difficult to allow time and space for small-scale prototyping and iteration. Public managers need to insist to politicians that it makes sense to do at least some rudimentary real-world testing before major programmes are implemented. In addition, they must secure resources and competencies to actually do the prototyping – which, incidentally, they did in the LiveWork project in Sunderland. One approach could be to collaborate with social innovators, who, as was discussed earlier, may have a wider margin to experiment, at least in the early stages of the innovation process.

Credo 2: Challenge the status quo

Former partner in the consultancy CPH Design Anna Kirah calls it 'whydeology': when you confront a problem and examine possible solutions, keep asking 'Why?'. When you run out of things to ask 'why' about, you've probably found the solution you are looking for (Kirah, 2009). Using the word 'why' is not something government officials are particularly trained at. Rather, the instinct of most of us is to use the word 'because'.

Challenging the status quo is also about allowing ourselves to imagine a different future. Because it is future-oriented, design thinking helps us ask questions like 'What if …?' and 'Might we …?' (Kelley, 2005; Brown, 2009). By reframing the question, it guides us to make sure we are doing the right thing (solving the right problem) and not just doing things right (applying existing tools to solve what we think is the problem). Because design as a discipline is about solving problems within constraints, focusing on outcomes, many designers almost automatically begin a new task or project by challenging conventional thinking. And this is where innovation begins. If one asks a designer to design a chair, she will be likely to suggest that instead she designs a 'sitting instrument'. In the new Copenhagen Metro stations, this has meant that there are no chairs or benches, but instead simple, slanted structures that you can lean comfortably on for a few minutes until the next train arrives.

Credo 3: Value the citizen

As a general rule, designers are concerned with practical problems and practical uses. Because the design process starts with the concrete in the present, and similarly ends with the concrete in the future, design is concerned with people, practices and their context. What do people do today, what seems to work and what doesn't? What are the narratives that people express when they are invited to share their own experience of public services? What could be done to change things, and how would a new solution, product or service function in practice? Placing people's wants, needs and situations at the centre of the creative process is a powerful way to generate the insights that allow us to create with people, not for them (Sanders and Stappers, 2008). Creating with people enables us to understand how their place within the social fabric can be leveraged as a positive force for change. As Gillinson et al (2010) point out, there are at least two benefits of focusing on people, and seeing them at the heart of social networks: first, it builds people's social relationships into the heart of the way services are designed, in the recognition that 'it is the quality of human interactions that make them effective'. Second, it views people's relationships not only as a constraint, but also as a valuable resource. At MindLab, a project we did with the Danish Enterprise and Construction Agency to identify how entrepreneurs with high-growth potential might be helped to accelerate their business development proved this point: the entrepreneurs had no relationship or interest in receiving assistance from the public system of business support (it was, perhaps unfairly, viewed as uncool and without sufficient expertise). However, they were keen to listen to their more successful peers. We prototyped various ideas and concepts, testing them in face-to-face sessions with the entrepreneurs, and arrived at a solution they found valuable: to let government facilitate a system of networks among entrepreneurs that would help them leverage these relationships, and build new ones, where younger start-ups with high potential could benefit from peer mentoring and coaching. Two such nationwide networks were tendered and established in 2010.

As I will explore in more detail in Chapter 8, designers are often assisted by ethnographers and anthropologists (some label themselves *design anthropologists*) to harvest detailed qualitative data from people through fieldwork such as observing, participating, probing and interviewing. This type of ethnographic research is only part of the co-creation process, but it can be an eye-opener as it helps us focus on the subjective, qualitative and emotional factors that are often the most important in driving outcomes. At MindLab, we call this a process of obtaining 'qualified inspiration'.

Credo 4: Be concrete

Applying more specialist design skills in the innovation process helps keep it concrete. Designers can visualise and build physical or virtual prototypes to make problems and potential solutions tangible. For instance, design consultancy Zago helped the United Nations headquarters in New York visualise the meaning of the CO_2 per capita figures in the reporting from the UN Panel on Climate Change. To make the relative CO_2 production tangible to visitors to the UN headquarters, Zago displayed the per capita production of selected countries as beanbags. Needless to say, countries like the United States and China were endowed with giant (9 ft tall) beanbags, whilst countries with lesser output per head were displayed with beanbags the visitors could easily sit on. Zago was also instrumental in helping former US Vice President Al Gore with the powerful and illustrative graphics in his documentary *An Inconvenient Truth* (Zago, 2010).

In a perhaps even more difficult context in terms of the level of abstraction, MindLab helped the Danish tax ministry visualise the concept of 'how citizens perceive their legal rights'. The task was to gain a deeper understanding of how citizens subjectively feel about factors relating to the tax authorities like fairness, equality before the law, transparency and security. We commissioned three contemporary artists to each create a work that could trigger reflection and dialogue amongst citizens, and between citizens and civil servants. The finished works were used as visual prototypes and presented for a group of citizens in a facilitated art reception, where the project team could harvest their impressions and dialogue. The output was used for reshaping how the ministry measures citizens' perception of legal rights, and today one of the works (a video installation) is part of the curriculum for training new tax and customs staff. Using art to drive creativity and innovation was, incidentally, not new to the ministry, which had previously experimented with artistic methods as an internal development tool (Danish Ministry of Taxation, 2007).

The power of visualising sizes, relationships and impacts in a different form than Excel spreadsheets should not be underestimated. By anchoring abstract figures, relationships and practices in the shared experience of something concrete, visualisation enables exactly the kind of transdisciplinary collaboration that is central to co-creation. It also enables better dialogue and consensus-building between professionals and citizens. An example of a concrete and highly effective design tool for capturing both analytic and interpretive modes is the *service journey*, which, amongst others, LiveWork used in their work for Sunderland City Council. Essentially a sequential map of the individual steps and interactions in a citizen's 'journey' through a government service process, service journeys focus both on the 'objective' efforts made by the system to conduct service and regulation, and on the key subjective emotional experiences of citizens on their travels. Service journeys are described in more detail in the following chapters.

Paradoxically, while the population and, to a significant extent, politicians are highly influenced by such visual and physical tools, bureaucrats hardly ever produce them as part of their own policy or service development process. At most, graphic designers are called in for final communication of the result. That misses the point. Visualisation, both graphic and video, is a powerful creative tool throughout the design process (Ylirisku and Buur, 2007).

These four credos are only a first stab at trying to demonstrate what potential design thinking might hold for government. Although more organisations are beginning to embed design thinking in public services, we still have a long way to go.

Challenges to design in government

In spite of the arguments in favour of design thinking in government, a number of challenges and barriers remain. One is the question of whether design thinking is simply a fad. As Lucy Kimbell of Oxford's Saïd School of Business has pointed out, 'In popular culture, everyone might be a designer but in management practice, it seems, everyone should be a design thinker' (2010). Kimbell proposes to take the 'thinking' out of the design discussion and focus more empirically on how design is practised ('design-as-practice'), seeing design as a situated and distributed accomplishment in which a number of things, people and their doings and sayings are implicated.

However we define it, design as a practice in government has consequences both for public servants and for designers. The first obvious challenge is for public managers and project managers who are charged with innovation projects to start considering themselves not (only) as civil servants, but as design thinkers. What will it take for an experienced policymaker in central government, or a head nurse in a hospital, to embrace that role? What are the tools, skills and competencies required, and how do they fit in the broader context of driving innovation in government? People with a formal design background themselves may have difficulty working transdisciplinarily, understanding sufficiently clearly how their own skill set matches with those of lawyers, economists, teachers or health professionals. Designers (also) need 'T-shaped' competencies, combining the 'vertical' ability to deeply master a skill with the 'horizontal' ability to connect and collaborate effectively with other professions (Kelley, 2005; Brown, 2009). The designer has to be comfortable working not with other designers, but with people with a very different mode of working than themselves. Another dimension, as Kimbell (2010) points out, is that if design must be viewed as a practice situated in a concrete context, then designers working in government will encounter a relatively unfamiliar territory of law, bureaucracy, administrative processes and the political nature of decision-making. It may be the trained designers who are first to lose their patience with the drawn-out and seemingly endless timelines of public sector decision-making processes. How do we keep motivation, enthusiasm and momentum going in such an environment?

Another challenge is for the project manager-designer to shift from the more familiar role of being 'the solver of problems', to being the one who empowers others to do the solving. 'Designers in the future will make the tools for non-designers to use to express themselves creatively' (Sanders and Stappers, 2008, p. 10). As I will explore further later in this section of the book, the co-creation process is essentially *orchestrated*, not led or managed. The designer, and for that matter the public manager, must perceive herself more as a coach or facilitator, and less as a director of the process.

Designers must also recognise that wicked problems are, by definition, not finally 'solved' anyway. Likewise, designs are played out long after the designers exit the process. In her recent work on design, Lucy Kimbell introduces a second perspective that she labels 'design-in-practice', and which addresses this point – designs, even when they are physical objects, keep on 'living' in other contexts and uses: 'When the designers have finished their work, and the engineers and manufacturers have finished theirs, and the marketers and retailers have finished theirs, and the customer or end-user has engaged with a product or service artifact, the work of design is still not over' (Kimbell, 2010). Kimbell's argument is that through their engagement with a product or service over time, users continue to be involved in constituting what the design is. This of course raises the question of how the designer can help make the design as valuable as possible throughout this 'downstream' process. This argument is strikingly close to Eggers and O'Leary's (2009) argument that we need to integrate policy design with implementation.

Applying design thinking to public services and policymaking is not going to be easy. It is still considered radical in most countries. But if public managers really, *really* took the four credos to heart, it could be the beginning of a revolution in government.

How to do it

Introducing design thinking in government is likely to be a long-term process. Although more and more examples are emerging from the work of leading design firms, social innovators, public agencies and innovation labs, we are only witnessing the beginning of what could become a paradigm shift in how we conduct public sector reform. However, public managers not only lack the skills to start practising design to power new policy and service innovation, they lack the basic awareness that design has something to offer. Placing design thinking, and design practice, more squarely at the heart of how government is shaped in the 21st century is, therefore, first and foremost an exercise in creating a consciousness of what it is, and what might be its potential. The following elements could help pave the way.

Educate in design thinking

In addition to a more general awareness of the public sector innovation landscape, project managers must be educated in design thinking. The more experimental, iterative, challenging, people-centred and tangible nature of design processes must become a part of the core curriculum of how we educate project managers in public organisations. More fundamentally, together with the basic innovation terminology introduced in Chapter 2, we should build curricula on design thinking and co-creation into all levels of education that lead to public sector careers: executive programmes, graduate and undergraduate modules in public administration, and in training for professionals in key fields such as health care, education and social work. In the UK, the Design Council has launched a mentoring and coaching programme for public managers, and the NHS Institute for Innovation and Improvement has undertaken to train professionals systematically in innovation processes, drawing extensively on the ideas behind design thinking. Likewise, in Denmark, MindLab runs a biannual, cross-ministerial project management course in citizen-centred innovation that draws heavily on design principles. As a public manager the question becomes:

- *Have I articulated why and how design thinking can be an appropriate way of helping us drive our innovation efforts?*
- *Do my staff have access to training or skills development in the field of design, for instance service design?*

Institutionalise design thinking

The principles of design thinking should be built more explicitly into the project models that are used by public sector organisations. Formal process models for 'how we do things', giving a mutual frame of reference as to where the team is in the process and what is the activity, can be a helpful tool to underpin transdisciplinary work. Another approach is to create and disseminate method descriptions to project teams:

- *To what extent might we institutionalise design thinking in the formal processes we already have in place?*
- *Could we inspire our staff through creating (or even better, sharing existing) tools to assist them running design-led activities?*

Recruit and source

Designers should increasingly be hired to be part of project teams on a range of assignments other than 'traditional' graphical work and product design. To the extent that more public organisations establish innovation labs or dedicated innovation teams, designers should be a natural part of the competence structure, bringing 'emerging' design skills into play. Finally, public organisations should be much more open to include strategic design firms on their shortlists when they tender development projects and research:

- *Could it be helpful for us to hire designers as part of our effort to create a more innovative organisation? If so, how do we ensure that they will thrive and become part of our professional environment?*
- *Have I as a public manager considered whether service design firms or design researchers could be relevant bidders the next time we tender for a new development project?*

Design thinking is a way of understanding the foundations of co-creation. Citizen involvement is a way to power the process, gaining insight into how people live their lives, and how that matters to public services. That is the theme of Chapter 8.

8

Citizen involvement

'Suspend judgement and connect to wonder.' (C. Otto Scharmer, Senior Lecturer, MIT, 2007, p 133)

'You have to be healthy to be able to manage a work injury case.' This statement by an injured citizen became a significant trigger of change for the Danish Board of Industrial Injuries. The agency is by any standard a very professionally run government agency. It has a sharply formulated strategy, effective performance management systems, has digitised much of its internal and external processes, and implemented lean management, speeding up case flows and increasing case quality. However, when the agency in collaboration with MindLab conducted in-depth ethnographic field studies of four citizens with a work injury, observing their meetings with state and local government officials, and videotaping citizens at home telling their case stories from A to Z, the results were surprising. Some of the agency's service efforts had the reverse of the intended effect: an on-site 'travel team' that could settle cases quickly was perceived by citizens as confusing and made them uncomfortable. A temporary payment to offset the often quite long case duration triggered frustration, because citizens mistakenly thought it constituted the final insurance settlement. With the citizens' permission, the Board not only used the video footage to analyse and create solutions to the specific problems citizens experienced, by reorganising service processes and communications, they also used the video clips as a burning platform for additional systemic change throughout the organisation, engaging both top executives and front-line staff in the process.

When civil servants experience first-hand what citizens experience, from the citizens' point of view, it is often a significant eye-opener (Bason, 2007; Bate and Robert, 2007; Bason et al, 2009). Even the most professional and service-minded organisations can have major blind spots for the simple reason that they are not who they serve. Placing citizens at the centre of the innovation process is to see one's efforts from the outside in (Boyle et al, 2010). It is to recognise that citizens are experts in their own lives and nobody – *nobody* – else can claim that role. But it requires that we suspend our own judgement of who people are and how they experience the world, and allow ourselves to connect to the wonder of personal experience, truly seeing it for the first time (Scharmer, 2007). This is what I call professional empathy.

Over the last decade or so, new approaches to placing the citizen's perspective at the centre of government innovation have shown an ability to open the eyes of public managers to the reality 'out there'. Public organisations, such as the NHS and the county of Kent in the UK, the French Regions, US federal agencies, and Danish central government, have started bringing in anthropologists and designers, who represent two very different skill sets, but which supplement each other in capturing the perspective of end-users. Bureaucrats are also venturing out to see real-world practices for themselves. For instance, the European Commission's Directorate-General for Innovation and Entrepreneurship in Brussels requires that managers spend one week every year at a private enterprise, to get a first-hand impression of daily life in the kinds of companies that they support and regulate. At MindLab, we make a point of always bringing our civil servant colleagues with us when we conduct field research, immersing them in the context of the services they regulate or deliver.

This chapter considers the theory and practice of citizen involvement in the innovation process. Building further on the principles and *credos* of design thinking from the previous chapter, we will examine the following themes:

- What value can citizen involvement bring to the innovation process?
- What is 'professional empathy'?
- What are the three myths of citizen involvement?
- How can citizen involvement be organised and conducted in practice through disciplines such as ethnography and design anthropology?

What is the value of citizen involvement?

Some of the key insights that conscious, explicit citizen involvement can give decision-makers, and which can be powerful drivers of innovation, are illustrated by these questions:

- *What is valuable?* A better understanding of which elements of current or future public interventions are valuable to citizens in terms of service and outcomes, identifying the key resources and drivers that may impact behaviour change, and pinpointing the relevant contribution(s) of government.

- *Can less be more?* Insight into what might not be valuable to citizens at all. We can thus either terminate existing services, or avoid creating new ones that would have negligible effect.
- *How do we create synergy?* Helping decision-makers see how the regulations, programmes and interventions for which they are responsible fit into the context of people's lives, and how they relate to the host of other interactions they have with other public organisations, businesses, family, communities and so on. This can enable the creation of much smarter, 'holistic' interventions at systems level, where the interplay between public bodies (and other actors) is truly experienced as 'joined-up' from the perspective of citizens or businesses.
- *Where is co-production possible?* As will be discussed later, citizen involvement can help identify where and how citizens or communities themselves have the resources, motivation and skills to undertake part of the job that government is currently carrying out, or wishes to be carried out.

These types of value are triggered from the direct, concrete insight into how citizens live their lives and experience their interactions (or lack of interactions) with government in that context (Parker and Heapy, 2006; Parker and Parker, 2007; Bate and Robert, 2007; Bason et al, 2009). As Gillinson et al (2010), amongst others, have pointed out, it is often by taking departure in the relationships with citizens, and redefining them, that public organisations can create more radical efficiencies, generating better outcomes at lower cost. Interestingly, it is striking how little it often takes to generate the 'professional empathy' that is the basis for such insight.

About professional empathy

How could the involvement of as few as four citizens become a powerful change agent for the Board of Industrial Injuries? Answer: by bringing the rich context and reality of actual citizens, real people, into the heart of the organisation. Exactly because the type of knowledge that the video footage introduced allowed for interpretation, for an emotional connection and for an intuitive *recognition of*, or *knowing*, what is right.

Involving citizens in the innovation process is, thus, not about increasing democratic participation or legitimacy through the act of involvement in itself. It is about finding better solutions to achieve politically defined visions of the future. Even though citizens may often be very motivated to contribute their time and expertise, and indeed experience that their participation is meaningful and empowering, that is not the main point. The point is that public sector organisations desperately need citizens' participation to *better understand what they experience, how their experience could be improved and their behaviour might be changed.*

Managers and staff of government departments and agencies are hardly representative of the population. But they may very well forget that. As a manager in a UK central government agency said to a group of visiting policymakers from Denmark, 'If you ask our colleagues here who they think about when they develop a new service, the answer would be "a white male in his mid-forties, with a higher education, living in London"'. Civil servants are rarely themselves users of the services they supply or regulate. Few social case workers have tried being an alcoholic, homeless or having a handicapped child. Not many officials who regulate or service private businesses have ever run an enterprise. At a presentation I gave to a group of health professionals in managing positions, many of them said they knew what it was like to be a patient because they had been ill and used the hospital too, at some point. I then asked how many of them had tried to be a Somali immigrant female patient with no Danish language skills? The group, consisting only of ethnic Danish persons, fell silent.

What we need to know as public innovators is: Who are we developing this for, how do they live their lives, what is important to them, and what motivations, practices, relationships and resources do they have that may help or impede the outcomes we are seeking to achieve? We also want to know: Have they themselves identified solutions that we could learn from or implement directly?.

How do we find the answers to such questions? First, we must experience first-hand what it is like to be at the receiving end of public services. As C. Otto Scharmer, a Senior Lecturer at MIT and author of *Theory U* (2007), points out, managers in both public and private organisations usually 'outsource the legwork' of knowing citizens or customers to external consultants or researchers. There are core areas, including innovation, where government staff themselves must be a highly active part of the process; they must learn through their own first-hand experience, not through someone else's. Without a direct connection to the context of a situation or interaction, we cannot see and feel the real issues, problems and potentials (Scharmer, 2007). For instance, when MindLab helped civil servants venture into the field to better understand how business people subjectively experienced administrative burdens, they obtained a first-hand emotional connection with what it means. When a senior accountant in a company broke down in tears in front of the research team because the interview triggered memories of a traumatic experience of government tax control 10 years earlier, it helped make it clear what government red tape can mean to people in practice.

The second part of the answer is that we must create new solutions *with* people, not *for* them (Sanders, 2006; Sanders and Stappers, 2008), orchestrating the process on the basis of the credos of design thinking. Ultimately, it is people who are at the receiving end of public policy, regulation, administration and service delivery. As discussed earlier, we may call them 'users', 'clients' or 'customers' (Tempoe, 1994), but 'citizens' is a better term (Bason et al, 2009). As discussed in Chapter 3, citizens have particular expectations, obligations, rights and powers. However, it is also important to remember that the role of citizen is but one of the many roles we all have, every day. We are also fathers, mothers, sisters, brothers, children, workers and lovers (Kirah, 2009). We are citizens too, but that may only be something we think about on election day, when we file our tax return or at the school's parent–teacher conference. Or when we get trapped in government bureaucracy, or highly dependent on certain services, our identity suddenly recast as citizen, client or even victim. Our current thinking in public services means that such highly vulnerable people and families rarely are able to effectively exit their dependency on public support.

Paradoxically, government either takes up very little space in people's consciousness (and thereby much less than administrators think), or very much of it (and they are thereby almost defined in terms of their relations with government). Knowing how specific interactions are experienced by people is fundamental. We must therefore never forget that it is by seeing and knowing *people* and the wholeness of their lives, as they experience them, that we discover the insights that might lead to new innovative solutions.

The three myths of citizen involvement

Throughout this chapter I will argue that citizen involvement is a powerful enabler of public sector innovation. But what do the sceptics say? Once I gave a presentation to an international workshop organised by the Austrian Ministry of Finance. During our talks, I shared how we at MindLab used videotaped interviews with citizens, and how one agency was currently using raw footage from such interviews as part of its change efforts. An Austrian official was deeply disturbed, although I underlined that we had obtained citizens' approval to use the material: to him, it was clearly unthinkable to use *videos of citizens* for inspiration, as part of analysis or to inform decision-making. There are quite a lot of objections and even fear about the involvement of citizens in the co-creation process. The 'fear of video footage' is one kind. At MindLab, we typically encounter three types of arguments against the active involvement of citizens in public sector innovation (Bason et al, 2009):

The fear of 'citizen dictators'

By involving citizens or business representatives explicitly through fieldwork or in workshops, allowing them to express their experiences and ideas, aren't we depositing our decision-making authority with them as well? The answer is, of course, that we are not involving citizens formally as part of a decision-making process, but as contributors to an innovation process. Ultimately, decisions are reached through deliberative democracy, and in most innovation projects by presenting solutions and options to steering committees or political bodies, which make the final decision. In addition, the purpose of involvement, as we saw earlier, is often not to ask citizens about which ideas they *like*, but to explore which ideas will *work*.

Citizen involvement requires too many resources

Doesn't it take too long, and isn't it too expensive? As the UK Customs and Revenue (HMRC) customer insight unit says, however, 'If you think knowing your customers is expensive, how expensive do you think it is not to know them?'. Or as I discussed in Chapter 7 on design thinking, it may be worthwhile to fail early to succeed sooner. The cost of just developing solutions behind a desk, 'rolling them out', as if implementation is like a carpet one can just roll out over the landscape of front-line workers, and then realising through citizen complaints, rising costs and lack of results that the solution didn't work, is much, much more expensive in both economic, human and political terms. Citizen involvement is a cost-effective means of ensuring that new solutions really do meet users' needs, and that they hit the target in terms of service improvements and better outcomes.

Citizen involvement creates unrealistic expectations

Now that we've involved them, and we've generated new ideas and solutions together, don't they expect something to happen? This is a valid argument. When people allow researchers to access their home or workplace, or choose to spend time participating in a workshop, they have a legitimate expectation that it serves a purpose. On the other hand, most citizens and business owners understand that there is no guarantee that just because a group of civil servants may think an idea is good, it will not be judged the same way by top management or, at the end of the day, by politicians. What is necessary, then, is to clarify expectations. That usually isn't hard to do. At a workshop at MindLab for business leaders across more than 20 companies, we started the session by saying that while we were pleased they had chosen to spend the day with us, we couldn't promise them that any of the ideas developed that day would be turned into practice. What we could promise them, however, was to take the process and their input seriously – and to report to them what, if any, ideas we would continue working on. They nodded almost simultaneously, and we went to work.

Co-creating, co-producing

Citizen involvement is, at its core, about a paradigm shift in the relationship between people and government. The shift originates from the increased need to focus on how behaviour can be affected to drive outcomes, and from the external pressures on government to perform. More fundamentally, it is a shift from an underlying public sector tradition of expert-driven creation and delivery, to a mode of co-creation and increased co-production (Hartley, 2005; Boyle et al, 2010). While co-creation is about the development, or *creation*, of new solutions *with* people, co-production is about the leveraging of people's own resources and engagement to enhance public service *delivery*. In other words, co-creation concerns how new solutions are designed; co-production concerns how they are executed.

It should be said that some research does not distinguish explicitly between 'creation' and 'production'. For instance, in a recent study of co-production, Boyle et al (2010, p 23) emphasise that the new paradigm is characterised by the transformation of 'the perception of people from passive recipients of services and burdens on the system into one where they are equal partners in designing and delivering services'.

The shift towards co-production

Many public organisations supply services based on the same blueprint, or paradigm, that has lasted since the formation of the modern public

Figure 8.1: Towards a new paradigm

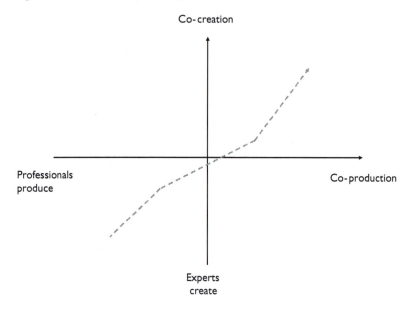

sector in the 1960s and 1970s, while the population's educational level, skills and access to resources, including new technology, has changed dramatically (Florida, 2002; Osborne and Brown, 2005; Hartley, 2005; Leadbeater, 2009a). Meanwhile, the problems and challenges in society have become more complex and long-term – from the rise of obesity and chronic disease to climate change. This means that the need and potential for new forms of co-production is on the rise:

- In health care, we have witnessed a shift from a focus on 'curing diseases' to 'enabling quality of life'.
- In employment policy, the effort has shifted from 'finding people a job' to 'enhancing employability'.
- In enterprise policy, government regulation is viewed less as just a barrier, and more as an opportunity for increasing competitiveness. As academic and former US Secretary of Labour Robert B. Reich has described, intelligent regulation and incentive structures can help businesses adapt quickly to a green economy (Reich, 2009).

The social sector is perhaps seeing the most remarkable shift towards recognising citizens' resources and potential, rather than mostly viewing citizens as victims of social injustice. For instance, the state of Oregon in the US has successfully introduced personal budgets for mental health patients (Cabinet Office, 2009). In New Zealand, a growing number of regional District Health Boards are employing a framework called *Knowing the People Planning*.This is a set of public management tools that helps mental health service users evaluate and plan services themselves, and improves and personalises individual care plans through identifying consumer needs.The approach is based on ten key features, which balance citizen needs with a set of service principles for public managers and staff (King and Welsh, 2006). In Victoria, Australia, the government created, in 2002, a Department for Victorian Communities, which was to be an advocate for an approach to the development and delivery of policies focusing on communities of interest and places, through the medium of communities of location. In other words, it was to do something in and with communities. The organisation was simply designed to co-create and co-produce solutions with communities and citizens – and turned out to be able to do this rather successfully (Hess and Adams, 2007). In Denmark, the city of Vejle, for instance, has reduced local immigrant ghetto crime rates by 60% by engaging with citizens through positive (appreciate inquiry) approaches, recognising their own resources and giving them great freedom to implement new solutions. The city of Vejle won the 2009 Innovation Prize of the Danish Association of Local Government for the project (KL, 2009). In Brazil, Restorative Circles, a community-based justice movement supported by the Ministry of Justice, has helped reduce violent crime dramatically through new approaches to conflict resolution in crime-ridden neighbourhoods. For instance, after introducing conflict resolution in a school, their approach helped produce a drop of 98% in student arrests that led to court appearances (Gillinson et al, 2010).

The shift towards co-creation and co-production takes place at different rates and in very different forms across government. In Chapter 5 on organisation and e-innovation in government, we saw how social media holds obvious potential as a platform for co-production.When government leverages its information advantage to let citizens get in touch with each other about similar problems or opportunities, co-production can take place. Providing mobile tools like portable lung monitors to patients forces a shift in the citizen–government relationship, casting patients, nurses and doctors in new roles. Letting unemployed people fill out their own online CVs and providing job search databases, as is now standard in most modern labour-market services, allows citizens to take more effective control of their own job search process.

However, non-technological processes, such as *joint care* in hospitals, where patients are treated in batches and collectively empowered to take part in the recuperation process, dramatically shortening hospital stays, are also expressions of co-production (Bason, 2007; Cabinet Office, 2009). Given the key challenges of increasing citizen expectations, ageing and scarcer resources, co-production appears to be a highly attractive way forward. Successful co-production designs promise productivity gains with no reduction in service experience, or most likely even an increase, since citizens tend to value something they take an active part in producing.

Involving to co-create

How do we identify new opportunities for co-production, and how do we design exactly the right technological and social systems and 'choice architectures' to achieve the desired outcomes? *Co-creation* with citizens seems like the only feasible answer. Before we turn to the overall co-creation process in Chapter 9, however, let's examine what forms citizen involvement could take.

Figure 8.2: Four types of citizen involvement

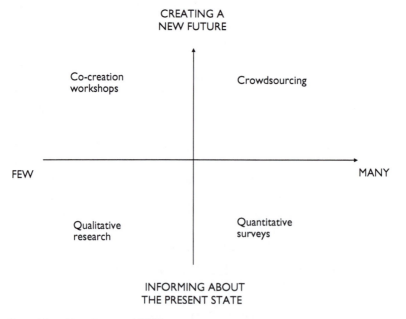

Source: Adapted from Bason et al (2009)

One can distinguish between two purposes of involvement: involving citizens as informants, helping to understand what the present (or past) situation is, and involving citizens as co-creators of a new future. One can also distinguish between involving the few (say, from four to 50 people) and the many (hundreds, thousands or, in principle, millions through *crowdsourcing*). I will focus on how non-traditional methods for data collection and citizen involvement can give us different kinds of knowledge and insight as drivers of public sector innovation.

Informing about the present state

Since the early 1980s and the rise of new public management, most public departments and agencies have expended some effort in trying to measure citizen satisfaction through either quantitative surveys, qualitative research or both. The surveys have often taken the form of paper-based or, more recently, electronic questionnaires with some mix of closed and more open-ended questions (Pollitt, 2003). If any qualitative research was undertaken, it may have involved case studies and personal interviews and/or focus groups. However, ethnographic research, such as participant observation and ethnographic interviews, has not, until recently, been at the centre of the methodological toolbox. And civil servants and public sector professionals have not, typically, been immersing themselves in the first-hand experience themselves (Bason et al, 2009).

In order to move from just understanding the present and citizens' stated needs, we need to employ other methods than usual. While traditional surveys and focus groups tend to capture what people *say* they want and do, ethnographic research and design methods help uncover what would actually benefit people by grasping the world from their perspective, emphasising what they *do*, the context they do it in and connecting the 'text' and 'context' (Rubow, 2003), for instance, as when 40% of shoppers entering a supermarket say they always buy organic vegetables, but a peek into their full shopping bags shows that only 15% of them actually did so.

Finding your inner anthropologist

We have to dig deep under the superficial information we often base our decision-making on, and introduce a different way of knowing and different types of insights (Martin, 2007). We must introduce exploration and wonder to our toolbox as public innovators. The anthropologist is prepared to take the time and effort to be a part of people's daily lives to look for what is surprising, seeing the extraordinary in the ordinary (Kelley, 2005; Brown, 2009). The method and focus always follow the premises and experiences of the people studied. As Copenhagen University Professor Kirsten Hastrup states, the ethnographic researcher doesn't talk first, but is there to find out which questions it makes sense to ask (Hastrup, 2003; see also Marcus, 1995; Bernard, 2006).

Ethnographic research, the anthropologist's research method, helps us see actual behaviour patterns and explore implicit needs, uncovering rich subjective and contextual data, which in turn can feed into the co-creation process. While traditional ethnographic field research could take months or years, highly condensed 'ethno-raids' of days or even hours are increasingly used by researchers to accommodate the tighter time frames of both public and private organisations. At MindLab, we rarely have the luxury of being able to undertake very long research phases; however, even with a short 'raid', useful insight can almost always be generated.

Ethnographic research focuses on understanding the world from the perspective of the study objects. The process can be extremely *open*, such as 'documenting a day in a person's life', or it could be more *focused,* such as 'mapping the citizen's journey through a specific public service', or, finally, it can be *challenging*, by testing explicit hypotheses about what is perceived to be the problem. This ongoing dynamic interplay between opening, closing and challenging is part of what makes ethnographic research such a good fit with design thinking and the iterative process of co-creation. The approach becomes an active learning process; a process with the purpose to change the researcher's perspective and understanding of the different contexts and create new grounds for reflection (Hasse, 2003). To give a sense of what the ethnographic research might entail, here are four types of research that have shown their value to public sector organisations (Bason et al, 2009).

- *Observation (shadowing).*

This is the simplest and most open form of field research, where the method is to observe a person or a physical place over time. Whatever takes place is captured. Even though the idea is to be a passive observer, the anthropologist is aware that through her very presence she becomes part of the context of the observed. Whatever is observed is, in the end, subject to two dimensions of subjectivity: the selective focus of the ethnographic researcher and the interpretation. So observation is never 'objective', but provides a perspective of what people themselves experience. Well-conducted observation research can be a source of wonder, and might generate a wide range of new questions to be explored. Video, audio, photos, written notes are typical means of capturing data from observation studies. For instance, part of the Danish Board of Industrial Injuries' citizen injury project was to observe meetings between citizens, local government representatives and agency staff. During the meetings the observer noted all dialogue and actions, capturing the exact moments when something that was done or being said by the officials triggered negative responses from citizens. This enabled the researcher, after the meeting, to explore further why the citizen had certain reactions, through direct interviewing.

- *Contextual interviews.*

Qualitative interviews are already used in much of the public sector. However, the contextual, or ethnographic, interview has several distinguishing characteristics. First and foremost, the interview takes place in the setting (context) people actually live or work in. Second, the interview guide is quite open, addressing a broad thematic level rather than specific questions. Although there is some structure and preparation, the interview aims at following the interests of the citizen, emphasising flexible, in-depth questioning and seeking illustrative stories and descriptions. This allows for a broader and richer dialogue with the interviewee. For instance, it could be to ask for a tour of the company and to be shown sites or people that are mentioned in the interview. Or it could be to ask the interviewee to show a folder, demonstrate an IT system or some other resource that is brought up. When MindLab researched how government control is perceived by small business, our researchers purchased rubber boots and full-body work outfits to visit a pig farmer on the small Danish island of Femø, videotaping the interview and being shown around not just the office, but also the farm. Why go to all the trouble? Because people's experiences are often tightly linked to the environment in which they live and the daily practices that are important to them.

- *Retrospective review.*

Here the focus is to uncover a chronological narrative about an event or series of events. The interviewee is asked to tell the story, recreating the dynamic of the past. The researcher probes by asking 'What happened then?' or 'What happened before that?'. The value of this form of interviewing is that it enables the researcher to discover surprising transitions or breaks in a series of events that might be hard to capture without such an open format. The interview can also uncover how events triggered subjective experiences and emotions, for instance by asking 'When that happened, how did it make you feel?'. The retrospective interview is a key tool in charting the *service journeys* that citizens or businesses experience in interaction with the public sector. It can be extremely powerful to hear, in a citizen's own words, how a service process was experienced.

- *Cultural probes.*

When MindLab was asked to help a team of civil servants to understand the drivers and motives of highly successful entrepreneurs, we asked selected business owners to send us photo (MMS) messages over their mobile phones, documenting their daily work and thoughts. With regular intervals, we would text small tasks to them, such as 'Take a picture of something that symbolises your ambitions for the company', or 'Take a picture of something that makes you proud'. The business owners would then take a picture of a situation or object, 'tag' the picture with a brief message (why did they choose exactly that image?) and MMS it to MindLab's project manager. Cultural probes are various tools, ranging from mobile phones to journals or disposable cameras, that enable informants to document their daily lives. The advantage of probing is that it can be done by people themselves, and so it is potentially a cost-effective means of harvesting large amounts of data. An obvious challenge, and a source of bias, can be that people are more motivated to document what they find interesting or positive about themselves – and may not want to contribute with problematic or critical material.

From observing how senior citizens live their lives to better sustain independent living, to engaging primary school students, parents, teachers and administrators in photo-documenting what is wonderful about their school, ethnographic research helps capture (and sometimes engage) citizens in new ways. The purpose is to gain exactly the kind of rich, contextual, emotional and intuitive form of knowledge that can supplement our analytical modes of 'knowing'.

Quantitative surveys

As a tool to provide rich citizen input to the innovation process, triggering the 'qualified inspiration' we so desperately need, quantitative surveys are not the most effective. However, quantitative data can obviously be required at various key stages in the innovation process, answering questions such as 'How many citizens are in the target population in the first place?', or 'Given what we now know, how many people would this solution be relevant for, and what would it cost?'. These are questions that most innovation projects will need to answer sooner or later. In combination with ethnographic research, mining existing databases or conducting surveys can be a very relevant supplement.

Creating a new future

Using ethnographic methods to understand reality and see it through the eyes of citizens is only the beginning of the process of innovation. The next challenge is to transform the empirical findings into insights and new future concepts through a process of co-creation.

As I will discuss in more detail in the next chapter, the task is to *orchestrate* a process that involves a wide range of people. For the purpose of the present chapter, I will mainly consider more specifically how citizens can be involved (and how they perhaps shouldn't be involved).

Co-creation workshops with citizens

When speaking of citizen involvement in public sector innovation, most people think it is about asking citizens for their ideas. But, as should be clear by now, 'involvement' is more fundamental than that: it is about understanding how people live their lives, in what context, what is important and meaningful to them, and *then* exploring what kind of changes might add more value. Citizens are usually not experts in public sector regulation or administration. They can't and shouldn't be expected to be better than public professionals at identifying the specific technical or legal solutions that could address their needs or problems. (An exception is the concept of *lead users*, which I will examine later in this section.) However, citizens can be extremely good at helping civil servants understand whether a proposed solution might work for them in practice. Co-creation workshops are about involving citizens in meaningful, concrete ways to actively explore possible futures together with all other relevant stakeholders. A key method here, inspired by design thinking, is to introduce *prototypes* of potential solutions that citizens can relate to and provide direct feedback about.

For instance, when MindLab worked with the Danish tax authorities to create new solutions for a next-generation online tax service, the developers thought that a mobile (SMS) texting version would be something citizens would like. If the tax agency had asked citizens through a standard quantitative questionnaire, many would probably have answered that it would be neat to have their tax return at their fingertips while on the move. But instead of conducting a survey, we sketched a visual 'storyboard' that, like a movie script, showed scene by scene how the SMS tax service might work in practice. When citizens were taken through this simulated service experience, and probed about how they would in practice use their mobile phone to enter data while sitting on the subway or in the car with their salary statements, stock transcripts and so forth, the service suddenly wasn't so attractive. With this feedback, systems developers chose to postpone the solution, saving millions that could be returned to taxpayers, or channelled to other and more pressing development needs.

In another co-creation workshop, leading companies – ranging from multinationals to small successful upstarts – engaged with policymakers to develop a coherent strategy for how the Danish government's national innovation policies could become more business-oriented. In preparation for the workshop, MindLab's team had generated five fictive company profiles, based on vast amounts of quantitative and qualitative data about business segments, experiences of current innovation policies and programmes, and market challenges. In the workshop, teams consisting of both business representatives and civil servants were given the company profiles, and asked to explore what their key needs were, and what government could do to strengthen their innovation ability. Through the facilitated workshop, companies and policymakers jointly identified opportunities, generated several hundred ideas, prioritised the solutions and developed concrete concepts. The output was a catalogue of policy initiatives that the civil servants could examine further, and build into the strategy. Often, it is much easier and more valuable for citizens and businesses to relate to something concrete and tangible that they can provide feedback on, rather than being asked to propose solutions to complex problems from scratch.

Lead users

Have some citizens and businesses become so expert at using public services that they begin adapting their own behaviour in advanced ways, or modifying the public solutions, to fit their needs? If so, they are what MIT Professor Eric von Hippel, author of *Democratizing Innovation* (von Hippel et al, 1999, 2005), calls *lead users*. In the private sector, lead users are not only the early adopters of new products, they also modify or develop entirely new ones. In some fields, such as medical equipment, research shows that users such as doctors and nurses innovate more (and more radically) than companies (Lettl et al, 2008). The challenge becomes to connect lead users, or user-innovators, with the businesses that can further develop and produce the products at scale.

In the public sector, there are other dynamics to the lead user concept. First, the public sector delivers services and enforces regulation, some of which isn't necessarily something people demanded in the first place. We've already seen that this challenges the rather one-dimensional notion of 'user'. Second, there often isn't a market incentive to develop a new and potentially costly public service. However, even though they may not modify or invent public services, there is still some potential in the lead user concept:

• *Engaged citizens.*
People who engage themselves extraordinarily in public service provision become 'expert citizens', and can provide a more substantial, considered input. Examples could be members of parent–teacher boards in schools, members of boards of retirement homes, volunteers in social organisations or social entrepreneurs (who we addressed in Chapter 5). When ethnographers studied how the motor vehicle registration process worked in Denmark, they found that while ordinary citizens encountered lots of confusion in their registration or deregistration process, car dealers (who were expert users) had adapted in various ways to the intricacies of administrative inertia and bureaucratic forms. This gap between what 'ordinary' users did and 'experts' did, could be used to identify potentials for improvement. In the health sector, a woman with a rare cancer disease discovered that while there were no other patients in Denmark with that particular diagnosis, there were several in the UK and the US. She gathered the resources to create an online patient network for that type of cancer, sharing experiences across the globe with treatments and coping with the disease.

• *Systems solutions.*
Companies develop systems and processes that help them meet requirements from the public sector (Seddon, 2008). One example could be the quality control systems in food-processing companies, which entail the same kind of control that public authorities carry out. Might food safety agencies learn from practices at leading companies, and could such practices be adopted by the agencies as part of their routines, or could they be spread to other firms? Another example, which we encountered at MindLab, was how to help qualified foreign workers move to Denmark. A key challenge in that field, MindLab discovered through interviews with HR managers in major companies, was that there was no single place where a foreign worker could go

online and see – step by step – what to do in order to meet formal government requirements when moving to Denmark. Moreover, much of the available information (and the forms) were in Danish. However, as a response, some multinational firms had, over time, built their own online to-do guide as a service to prospective foreign staff. The Danish government could, in principle, buy or borrow such a guide and make it its own.

We need to adapt the concept of the lead user to the particular context of the public sector. But that does not mean it doesn't have value as an approach to discovering existing solutions that might just be copied by government and provided on a much broader scale.

Crowdsourcing

As I also discussed earlier, private enterprises are increasingly opening up their innovation processes along the concepts of 'open innovation' and 'open business models' (Chesbrough, 2006a, 2006b). Some do it by systematically spinning off ideas and business opportunities as development projects go through the innovation 'funnel', essentially poking holes in the otherwise hermetically sealed funnel, as if it were Swiss cheese. Others take an even more radical approach. Some years ago, pharmaceutical giant Eli Lilly launched *Innocentive*, a website that offers rewards for solutions to R&D problems that are posted online. Consumer goods giant Procter & Gamble's *Connect & Develop* strategy has successfully connected the company's own product development teams with external researchers, thereby massively expanding the company's innovation capability. Philips, the Dutch electronic consumer goods producer, has equally turned its development approach on its head, transforming its secretive culture and symbolically tearing down the fences around its main research facility, creating a dynamic campus right next door for high-growth enterprises and collaborators. The idea with crowdsourcing, which plays on 'outsourcing', is to invite the masses to join the creative process, typically enabled by some type of internet-based platform (Howe, 2008). Rather than seeking out *lead users*, which may resemble looking for the proverbial needle in the haystack, could it be more effective to simply publicise problems or challenges, and allow potential innovators to make themselves heard, suggesting their solutions? Tapscott and Williams (2006) argue that the potential of involving millions of people through the internet in collaborative ideation and innovation is huge. They emphasise four dimensions of mass collaboration: openness, peering, sharing and acting globally. Fora such as Innocentive are, in Tapscott and Williams' view, the first virtual trading floors in an emerging global idea bazaar' (2006).

A few front-running public and social innovators are now embracing the potential of crowdsourcing for the public good. As mentioned earlier, The Australian Centre for Social Innovation (TACSI) has established a nationwide innovation contest titled the *Bold Ideas, Better Lives Challenge* that invests AUD 1 million in *crowdsourcing* new ideas for radical social innovations. People and organisations are encouraged to participate through ads in major newspapers and on the TACSI website. TACSI will invest in maturing and implementing up to 10 of the most innovative ideas. Likewise, Singapore runs the Enterprise Challenge, where the government invites citizens and businesses to suggest ideas for improving the public service, and awards grants to prototype and test them. And the UK's Nesta Public Services Lab has similarly invited innovation through competition. By encouraging large-scale external participation in their innovation efforts, these organisations are opening up to not just a few people, but to thousands or millions of potential contributors.

In spite of these examples, one wonders why we don't see more major government-run websites quite like *Innocentive* that post public problems and offer rewards. There may of course be ethical or political considerations involved – how much should a solution for a (usually free) public service be worth? Isn't it part of a citizen's obligation to contribute with ideas they may have? Nonetheless, it seems a bit paradoxical that businesses that are in a competitive environment open up their innovation process in quite radical ways, while public organisations, most of which are not competing and not subject to intellectual property concerns, do not. It may simply be that the competitive pressure that private firms are under forces them to a much quicker adoption of new innovation models that at first seem challenging or even frightening (are we putting our company's future in the hands of R&D people *outside* the firm?).

One public initiative that captures at least part of the idea of crowdsourcing is the Obama government's data.gov initiative, which opens up thousands of government databases to the public domain, and provides online tools to process them. By giving data back to US citizens and businesses, the hope is that they will find innovative ways of using them, either privately or commercially. Another dimension of *crowdsourcing* for innovation is the potential in social media, where citizens don't just propose ideas, but develop their own platforms and solutions and start using them, more or less independently of the public sector. An example is *Fix my Street*, the independent website that I mentioned in Chapter 5.

Finally, as James Surowiecki (2004) points out in *The Wisdom of Crowds*, aggregated information amongst groups of citizens or consumers can in many instances lead to better, faster and more objective decisions than individuals are capable of. Could public sector innovation capacity be boosted by new forms of smart involvement of the masses, using online 'web 2.0' platforms? In a very low-tech way, existing fora for citizen–public sector interaction such as parents' or relatives' boards for schools or handicap institutions are potentially platforms for innovation. However, often they are rather bogged down on day-to-day administrative matters and budget discussions, not living arenas for neutral dialogue on reshaping public services. The purpose of many such boards is often representation and legitimacy (which of course is valid enough), not innovation. But the potential may be there: what would happen if all of such boards were energised to be local innovation platforms, co-creating new solutions in a collaborative spirit with administrators, citizens and professional staff?

When citizen involvement meets the design process

As illustrated in Figure 8.3, the methods I've reviewed apply in various ways to the design-thinking platform I showed in Chapter 7, combining the design-process methods with citizen involvement.

Figure 8.3: Forms of citizen involvement in the design process

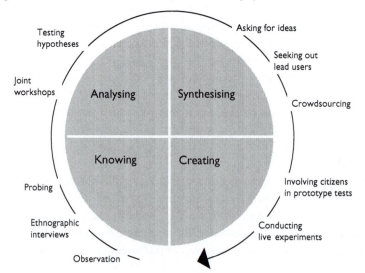

I will discuss the model in the context of the co-creation process in more detail in Chapter 9.

How to do it

This chapter has shown how to involve citizens in the public sector innovation process. Placing citizens at the centre of the innovation process holds a number of challenges for public managers and staff, who have to learn to put their own professional backgrounds and experience on hold, and allow themselves to discover a different reality than their own. We often lack the recognition that there are other ways of involving citizens, and we lack the tools to do it. Rather than define problems *for* citizens, we must examine problems *with* them. Paradoxically, the fields where we often perceive and defend citizens as weak and in need of help, such as social or health services, are the fields where we are not yet good enough at systematically listening to them. Public managers have a special responsibility here, to step out of the more collegial culture in many professional environments, such as schools, day-care institutions, care homes and hospitals, and to insist on exploring how citizens experience the public sector. This takes courage. When citizens are invited into the public organisation, 'People get nervous' (Parker and Heapy, 2006). The key to-dos of citizen involvement, which public managers must take to heart, are the following:

Involve citizens for deep understanding of experience

The potential for discovering new ways of generating value, and of driving more radical change in public sector organisations, starts and ends with the citizens and businesses. The approaches described in this chapter show how ethnographic research and design methods can help public managers obtain a different type of knowledge, and thus a much more concrete but also intuitive understanding of people's experiences, challenges and resources. Involvement brings us closer to 'the users as they are used' through interactions with government. Public managers must recognise their responsibility to lead this process of end-user involvement and co-creation, and ask questions such as:

- *What is the case for increased citizen or business involvement in the way we create new solutions in our organisation?*
- *How might we start taking the first concrete steps to immerse ourselves to better understand how citizens experience what we do with (or to) them?*

- *Have we identified possibilities for educating some of our staff in methods for citizen involvement?*
- *Who might be our pioneers in venturing out to conduct citizen-centric research?*

Have the courage to see and act on citizen-centric knowledge

There is no point in using the resources to involve citizens in public sector innovation if it doesn't have consequences. But when people get nervous, the most obvious choice is to not allow the new kind of knowledge that is generated by qualitative, in-depth research to become a serious part of the decision-making process. The best way to overcome this barrier is to allow the raw data material – video or audio clips of interviews with citizens, quotations, visual mappings of service journeys – to speak on their own. The real challenge is to let the reality for citizens become a direct input to the process, in balance with quantitative data and a host of other considerations. In essence, this is an orchestration challenge, which I will take a closer look at in Chapter 9. Public managers should consider the question:

- *Do we have the courage to actively use context-rich qualitative data as an explicit input to our decision-making process?*

9

Orchestrating co-creation

'Bringing co-creation into design practice will cause a number of changes to occur. It will change how we design, what we design, and who designs.' (Elizabeth Sanders and Pieter Jan Stappers, 2008)

During the past few years, a new term has entered the Danish government's efforts to drive regulatory reform and make it easier to start and run a small business: *burden-hunting*. Widely reported in the business press, civil servants ventured out to conduct on-site field research, engaging with company owners, finance officers and accounting staff to better understand what it is like to own a business and to be at the receiving end of bureaucracy and red tape (MindLab, 2008). These civil servants, from across three different government departments, had been trained by MindLab in ethnographic research techniques and, through a process of co-creation, invited companies to be part of the development and testing of new policy and service solutions. In March 2009, when the strategy was finally presented to the public by (then) Vice Prime Minister Lene Espersen, it took place in the rugged facility of a medium-sized Greyhound bus operator that had itself been subject to an on-site visit by the burden-hunters. A number of the innovative policy initiatives launched that day, including a new single account number for all payments to public agencies nationwide, would not have been possible without the burden-hunters' efforts. The approach was so successful that, in 2010, the Danish Ministry of Finance proposed that a new programme to identify and remove administrative burdens for citizens should also build, to a high degree, on the 'burden-hunter method'.

Co-creation is the explicit involvement over time of people to identify, define and describe a new solution (Scharmer, 2007; Sanders and Stappers, 2008). Building on the foundation presented in Chapters 7 and 8, co-creation is about orchestrating a design process with citizens, businesses and other internal and external stakeholders. This entails reconceptualising citizens not as subjects, but as equal partners in design and delivery, and recognising people as assets (Bate and Robert, 2007; Sanders and Stappers, 2008; Boyle et al, 2010;

Gillinson et al, 2010). For the public manager or project manager, the key challenge is how to effectively facilitate the process, recognising that 'the entire journey from idea to results is fraught with danger' (Eggers and O'Leary, 2009, p 85). How do we reap the benefits of this new paradigm of public sector innovation? This chapter zooms in on the following questions:

- What are the elements of the co-creation process, from systematically questioning problems to idea generation to selection, prototyping, iteration and ultimately scaling and learning?
- How can the the process be orchestrated in practice?
- What is the potential of co-creation as a new paradigm of public sector innovation?

A process for co-creation

In Chapter 2, I considered the process of moving ideas from exploration of 'mystery' over implementation to the creation of value: starting with hundreds or even thousands of ideas, moving the ideas through the knowledge funnel towards selection and maturation of the ideas that work and might even be turned into a reliable method of delivery at scale (Martin, 2007). We've also seen how the innovation process itself can be opened up in the form of more collaborative ways of working, and how the political context, strategy, organisation, people and culture can limit or foster the capacity to create and execute ideas to generate value.

In this section of the book, I've considered how design thinking provides us with not just an overall way of balancing analysis versus synthesis, but also with four credos that in more concrete terms can guide the process of innovation in a new direction: more experimental, iterative, concrete and citizen-centred. And we've seen the various new forms that citizen involvement can take, in particular inspired by ethnographic research methods.

How then do we combine the fundamental assumptions and credos of design thinking with the methods of citizen involvement in a coherent, orchestrated process of co-creation? I suggest an approach involving the seven activities of *framing, knowing, analysing, synthesising, creating, scaling* and *learning*, which expands on the models I introduced in Chapters 7 and 8.

In this chapter I consider each element in detail. It is important to note that as a process, they do not necessarily fall in a neat, sequential order. To the contrary, co-creation entails a continuous openness to the possibility that the order shifts or overlaps, and that it may well be necessary to revisit activities that have already been addressed once or twice (Brown, 2009). As the arrow in Figure 9.1 suggests, co-creation is an iterative process overall – and so it goes for each of its sub-elements.

Figure 9.1: The co-creation process

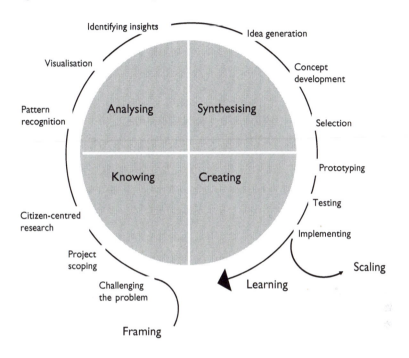

Framing

Innovation doesn't start with an idea. It starts with thinking in a different way about the problem or by identifying a new opportunity.

Challenging the problem

A key activity of the co-creation process is to understand what the problem or opportunity might be about. As mentioned, some call this phase the 'fuzzy front end', or simply the 'front end of innovation'. This is where the fundamentals of the process are determined, 'fuzzy' signifying a high degree of early uncertainty and complexity (Koen et al, 2001; Sanders and Stappers, 2008). This is where the design credo of 'challenging the status quo' comes into play.

In their work on radical efficiency in public services, Gillinson and her *Innovation Unit* colleagues show that it is when individuals and organisations gain an entirely new perspective on their challenges – in particular through new insights and new understanding of 'customers' – that services can be redesigned to be different, better and lower cost, generating true paradigmatic innovation and savings of up to 60% (Gillinson et al, 2010). These kinds of gains are not the result of mindlessly cutting a few percentage points of government budgets annually. They are the result of casting away existing 'mental maps' of what we are delivering and how we do it, and replacing them with new ones.

This means that the framing of the problem has to start with people, their needs and the outcomes we are seeking. However, the culture and practice in many public sector organisations is to readily accept what 'the top' – whether that is politicians or top management – defines as the problem or the task (Bason, 2007; Eggers and Singh, 2009). As a public innovator it is necessary to immediately ask questions like 'Why is this important?', 'Why is it a problem?' and 'Who does it affect?', even though a report, a memo or a policy statement seems to provide the answer. In that sense, we have to think of the role of the innovation team as the 'loyal opposition', just like the role of the innovation lab I discussed in Chapter 5. Loyalty and an understanding of political motivations and priorities must be balanced against rigorous questioning and reframing.

The kind of innovation challenge obviously differs immensely depending on what type of problem or opportunity it is. In Chapter 2, on the innovation landscape, I introduced a typology of the value and type of public sector innovation, distinguishing between four innovation types: administrative, service, policy and democracy innovation. Each type involves particular framing challenges – but all benefit from involving multiple actors in the process of problem definition. The task is to be aware of what kind of innovation challenge is being addressed.

Administrative innovation happens close to operations, and might involve implementing a lean project, a new IT system or some other type of change in work flows or organisation. The framing challenge here can be to identify the (true) champions of the project, resources and motivations for the change, and what kinds of resistance or scepticism there might be throughout the affected parts of the organisation.

Service, policy and *democracy innovation* might be initiated from external demands, by government or top management, it may be employee-driven or it may arise from citizen-centric insights. No matter the source, it is not always clear who the end recipients of the policy or service are. *Wicked* problems that are not clearly defined, where the nature of the problem in itself is open for debate, where there are multiple possible solutions and (not least) where the problem will most likely never go away, characterise many public sector innovation challenges; framing becomes a key discipline to help us see old, intractable problems from new perspectives.

Creating problem trees and establishing theories of change are useful techniques for challenging the problem. Problem trees help identify the root causes of the problem and identify its key consequences. Theories of change are a way of mapping the expected chains of causality in current or planned public programmes and interventions. A key question to ask is: 'Who is ultimately going to benefit from this effort, and how?'. As other activities in the co-creation process are carried out – in particular citizen involvement – new insights may emerge that help us further reframe the starting point.

An effective process of loyally challenging the problem needs the right mix of people. A kick-off workshop where a broad, diverse group is involved in systematically discussing the problem definition can be very helpful. At MindLab, we sometimes do two kick-off rounds: one where the core team tries to come to grips with how we feel the problem could be framed, and one where we invite a larger group to help us see it from more perspectives.

Project scoping

Once we understand what kind of challenge we are addressing, it is time to design the co-creation process. Given the open-ended nature of innovation, there are obviously limits to how precisely the process can be scoped. However, it is usually possible to lay out an overall time frame, key activities and (not least) who is involved and how many resources it will roughly require. Another scoping activity is to collate the necessary data to determine a baseline of the current value being provided by the organisation to the target population, to the extent this is at all possible. Such a 'value baseline' or 'balanced scorecard' is necessary for determining whether the innovation produced the intended value or not, for instance by increasing productivity, service experience or outcomes (at the latest, it should be established immediately before a solution is implemented).

Establishing the *core team* is key, as it is to identify the overall group of actors – internal and external – that must be part of the co-creating process. Stakeholder analysis can be a starting point, as can 'snowballing' methods of identifying actors to include in various phases of the project. The project team should include a diverse set of disciplines and professions – among them a mix of public administrators, professionals, social researchers and design thinkers, as described in Chapter 6.

Often, it is most efficient to keep the core team very small, particularly in the earlier phases of the innovation process, in order to allow for optimal interaction and communication between team members, energising the creative process. Such teams should not, as a rough guideline, exceed more than six to eight people.

The *broader group* of involved actors, which will become part of the co-creation process as it unfolds, should be chosen to reflect a consideration of both internal and external resources. What is particularly important to balance in determining this wider involvement is essentially two needs: the need to include the stakeholders that are crucial to ensure ownership and implementation throughout the process (Attwood et al, 2003; Ackoff et al, 2006); and the need to include people who can help increase divergence through the diversity of backgrounds, experiences and expertise they possess.

The broader group, for instance, should include managers and staff in the host or client organisation, key individuals from other public bodies that have a stake in the project, social innovators from third-sector organisations, external experts and academics. Explicitly identifying such 'wild cards' that could contribute with new angles and perspectives to the project can in itself be a driver of innovation. Note that I am not suggesting that citizens, business representatives or other recipients of policy are necessarily asked to be part of the entire co-creation process. Sometimes they can be, but more often than not they are invited into the process at very specific stages, particularly in the 'knowing' and 'creating' phases.

Knowing

Really seeing the world as other people experience it, not as our mental maps might have constructed it, is a key part of the co-creation process. As we saw in the previous chapter, getting to know the problem through a citizen-centred lens requires a real curiosity and willingness to spend time with the people that the service or policy concerns. The co-creation element of this activity is essentially about obtaining new insight through conversations with people.

Citizen-centred research

This is where the in-depth qualitative research and citizen involvement that I described in detail in Chapter 8 come into play, grounding the creative process in a deep understanding of citizens' lives and the contexts in which they are lived. Before applying the tools of 'professional empathy', however, we must start by asking: 'What do we know already?'. We have to chart the existing knowledge landscape, data and evidence, and identify the key blind spots we may have. We must be aware of what we don't know, and what makes us curious.

If there is one thing many public organisations are good at, it is assembling data. Accessing existing data and information in public databases, as well as previous analyses, evaluations and other reports through rigorous desk research must be done at the earliest phase of the project (van Wart, 2008). As mentioned earlier, this type of data can also feed into the establishment of a 'value baseline'.

Looking beyond the organisation – checking whether other public agencies hold data that might be relevant – is a key task at this stage. Information is often not regularly exchanged across government departments and agencies – which may partly be due to legislative limitations on data exchange, but may also simply have to do with organisational blind spots. For instance, when two public managers from Australia visited Denmark on a study trip, they interviewed two different, but related, government agencies with overlapping target groups. To their surprise, the Australians realised that each agency held data of key relevance to the other, but didn't share it systematically – yet. Sometimes it really is necessary with an outside view to gain a new perspective on one's own practices.

Another approach is to involve external experts with deep practical or academic knowledge and experience in the field in question, or in seemingly unrelated fields in the private sector, and harvesting their input (Bessant, 2005). Such external views or insights may have very significant relevance. In their research on the drivers of more *radical efficiency*, Gillinson et al (2010) emphasise that new insights from other sectors, or finding old ideas in new places, are among the strongest catalysts for creating different and better outcomes. Harvesting such knowledge, once potential contributors have been identified, can be done through 'expert interviews' or joint workshops, for instance.

In spite of mapping existing knowledge and identifying gaps, there is one thing that these exercises cannot do for us: they won't tell us what we don't know that we don't know. Often, the insight needed to innovate is answers to questions we didn't realise we were asking.

For example, when the Danish Enterprise and Construction Agency wanted to know how it could accelerate the growth of small and medium-sized businesses, the agency thought it was asking 'How do we help these business people make more money?'. Through qualitative research, using in-depth interviews, observation studies and cultural probing, it turned out the question it needed to ask was: 'How do we help these people realise their dream?'. Realising a dream was the main motivating factor for these entrepreneurs, and it was only when the co-creation project revealed it that the agency could design and implement an effective and relevant service process.

No matter the amount of quantitative data, international best practice, insight from other agencies, and cutting-edge research that is available, there is often no substitute for venturing out into the field and observing, listening, participating, exploring and letting ourselves be surprised by the complexity and humanity of people's own experiences. This cannot be replaced by numbers, and it cannot (only) be outsourced. Flip back to Chapter 8 to see how it might be done.

Analysing

In the co-creation process, the analytical phase is essentially about transforming data into structured knowledge. In this section I am assuming that the data concerned are highly qualitative, having been generated through ethnographic research. However, there can (and should) of course be a wide range of other kinds of data, from mining databases, conducting surveys, reviewing academic literature, checking existing evidence, running crowdsourcing exercises and so on, that feed into the process, basing the new insights on the sum of available knowledge.

The process of analysing rich, qualitative data must be collaborative. The team that has collected data first-hand must also be the team that organises the data into meaningful categories and expressions.

Pattern recognition

Many ethnographers and some participatory designers call the process of structuring data *pattern recognition*. The term is quite precise: we must try to reveal the deep underlying patterns and structures of belief, behaviours and experiences that our data hold. What are the findings that emerge? Mapping qualitative field data is a bottom-up process that is not guided by strong hypotheses or assumptions (Bason et al, 2009). It is guided by the inner coherence and meaning in the material that has been collected. The approach is inductive, not deductive (Nachmias and Nachmias, 1992). We must allow ourselves to be surprised, even baffled, by the data and the patterns they reveal. We have to suspend judgement. Even so, we must at the same time recognise that any process of analysis is subjective, and there will necessarily be an element of personal interpretation. The key is not to ignore this, but to be aware of our own biases and prejudices as a condition of the process – and thus take account of them.

From ethnographic, qualitative fieldwork, there will typically be at least 50–100 significant statements (in the form of notes, photos, sound or video clips) from each interviewee. Each member of the research team contributes with this material, in a format that is practical, such as printouts of interview transcripts (cut out into individual statements or sentences), photos, cards representing key video clips and so. Computer software for qualitative research, such as *Atlas.ti* or *NVivo*, can be used to *tag* the data and help systematise, sort and search. Often, however, a hand-held approach is more effective, especially if there are only 5–10 interview sources.

The research team then map all the individual statements and experiences, for instance on a large whiteboard, and enter a process of structuring them in mutually exclusive groups or patterns. This typically involves a lot of dialogue and discussion between team members about the meaning and significance of individual bits of data. It takes time; usually not less than a full day, sometimes more. The key is to carry out the exercise collectively and to do it in an intensive session, not spread out over time. This dilutes the analytical edge and it becomes more difficult to remember vivid details from the fieldwork. The result of such a pattern-recognition workshop is essentially a map of key clusters of statements, where each is labelled with some overall theme that addresses what the finding is about. For instance, when we at MindLab categorised how citizens experienced roundtable meetings with state and local civil servants, a group was titled 'Confusion about the purpose of the meeting', and all relevant statements about this topic would be clustered.

Sometimes there are different ways of structuring the patterns. One might be themes, one might be steps in a service process, and one might be how certain groups (segments) experience a service or public intervention. Thus, it may be that several maps are made, each 'cutting' the data differently, leading to multiple angles or innovation paths. The themes that have been identified are then brought into play in the next step, further visualising the findings and interpreting what they imply for the organisation, creating insights.

Visualisation

A key contribution of design skills in this phase of the co-creation process is to visualise people and processes, helping decision-makers to see citizens and services in context and facilitating collaboration across agency and professional boundaries. Most government organisations stick to abstract (quantitative) segments of users/customers/citizens – leaving them with a rather one-dimensional picture of what characterises their target population. Visualising people can be done by building *personas* out of the individual data material that has been harvested, where possible combining it with quantitative data from existing databases or from surveys (Pruitt and Adlin, 2006; Bason et al, 2009).

Personas are holistic, rich archetypal descriptions of the citizens, businesses or institutions that the agency serves. A persona thus expresses the values, beliefs, practices and daily life of the person or business. It may also express quantitative measures such as age, how much time the persona spends on average on a service, their typical personal income, how many persons in the segment in total (if known) and so on. Most important, the persona will display the kinds of findings that are harvested from qualitative research: what motivates him or her? What benefits are there from the given service or intervention? What are the resources and barriers at the personal level? A persona is made living and personal by giving the person or organisation a relevant name.

As an analytical tool, the persona can be highly effective in bridging the gap between quantitative segments and the more emotional and (not least) memorable qualitative knowledge. Personas can be used actively in the innovation process to develop new solutions and even to test them: 'Would this be a relevant solution for John?', 'How would John's own resources help us achieve this goal?', 'Does he have challenges or barriers we need to take into account?'. The dialogue over potential solutions and desirable futures becomes much more alive, creative and not least concrete (Madsen and Nielsen, 2008). Often, not only decision-makers at central level but also front-line workers who interact with citizens daily quickly recognise personas, engage themselves in developing and adjusting them, and start speaking about them as real people. Personas simply help place citizens at the heart of the innovation process.

Another reason it is key to involve front-line workers in the creation process is that the ownership they develop over the personas can feed into how they manage daily service delivery as well as professional development. For instance, when a public library in Aarhus, Denmark, created personas through substantial engagement of its front-line staff, the staff subsequently used them to regularly discuss service strategies and for training (Bason, 2007).

There is the argument that personas may not always be an appropriate substitute for 'real people' (Bason et al, 2009). Why seek to reduce the richness of people's lives into archetypes in the first place? One argument can be the need for attaching personas to quantitative segments, thus matching descriptions with the key question of 'How many are they?', and the associated 'What would the cost and benefits be to introduce this service to this persona?'. Another argument against using true personal portraits is anonymity. For pure inspirational purposes, however, 'real people' may be better. I once discussed this with a concept developer at DR, the Danish Broadcasting Corporation, who said personas tend to make reality a bit too 'round and vague'. But innovation needs sharpness. He then drew two figures on a whiteboard, the persona being all blurry. The 'real person' he drew much sharper. And then he drew a balloon on a string in the person's hand: 'See, suddenly this person is interesting. The balloon is surprising. And surprises are great innovation drivers'.

Another key visualisation tool that also emphasises citizen-centric processes is *service journeys*. A service journey is a visual map of the individual service interactions with government over time, with the citizen's actions and experiences at the centre (Parker and Heapy, 2006; Bason et al, 2009). At MindLab, service journeys are an indispensable tool in most of our public service design projects. A number of features in service journeys are:

- Displaying a service process from an *outside-in* perspective, placing people using (or not using) the service at the centre, recognising that it is the individual's interaction with public services and experience of the service that is of interest.
- Capturing the *entire* service process chronologically from A to Z, showing all steps along the way, sometimes down to hours or minutes.
- Including *all* actors of any relevance (positive, negative or neutral) to the process, thus placing the service interactions in social context.
- Focusing not only on what happens in individual steps or interactions, but on how it is subjectively experienced – how it *feels*.

Service journeys are at their most powerful when they map what *actually* happens and how it is experienced from the citizen's perspective, really visualising the complexity and context of service interactions. However, service journeys can also be shaped as the 'ideal journey', in terms of how we (today) think it looks, or what we would want the future process to look and feel like. It can be quite revealing to compare ideal and practice, identifying surprising gaps and differences, and addressing them. As I will consider later in this chapter, creating future 'ideal' service journeys is essentially a concept-development tool.

What about the public sector (internal) side of the journey? Of course this can be mapped as well, as is often done in lean or business process re-engineering projects. As part of a co-creation process, however, there should always (also) be an outside-in perspective.

How are service journeys established? They are established through rigorous interviewing of citizens or organisational representatives, as well as with the relevant public employees and other stakeholders. Methodologically, service journeys are uncovered using retrospective techniques, but also through observation studies and longer-term fieldwork, triangulating with known regulation, formal descriptions of administrative processes and service provision and so on. It should always be ensured that the service journey is validated through several sources, and it should be taken into account that local implementation of a service process may vary greatly. Sometimes it may not be possible to establish a 'standard' process, and several different journeys, either differing by personas, geography or type of service provider, must be created. Service journeys and personas often work well together, because it is possible to vividly show how specific people experience different service flows.

For instance, in the 'Land of Rules and Regulations' project, the Dutch government mapped the key 'administrative burdens' and service experiences that citizens have with public bureaucracy, combining a 'map' of citizens' journeys with rich descriptions of the human living the actual journey. The Dutch even added clear quantitative measurements to their descriptions of nine particular citizens, each with their own challenges and journeys. According to the analysis, for instance, a single, unemployed mother spends 71 hours and 59 minutes per year handling seven different authorities' information and interaction requirements, including letters, phone calls, meetings and so on. A family with a handicapped child hits more than 125 hours of dealing with red tape. In comparison, a 'regular' Dutch citizen spends just 27 hours and 42 minutes on government regulation per year (Ministry of the Interior and Kingdom Relations, 2006).

Finally, because service journeys can map not just interactions, but also the entire context and other actors, they describe the system as well as relationships. Thereby they can help us not only redesign interactions, but consider the entire system architecture. This can help us create smarter interventions that strengthen outcomes. Are there additional actors who might have an impact on service experience and outcome? When we at MindLab visualised the service journey of citizens with a work injury it turned out that the partner or spouse was a key source of advice. Should, then, the Board of Industrial Work Injuries not think about how it could (also) communicate with the partners, if they have a big say in the decisions made by the injured?

Personas and service journeys are visualisation tools that can give direction and substance to the co-creation process. Should citizens themselves be involved here? Perhaps not when describing personas. Citizens may feel that personas reduce them to archetypes and some elements may feel clichéd, even though they are based on rich triangulated data. To validate and further develop service journeys, however, involving citizens or other users can be highly relevant. They can contribute by adding further precision, or to expressing what emotions and behaviours were triggered by certain interactions. For instance, as I discussed in the previous chapter, when the service design firm LiveWork carried out their employment project for Sunderland, England, the resulting redesign of the system of employment was possible because LiveWork took its departure from the citizen's perspective (LiveWork, 2006).

Identifying insights

To identify insights is essentially to bridge the gap between analysis and synthesis: how should we interpret our findings? What do they mean to us? What do they imply for what we are seeking to achieve as an organisation? Where does it hurt? When Pam Nyberg, design principal at the appliances firm Whirlpool, said at a seminar that 'co-creation is to overcome a world of pain', part of what she meant, I believe, is that the process is tough to lead. But part of what is painful is also to really *see* the implications of people's experience, context and practice on what one is already doing. A strategic design firm in Copenhagen says that if their clients don't cry when shown the research results (much of which is based on ethnographic research and design thinking), they haven't done their work properly. Perhaps it shouldn't be a criteria to get our public sector colleagues to cry, but it should clearly be a measure of success that the insights generated through user research and analysis *matter* (Bason et al, 2009).

Who should be involved in interpreting the significance of the findings, and turning them into insights? It certainly should be the top- and medium-level decision-makers and strategists, who 'own' the objectives, tasks or strategies of the organisation; they can help the team understand how the findings relate and perhaps clash with official objectives and visions. It should certainly also be practitioners, those who carry out service or regulatory activities, and who have most likely in some way or other been involved in the data-collection phase; they can interpret what the findings mean *practically*. When MindLab helped the Board of Industrial Injuries create new approaches for citizens with a workplace injury case, we involved both the manager of the particular service unit and the staff who went out for the on-site roundtable meetings. As MindLab presented the findings, mainly in the form of short one- to two-minute video 'snippets' from citizen interviews, the officials were the key drivers in identifying exactly where the 'strategic meat' was. The process illustrated the power of the outside-in view, represented by the video material. While watching an interview, one workshop participant spontaneously burst out: 'Wow, this is an eye-opener!' The insights we gain might be called 'innovation tracks'. Like multiple train tracks, they lay down potential directions towards the distant future horizon.

Synthesising

Synthesis is about putting together, generating not just ideas, but growing, shaping and qualifying coherent, possible avenues or 'tracks' for innovation. Synthesis is about recognising what the desirable future solution might look and feel like. It has been quite precisely put by UK innovation broker The Innovation Unit, which states that 'best practice' is no longer enough – what we need is 'next practice' (Digmann et al, 2008). Academic C. Otto Scharmer, author of *Theory U* (2007), might formulate it like this: 'We must sense the future as it emerges'. And as discussed, Roger Martin of the Rotman School has emphasised: leaders must embrace *abductive* thinking – the ability to have a 'hunch' that something might work (2007, 2009). Several processes are involved in the synthesis phase: idea generation, concept development and selection. Because it involves a more intuitive and interpretive way of working, synthesising isn't an exact science – perhaps even less so than other phases of the innovation process.

Idea generation

Allegedly, in the midst of the financial crisis, in 2008–09, US Chairman of the Federal Reserve, Ben Bernanke, held so-called 'blue sky' meetings – a term he used for brainstorming sessions with the purpose of soliciting unorthodox ideas from any participant. Not surprisingly, this was a time of unprecedented challenges, and even central bankers were in need of a major dose of creativity (*Time Magazine*, 2009). Idea generation, or *ideation*, is probably the single activity most associated with innovation: collaboratively developing new creative ideas, applying imagination and energy to describe possible futures. And sticking lots of coloured post-its up on a wall.

MindLab's 'The Mind', a 100 square foot white oval room lined entirely with whiteboards, is an iconic manifestation of this notion. The room has no corners, so there's no excuse not to participate in the creative process. Even if idea generation isn't an exact science, it certainly is a discipline, and it can be done in quite systematic ways (Kelley, 2005). It is impossible to do credit to the field in this short subsection, but I will highlight a few of the principles and methods that we have found effective in driving public sector innovation – while addressing the key barriers too. Some of the most important principles underpinning the process of ideation are identical to the basic rules of brainstorming, such as:

- Ask 'What if …?' or 'How might we …?'.
- Suspend judgement.
- Go for quantity, not quality.
- Build on each other's ideas.

In the public sector, this means we are already up against several challenges.

First, in the analytical-logical world of many public organisations, suspending judgement is almost counterintuitive. Civil servants are usually trained to be professional sceptics, weighing arguments for and against, assessing cases and managing risk.

Second, going for quantity means allowing ourselves to throw entirely crazy, unproven and 'unrealistic' ideas out there, right in front of our colleagues or, even worse, in front of staff from another ministry, department or agency. The ideation process thrives on divergence, not convergence, and we *must* allow enough time, energy and effort to truly explore the corners of our imagination, as it bears down on a particular challenge (*McKinsey Quarterly*, 2008). Karl Ulrich, Professor of Operations and Information Management at the Wharton School at the University of Pennsylvania, has conducted research that shows that 'diminishing returns to scale' of more new ideas don't kick in until after between 150 and 200 ideas (Ulrich and Terwiesch, 2009). In other words, to be sure that the quality of ideas is as high as possible, as judged by the innovation team itself, the group has to develop at least 150 distinct ideas. When I mention this to public officials, they often look at me as if I'm crazy. But then we carry out a fast creativity exercise, and in half an hour they can generate the first 100 ideas, or more.

Third, public officials are adept at managing risk rather than leading innovation (although some might argue we aren't too competent at the risk bit either). It is a bit scary to articulate an idea that could involve numerous risks both in implementation and final execution. It might even be more than scary, it might be perceived as unprofessional. As discussed earlier, the culture and values in many public organisations are often not geared towards the creative process. How does the discipline of brainstorming radical ideas come to be perceived as being just as professional as drafting new legislation? The best answer is, I believe, that it has to be treated and carried out as a professional discipline that, just like any other professional endeavour, requires time, focus and, first of all, practice. In *Innovation in the Making* (2001), Danish academic Lotte Darsø describes how the key dimensions of *relationship* (trust, communication), *concepts* (for instance visual models, mutually understood metaphors), *knowledge* (both theoretical and practical) and *absence of knowledge* (such as not knowing that something is impossible, asking 'stupid' questions) are all ingredients of the ideation process. Innovation competence is to master all four dimensions and create an environment of mutual trust in which they can play out (Darsø, 2001). The role of the competent facilitator is to apply the methods and processes that mix these dimensions in an optimal way.

Here are a few methods that can help public organisations add power to the process of generating radical new ideas:

- *Mind setting.*
To kick off a creative process it can be necessary to help people shift from their analytical mode of thinking to a more intuitive mode. Mind-setting exercises are essentially aimed at helping to put people in the 'right frame of mind' or even the 'right emotional state' in the context of the topic or problem that is addressed. An objective can be to generate empathy about the situation or challenge. For instance, in a workshop for a pharmaceutical company about how to market a new anti-asthma drug, the facilitator asked the group of executives to each breathe through a straw for two minutes. The exercise made them acutely aware of how it feels to suffer from asthma, and helped them think more broadly about ideas for marketing. Another example is a workshop held at MindLab, part of crafting the Danish policy on climate change and business growth, where we placed a huge block

of melting ice in the middle of the room, amidst the tables with work groups. We wanted to remind the public managers what was at stake.

- *Thinking inside a different box.*

Rather than trying to think 'outside the box' (where is that anyway?), ideas can be stimulated by establishing a different box to think in. That is what Great Ormond Street Hospital in the UK did when they looked to Formula One pit-stop teams to learn how to carry out extremely fast handovers in the operating theatre. A top pit-stop team fuels and changes tyres on a car in around seven seconds. The doctors at Great Ormond Street Hospital asked how that process might be applied to their own reality. Watching, mapping and videotaping the Ferrari pit-stop team's efforts first-hand in Italy, the doctors saw the process as similar to the effort of surgeons, anaesthetists and intensive care unit staff to transfer the patient, equipment and information safely and quickly from the operating room to the intensive care unit (American Society for Quality, 2010). By engaging in a collaborative effort with the Ferrari team, the hospital not only designed a more effective handover process, it also reduced patient error rates significantly.

- *Conscious obstacles.*

In the early 1970s, Danish filmmaker Jørgen Leth was asked by (now) internationally acclaimed director Lars von Trier to remake scenes from one of his first and highly aesthetic films, accepting to obey certain very specific rules or obstacles. The resulting documentary, 'The Five Obstacles', follows Jørgen Leth's travails as he must deconstruct his beautiful film under the strict supervision of von Trier. The film illustrates that the creative process is driven forward not by freedom, but by obstruction. Just like designers thrive on challenging boundaries, filmmaker Jørgen Leths' creativity was stimulated as he tried to tackle increasingly obscure obstacles posed to him by von Trier, such as filming a scene of his tuxedoed self eating a three-course dinner in the middle of a Calcutta slum. Similarly, we can propose explicit obstacles to help drive the ideation process. For instance, what would happen if a certain public service process could only be digital, with no in-person contact at all? Or what if a case handling process that today takes nine months on average had to be done in less than one month? What if the rate of error in a hospital was to be zero? Consciously establishing obstacles reinforces divergent thinking, helping us explore the frontiers of what we thought was possible (Brown, 2009).

- *Temporary anonymity.*

Cross-agency collaboration in the public sector is becoming more and more necessary, as the governance model becomes increasingly networked (Hartley, 2005; Goldsmith and Eggers, 2004; Mulgan, 2009). But, as discussed, it is also often an innovation killer. So how do we help people forget what silo of government they represent, giving them back the freedom to propose a 'stupid' or 'dangerous' idea? As illustrated in the introductory case of the Danish climate strategy, a powerful enforcer of ideation processes across organisational and professional boundaries can be to make every participant temporarily anonymous. Software such as Group System's *Think Tank* and other non-commercial solutions can enable groups of individuals to brainstorm from each of their laptop computers, instantly documenting and viewing each other's ideas, but not being able to discern who enters which idea. This frees up much energy and creativity to take all ideas at face value, allowing civil servants from one department to build and expand on ideas that perhaps originate from another department, allowing a junior civil servant to strengthen the suggestion of a senior executive, and vice versa. Simple as it may seem, taking the hierarchy and power structure out of the collaborative effort can be tremendously liberating. At MindLab, we've used the method in both more analytical processes and in pure brainstorms; and we've involved from three to seven different ministries in the process simultaneously. The officials could develop on each other's ideas, across policy areas, in a spirit of collaboration and professionalism: let the best solutions win, not the most powerful ministry or highest ranking official. Creating anonymity across public bodies is like infusing an artificial dose of liberty to engage in each other's domains, to ask the 'stupid questions' and even to have fun doing it. It might even be the first step to building a more fundamental sense of trust among the participants, paving the ground for next steps and perhaps venturing into less anonymous collaboration.

- *Innovation labs.*

As discussed in Chapter 6, innovation labs, as physical or virtual platforms for creativity and ideation, can help set the scene for the co-creative process, and provide the thought leadership, skills, tools, spaces and technologies that can power ideation. In terms of enhancing the 'professionalism' of the ideation process, this is probably one of the potentially biggest benefits of dedicated innovation labs: imagine that there is actually someone in your organisation who treats innovation just as seriously as a discipline, in theory and practice, as you treat the budgetary or legislative process. Whether it is to help design a two-hour workshop or a three-month process of citizen involvement, innovation labs can provide the experience, tools and resources that make it possible. Just as human resources departments, at their best, support and strengthen the organisation's ability to recruit, retain and develop people, and just as financial controllers underpin the ability to conduct economically responsible governance, innovation labs increase the capacity to drive strategic innovation.

• *Physical and emotional space.*
No matter whether an innovation lab is available or not, physical space can help set the scene for ideation, as a creative platform, such as I described in the previous section. Taking people out of their daily business, lifting them out of the 'swamp' of daily routines, signifies that they are now entering a dedicated, creative process and can help increase motivation, commitment and concentration (Kelley, 2005; Hansen and Jakobsen, 2006). Introducing a sense of fun and 'serious play' can help stimulate creativity. For instance, toymaker Lego has developed an entire idea- and-concept development tool that uses Lego bricks for vision and strategy processes. Building the organisation's future service concept collaboratively with yellow Lego bricks instead of writing a memo might generate a bit more enthusiasm.

Rehearsing the future

I've only highlighted a miniscule fraction of the possibilities for running an ideation process. Just Google 'creativity tools' and around 50,000 links appear, many of which contain entire toolboxes. There is no lack of online resources; the challenge is to select the best and to consciously design the process.

It almost goes without saying that the format for much of the ideation work I've described earlier is the *workshop*. Gathering in workshops rather than in meetings, and producing something tangible, through a collaborative process, rather than exchanging views or positions, can be foreign to many. At MindLab, we had proposed to a senior director in a ministry that we could facilitate part of a cross-ministerial steering group meeting he was chairing, in order to ensure that all dimensions of the problem were covered. So we said we would run the meeting as a workshop and bring *post-its* along. That was the point when the manager said he really didn't see the need for any facilitation at all. Given that later stages of our joint project would involve somewhat more radical processes, such as bringing ethnographic research and video clips into play as part of the decision-making process, this was not a good start.

We chose to schedule a new meeting, where we shared our methods and work processes in detail with the director, providing case examples for illustration. His reaction was something along the lines of 'Oh, is *that* what you do?', and not only did he allow for a more open process in the steering group, including workshops, but also for the running of key video material at a later high-level meeting.

One of the most effective drivers of new ideas might therefore simply be the ability to meet and work together effectively in a different way. Establishing a simple template for designing workshops that combine various creative process tools is the first fundamental step to applying creativity systematically in the organisation. Creative workshops should be celebrated as occasions for shaping the future together. Often we make sure to take plenty of pictures or video during the process, capturing the feel and energy of the collaboration, sending the best shots and clips back to the group soon after.

A powerful way of viewing ideation workshops, which is emphasised by researchers at the Danish Design School, is to see each workshop as a 'design lab' where the participants through their collaboration not only imagine different futures, but start creating them by the very act of imagination (Binder and Brandt, 2008). Building on this perspective, Brandt and other colleagues from the Design School characterise such sessions as 'rehearsing the future' (Halse et al, 2010). Once you have been part of seeing and making explicit how things could be, you are already more prepared to also be an active part of that future. Video can be a strong ingredient in that design process (Ylirisku and Buur, 2007). For instance, at MindLab we have helped public servants enact new service processes using small (10 cm tall) cardboard figures of the actors involved (such as citizens, government agencies, health professionals), capturing the miniature 'plays' on video, and using the clips to vividly illustrate exactly how they imagine a new service should function. Once their initial reservations are overcome (the process often starts with a bit of giggling), public servants embrace the new reality they are creating. By prototyping a new service idea immediately in this manner, and capturing it to review and share with colleagues and managers, service design becomes extremely tangible. Such workshops are in many respects the engine of the co-creation process, driving it forward, setting the scene for collaboration. The power of workshops as a form of working and creating together in the public sector cannot, I think, be underestimated.

Selection

Throughout the various ideation stages, moving through the innovation 'funnel' from hundreds of ideas to the three concepts we want to pursue, a screening process takes place. The reason we need many ideas, perhaps 200 or more for each really good one, is that our assessment of the quality of an idea changes as we begin to describe it in more detail. What sounds like a great idea when it is described as a one-liner, might not seem so convincing when it is presented as a more elaborate one-pager (Ulrich and Terwiesch, 2009). And again the innovation team might be entirely disenchanted when it sees a thorough 10-page business case. Conversely, what does not sound particularly hot at first, may, upon further scrutiny, be a sound proposal. Because ideas, over time, can shift place in this hierarchy of 'innovation quality', we need many of them. But we also need agreed and transparent criteria for selection. Because design thinking prescribes an iterative, more open and flexible process than traditional 'stage-gate' processes, a selection is not necessarily final. We can revisit the previous step, grabbing discarded ideas and giving them another chance, or combining them in new ways.

What are good criteria for evaluating ideas? Of course it depends. But a few of the most common criteria are:

- Is the solution realistic – how likely is it that this can be done in practice, given constraints such as time, resources, skills, political concerns? Would it work for these people or businesses (personas)?
- What would be the potential impact (value) of the idea, if we implemented it?
- How strong is our evidence that this solution will work in practice?
- Strategic match – to what extent does the idea really address our core strategic objectives and goals?
- Quick win – is this something we could do extremely fast, and would it provide us with some positive response and branding, paving the way for longer-term efforts?

Often it can be helpful to draw a coordinate system, placing the two most significant criteria on the axes, and posting all the ideas in the resulting matrix. It could for instance be on the two dimensions of 'realism' and 'potential impact'. This gives a quick visual guide to which ideas may be worth continuing to work on (the most obvious ones being 'high impact, highly realistic', and the least interesting ones being 'low impact, not realistic').

Selection can also be done by asking the team to place their ideas on a dartboard, placing favourites close to the bull's eye, or it can be done by dot-voting, giving the team members dot stickers and asking for their votes on favourite ideas (again on the basis of a mix of specified criteria).

Perhaps the single most important point about the selection process is to never throw 'old' ideas out entirely, but to save them for later. For instance, even though the tax agency wasn't able at the time to implement some of the solutions MindLab helped them develop in a number of workshops with citizens about personal digital services, the agency kept all the resulting raw ideas and draft concepts as an inspirational catalogue for future use. When budgets became available in 2010, a number of the ideas were then fed into the project pipeline.

Concept development

Growing ideas from simple, individual words or short one-liners to mature, well-described and valuable solutions is what concept development is about. A concept is a coherent set of solutions, activities and benefits that are based on one particular 'pitch' or fundamental idea. A concept is tightly connected to the findings and one or more key insights. An example of a public service concept was 'capturing the dream', the overarching title for the project that MindLab carried out with the Danish Enterprise and Construction Agency, and which I mentioned earlier. The concept built on the finding that owners of small and medium-sized enterprises don't primarily run their business to become rich; they do it to live out the dream of building a success. The essence of the solution was that the public agencies in charge of supporting these businesses on their path to growth would have to meet the men and women not as capitalists out to 'make a buck', but as people trying to realise a personal dream. Taking departure in the 'capturing the dream' concept, MindLab and its partner, strategic design firm 1508, could shape a new communications and service process.

The language of 'concepts' is almost entirely absent in the public sector, even though it could easily be applied to both descriptions of how to change an administrative process, a service process, a policy or a form of citizen participation. A concept is a way to structure the objective, content and value proposition of a solution.

Some organisations have established a more or less fixed concept model, which means that a concept or new business model must be described according to a specific template or structure. For instance, in California, Menlo Park-based SRI International has pioneered the NABC model (Needs, Approach, Benefits, Competition), which establishes four categories that an innovative business proposition must be structured around. As discussed earlier, public organisations such as the BBC and Danish Broadcasting (DR) have to various degrees adopted the NABC model. The advantage of such a model is that once it has become an organisation-wide approach to or language for describing solutions, everyone knows how to use it, not just for concept descriptions, but also as a basis for decision-making. In politically governed organisations that are not as close to operations as the BBC and DR, the NABC framework may need to be modified, because it is based on the assumption of a competitive context; however, modified versions or other types of standard conceptual frames may be extremely helpful in embedding a practice and culture of innovation and concept development in the fabric of the organisation.

Concepts can be built around key personas, if they were identified in the earlier analytical phase of the co-creation process; this has the advantage that the concept description specifies how and to what extent it will service or help the different personas.

Any concept needs to state what *benefits* or value it proposes. In public sector innovation, that means specifying expected value across the four bottom lines. What kind of productivity improvements will happen (or will productivity drop)? In what way will the concept, if implemented, improve the service experience for citizens, businesses or other end-users? What are the proposed outcomes of the solution in the short, medium and long term? Are there democratic effects, in terms of increased or decreased citizen participation, transparency or public legitimacy? The ability to succinctly and precisely describe a well-grounded value proposition is not necessarily easy in a complex, conflict-ridden and ambivalent political context. But it is nonetheless the standard a good public sector innovation concept should live up to if it is to form a meaningful basis for decision-making.

Creating

The credos of design thinking give us a few more tools to sharpen our concepts before final decision and implementation. Through an iterative process of prototyping, testing and further adjustment, we are able to 'fail faster to succeed sooner', learning through smart errors in relatively controlled environments.

Prototyping

Applying prototyping to the public sector innovation process isn't just about using a different word for known practices such as pilots. It is, in my experience, about a radically different and more practical way of exploring future solutions at an early stage, and of shaping them in ways that allow fast, small-scale testing, iteration and learning.

In the public sector, a prototype can be a model of a new administrative process, a service journey or a policy initiative. What characterises prototypes, drawing on the principles of design thinking, is that they are highly tangible, either as graphical illustrations, as virtual or physical models or spaces, or as enactments. Service journeys, as I've considered earlier in this chapter, are essentially service process prototypes. They are often made visible through graphically illustrating all steps, interactions, events and experiences that make up a service. Another approach is not to illustrate the service as a diagram, but to illustrate it as a story. The story could simply be a text describing what happens and how it feels, using the tools of science fiction literature to create a 'story from the future' (often scenario planning is associated with such stories). A more visual approach to prototyping future services is to build a storyboard, like a Hollywood movie might be illustrated by graphical designers before the filming begins. Specialist graphic design skills are certainly helpful here – but not always necessary. Anyone can draw a story using stick figures and short explanatory sentences from the key actors in the story – enough for others to get an idea of the key steps and events.

Services can also be enacted. When we at MindLab ran a workshop with US design firm Zago to explore new solutions to climate change, the workshop participants played out different scenarios by miming them. In this process of enactment, which Zago calls 'body slamming', the participants are cast into not just imagining a future, but physically living it. In the workshop one of the groups believed that people would be motivated to use more mass transport, thus reducing CO_2 emissions, if only buses were more comfortable and individualised. So they enacted a day in a person's life, waiting at the bus stop, catching a smart new electric minibus and experiencing the higher service level of the CO_2-free collective transport of the future.

Sometimes physical models are the answer. For instance, when American Red Cross worked with IDEO to explore new ways of making temporary field clinics for blood donors more comfortable for doctors and donors, they built a full-scale prototype of the new portable facility they imagined. One of the new service processes, drawing on citizen-centric insights about what motivates people to give blood, was that donors would be given a card at the entry to the facility where they could write their personal story and share their emotional reasons for giving blood. The cards were then placed on a bulletin board near the entry to the facility, sharing these personal stories. According to IDEO, the objective was to design the 'emotional experience' of the donors (Brown, 2009).

Digital services are also easy to prototype. Graphical sketches or 'mock-ups' of home pages can be drawn by hand, illustrating the layout and specific functions. More advanced drafts can be drawn in PowerPoint or graphical programmes like *InDesign*. However, it can be a good idea to consciously keep the prototype looking 'raw' and unfinished. Our experience at MindLab is that the rougher a draft is, the easier it is to engage citizens or other users in a dialogue about how the solution might look and function. If the mock-up looks too polished, people will think it is nearly finished and that there isn't much room for changing it anyway.

What about prototyping policy? When a policy initiative consists of a number of elements such as regulation, expenditure programmes or particular services, the way in which each of those elements will play out in a real-life setting can be prototyped in its own right, using the approaches sketched out above. Policies might also be prototyped through future scenarios: what would the world look and feel like if the policy was realised? Which alternative futures might it help create?

It is usually extremely helpful to involve citizens as part of the prototyping process, obtaining their feedback and testing the ground for different options. A key strength of prototypes is that they allow for common understanding and dialogue about a proposed solution not only across internal disciplines and hierarchies, but also between the 'system' and 'users'. Sometimes the user feedback is not to build the service at all. For instance, when the Danish Labour Market Authority prototyped a new digital self-help service where unemployed citizens could schedule appointments with caseworkers online, it turned out that citizens had no need for such a service. Two workshops with carefully selected groups of unemployed people helped innovators gain a much better understanding of their real needs. As it turned out, fitting appointments into a packed calendar wasn't really the challenge the unemployed were typically facing (when you are unemployed there is one resource you have in abundance: time). But they did lack an online service that could sum up the activities they had agreed with the caseworker, job search strategies and to-dos. So instead of building the self-booking system, the Labour Market Authority chose to first create an online résumé and reference tool – utilising the resources of the unemployed more optimally.

Testing

In addition to being fast and cost-effective to carry out, a major strength of prototypes is that they usually don't create a lot of the types of questions and challenges that pilots and real-life trials do (Mulgan, 2009). Because pilots only involve part of the population, there will often be a question of citizens' rights and equality before the law. However, since prototypes cannot take account of all the relevant context factors that may be involved, and since there will be unforeseen elements in a real-life setting, moving from prototypes to 'live' pilots in small scale, for instance in geographically selected sites, might still be a relevant next step. Some public organisations go about their pilots in a highly systematic way, establishing randomised control trial set-ups to gain a strong evidence base that a new programme works (or not). A key challenge here is to be able to conduct and learn from pilots fast enough to be able to implement the new ideas before they become redundant. Another challenge is to not design pilots to simply ensure success; too often stakes become so high that a pilot must not fail, and so there is no learning. As Mulgan (2009) rightly points out, anything genuinely innovative is almost certain to not go quite according to plan.

Implementing

Once we are sufficiently confident that a solution will work, it is time to put it into practice. As I highlighted in Chapter 2, successful implementation is what bridges the generation and selection of ideas with the ultimate creation of value. The discipline of implementation has received extensive interest in the management literature, probably for the simple reason that it makes all the difference between *wanting* to do something in an organisation and actually making it happen. To a large extent, implementing innovative new solutions in the public sector, like the private sector, is a change management challenge. It is not the purpose of this book to cover in any detail the vast knowledge about implementation and organisational change processes; however, a few key points should be made that are of relevance to the public sector organisation and the co-creation process.

First, one of the central insights about co-creation that can hardly be overstated is that if you go through the process of creating a new solution *with* the people who are going to use it, the chances of successful implementation increase dramatically (Attwood et al, 2003; Ackoff et al, 2006; Binder and Brandt, 2008; Eggers and O'Leary, 2009).

Second, there really is no stage too early to involve people throughout the organisation who will at some point play a role in implementing and running the potential solution: systems developers, trainers, human resource professionals, communication staff, front-line managers and workers and so on. The level of involvement may vary over time, but you will want them on board *early*.

Third, in spite of high involvement, implementation can still be extremely challenging. It requires leadership and direction. A classic book like John Kotter's, *Leading Change* (1996), can be helpful in planning and engaging in small- and large-scale change projects. In an intriguing article, 'The Irrational Side of Change Management' (2009), Aiken and Keller of McKinsey, a consultancy, argue that change processes are viewed in one way by management and in a very different way by the people who are impacted by them. Understanding the kind of rationality at work amongst staff is a prerequisite for managing the change process well. They highlight nine 'counterintuitive' insights that can help increase the odds of implementation success. The insights are ordered around the four overall change management 'best practices' of *telling a compelling story, role modelling, creating reinforcing mechanisms* and *capacity building*. A common thread across these dimensions is the need to understand the uniquely human social, cognitive and emotional biases that can impede change efforts. A much better recognition of how people interpret their environment and choose to act is necessary (Aiken and Keller, 2009).

It is one thing to implement a solution within one organisation – be it large or small. That, in itself, can be difficult enough. In the public sector, however, at least when it comes to central departments, but also sometimes in agencies and institutions, the idea or concept is not to be implemented in the same organisation that created it in the first place. A classic example is the department that formulates a new policy initiative that some dozens or hundreds of institutions must take up and turn into reality. This essentially requires hundreds of near-simultaneous implementation processes to take place – transforming someone else's idea into practice. Another example could be a department or agency that identifies an innovative, valuable practice in one institution and subsequently wants all other institutions in the sector to take up the same practice as their peer. In public sector innovation terminology, this is what we would call *scaling*, and it is one of the toughest challenges we have.

Scaling

'Scaling' is a slightly misleading term, because it carries with it a connotation that it's an easy thing to do. It isn't. Scaling isn't a mechanistic process, like blowing air into a balloon and watching it expand accordingly. Scaling – ensuring wide take-up of innovative new solutions across geography and time – depends on people. Even if one public organisation has successfully demonstrated that a new practice, approach or method is highly valuable, there is no guarantee that it will ignite the interest of anyone else (Moore, 2005; Harris and Albury, 2009). In fact, this even counts for colleagues *within the same institution.* At a public school in northern Zealand, Denmark, two enthusiastic teachers had with great success introduced the concept of innovation and creative processes for kids in the lower grades – to the point where a class successfully did an independent presentation for the city's mayor and a room of more than 100 civil servants. When asked whether other teachers in the school had been inspired and adopted the same methods and practices, the answer was negative.

'Scaling', however, is no worse than other labels such as 'dissemination', 'take-up', 'replication' or 'diffusion'. All are terms that seek to capture the key question: how do we move from successfully doing something new in one setting, to doing it in all relevant settings? As Jean Hartley, who prefers 'diffusion', has stated: 'Whatever the language, there is still a lot to be learned about how diffusion takes place, and how and why innovations are adapted to different contexts and cultures' (2005, p 33). There are a number of barriers to scaling, which need to be understood:

• *Lack of 'pull' incentives.*
As I discussed in some detail in Chapter 3, because only few public organisations operate in full-blown competitive markets, the incentive to *pull* and actively adopt new solutions is usually not as strong as in the private sector (Moore, 2005). Scaling requires not only that an innovation is well documented. It requires that others in a position to leverage that innovation to the advantage of their own organisation and its constituents hear about it, understand it, like it, are motivated to try to adopt it, are able to create the internal coalitions to actively translate and adapt the solution within the organisation, and can muster sufficient enthusiasm and resources around it – in spite of the fact that the idea came from somewhere else. The intrinsic and extrinsic incentives to pull new solutions in from the outside are not always strong enough; and few organisations are actively scanning the horizon for others' ideas,

taking an open approach to innovation and having the leadership and culture to adopt new solutions effectively.

• *Lack of 'push' incentives.*
Conversely, there typically is no market-driven incentive to spend the necessary time and resources to *push* a new solution, trying to convince others that there is real value to gain by using your idea. If a public manager in one organisation spends one third of her time for half a year 'selling' an innovation, and a few others adopt it, what would be the benefit to her, other than possibly the satisfaction? As Tom Kelley has highlighted, car-maker Volvo, the company that invented the modern three-point seat belt, chose to share the invention with everyone who was interested. Why didn't they patent the invention? The company considered it too important for traffic safety to keep it for themselves (Kelley, 2005). What if more public organisations thought that way?

• *Lack of codification.*
There is no strong public sector tradition for conceptualising and codifying solutions, whether they are technological solutions, processes or professional in-person services, so that they can easily be shared and transferred. Part of it could be due to limited use of professional knowledge management systems; another part could be that there is no incentive since scaling isn't considered a relevant scenario. While a national bank might be interested in codifying solutions and processes so they could be scaled in connection with mergers, acquisitions or international expansions, many public organisations don't have those types of incentives.

How do we do it then? To scale innovation it is necessary to play a wide range of instruments, combining the different tools in the way most appropriate to the task. Let us consider the range of approaches.

Legislation

Legislating to ensure that all relevant actors adopt or comply with a certain solution seems like the obvious answer; however, it is but one tool among many. Under certain conditions, it is obviously the right tool. Geoff Mulgan and David Albury (2003) have pointed out that this particularly is the case when there is solid evidence that the solution can work independently of local context; and when there are sufficiently strong administrative systems for enforcement in place. In Denmark, for instance, the drive to spread the innovation of digital business-to-government (B2G) payments, getting 100% of business transactions with government online, was ultimately driven by legislation and centralised control. However, many ideas would be too small, too dependent on organisational context and conditions, not sufficiently evidenced, or otherwise not suited to enforce by law.

Creating demand

It is easier to scale innovations that are in demand. And scaling through a *pull* dynamic, rather than the traditional *push* dynamic, is usually the most effective. Haven't we seen enough pamphlets, websites and best practice guides being produced to no end (Harris and Albury, 2009)? Serious consideration must be given to the different types of incentives for organisations and individuals to become 'willing adopters' (Moore, 2005; Mulgan, 2009). One obvious point then, in the spirit of co-creation, is to ensure that at least some of those ultimately responsible for using or taking over the innovation are themselves involved in the innovation process (Harris and Albury, 2009). Being part of the process not only creates a sense of mutual ownership, it allows people to start thinking at a very early stage about how the solution might work for them in their particular setting, enabling them to begin 'rehearsing the future' (Binder and Brandt, 2008; Halse et al, 2010). It builds the foundations that later scaling must stand on.

However, it is often not feasible that more than a fraction of potential adopters of a public sector innovation are involved in the process. Some after-the-fact approaches may also be necessary. Can we take in specific measures that make adopting the innovation particularly desirable for everyone else? Are the benefits for us (for instance central government) of adoption by others so great that we might share some of the potential rewards upfront, as icing on the cake? Involvement of some of the potential adopters can uncover what might work as incentives, and help provide a realistic assessment of what it would require to generate real demand. If involvement of those intended to use the innovation is not feasible, it is a good idea to conduct interviews or fieldwork with the target organisations to understand their context and motivations. Prestige and recognition (and competition) might be as powerful drivers of demand as monetary incentives; what matters the most, and would work the best in the specific case, is up to you to discover.

Documenting results

Needless to say, the value of successful innovative solutions must be stated convincingly. There must be strong and clear descriptions of what the change is, how it was brought about, what it required, and how it created value on one or more of the four public sector bottom lines. Quantitative data that generate the sense of 'hard facts' are good; but powerful stories about the enthusiasm, energy and satisfaction the solution will deliver can be at least as convincing. Go for stories that include the numbers (Heath and Heath, 2007). Should an innovation live up to the rigour of 'evidence' (such as extensive evaluations or randomised control trials) to be sufficiently credible? That might be very helpful and relevant; but it also might well be that the immediate feedback and learning already generated by the host organisation is sufficiently convincing to allow others to get on board, knowing that positive outcomes aren't finally 'proven'; the context might change before the studies are finalised, or citizens may even be left to suffer while bureaucrats are awaiting 'hard evidence'. Given the dynamics and complexities of 'wicked problems', there are limits to how much we can trust evidence (Mulgan, 2009).

Sponsors and champions

For public sector innovations to be sustainable at scale, they often need sponsors and champions. It is necessary to identify organisations with the resources and critical mass to either implement the innovation itself at scale, or to actively help others do so. Sometimes the task is to find strategic matches and develop partnerships between organisations with great ideas (but few resources to leverage them) and organisations with fewer ideas (but the power, channels and capacity to make them happen). This is often the model advocated in the realm of social innovation, where (non-governmental) social entrepreneurs seek private or government sponsors to carry their solution to scale (Mulgan et al, 2006). But sponsorship is just as relevant in pure intra-governmental innovation.

An example is the Danish electronic transfer system for B2G data transactions that was mentioned earlier. The Danish tax authority had created and worked on the solution for nearly a decade, getting a penetration rate to the target population (all Danish enterprises) of only around 5%. The responsible manager then identified an opportunity to shift this innovation portfolio to the Ministry of Finance; a few years later the penetration rate, backed by law, was closing at 100%. The finance ministry simply had a more powerful position on the issue, and was able to leverage political backing for the necessary legislative measures to effectively scale the solution. (This story also illustrates the old point that it is amazing what can be accomplished if one is willing not to take credit for it.)

In particular more radical innovations can require a critical mass and gain the necessary momentum. As Osborne and Brown (2005) point out, more classic public bureaucracies may in fact be better at carrying through system-transforming innovation than smaller institutions in a market setting. If the task is long-term scaling of a significant innovation, it might even be relevant to establish an entirely new organisation or unit to do it.

Roadshows

Professional practitioners will (usually) be more willing to adopt something they see other fellow practitioners do with success. This implies that there is only one thing to do if one wants professionals such as teachers, doctors, nurses and social workers to take on a new solution. Show it, in person. Roadshows, where the originators of the innovation demonstrate the solution(s), are a powerful tool. One-way presentations at a few generic conferences aren't enough, though. There has to be a real effort to make sure that the right people participate, and the meetings must be framed for interaction, real engagement and learning. Visual tools such as video demonstrations can also be helpful, as can websites and online resources that people can browse after the event. The challenge here, as discussed earlier, is of course to allow the time and resources for the people who 'own' the innovation to actually promote it actively. Another challenge is scope; there is a limit to how far around a country a 'roadshow' can go; what could work in a relatively small country like Sweden is not as easy to carry out in the United States.

Communicating through professional networks and trade associations

Since there is a limit to how far roadshows can go, other professional channels might have to be employed. Often front-line professionals are members of unions or professional associations, and these organisations may have greater reach and deeper resonance with those that need to know about the innovation than a public authority (Mulgan, 2009). It can be a very effective means at least of spreading knowledge of an innovation to utilise the communication channels already used by the target group, and that might be recognised as a highly legitimate and credible source of information. For more hands-on dialogue and interaction there may be professional forums or subgroups where people meet and where it would be natural to share an innovative new approach.

Recognising managers as knowledge engineers

Strong and visionary leadership has regularly been highlighted as key in ensuring the adoption of something new. Professor and knowledge management guru Ikujiro Nonaka has pointed out that mid-level managers (and in the public sector, institution heads) often play a crucial role in connecting top management's strategies and objectives with the daily challenges and opportunities facing front-line workers (Mulgan and Albury, 2003). Because of this unique position, mid-level managers can potentially act as *knowledge engineers*, identifying how a solution can be tinkered with and adopted in a way that will actually work (Sanger and Levin, 1992; Nonaka and Takeuchi, 1995). The point, of course, is that for an innovation to be successful it must not only potentially contribute to the organisation's strategic goals, it must also be practically applied. And practical application (getting stuff to work) is something that engineers are very good at. To engage mid-level managers as knowledge engineers could mean to involve them meaningfully in the innovation process (for instance in prototyping/testing), or to build networks where they can be introduced at an early stage to the solutions(s), receive information, training or advice, and subsequently share experiences with the process of adoption. A key point is to allow the managers the flexibility to create their own subversions or adaptations of the solutions, generating ownership and laying the foundation for more sustainable scaling, driven by such champions.

The big challenge with scaling, then, is to understand that it takes a lot more than a website and pamphlets – and that legislation may not be the answer either. In between these two extremes there is a variety of tools that, used wisely in combination, may do the trick.

A slightly heretical thought on scaling here at the end of the section: what if we, in many instances, will never truly be able to achieve the kind of scale of innovative public solutions that we want? What if public organisations simply do not want to adopt 'best practices', but would rather shape their own 'next practice'? Could it be that the best way of generating the motivation and enthusiasm, and mustering the needed resources, is essentially to nurture the innovation ecosystem of consciousness, capacity, co-creation and courage in *all* public organisations? Rather than spending too much energy on 'diffusing' centralised solutions, should we set institutions free to (within boundaries of the law) create their own, from the bottom up? Even if it would sometimes mean reinventing the wheel? As Harris and Albury (2009) have argued, might it make sense to decentralise innovation resources, which sometimes seem abundant at central level, and allow local institutions more freedom and give them better tools to innovate for themselves?

We have to be realistic about what can be 'scaled' in the absence of the strong innovation demand that is generated by highly competitive market pressures. Even then, as many private businesses painfully realise, do employees still often maintain a 'not invented here' attitude. For instance, it took global consumer business Procter & Gamble years of work and hard metrics and incentives to achieve a culture where it was accepted that innovations could come from outside the organisation via its famed *Connect & Develop* strategy. No wonder public sector organisations, who are usually at no immediate risk of losing market shares or bankruptcy, find it hard to successfully adopt solutions created elsewhere.

Learning

Innovation is an iterative learning process – both at systems, organisational, project and individual level. As I discussed in Chapter 4, innovation approaches that are 'strategic-reflexive' and emphasise openness and learning may hold significant potential for public organisations. The same applies to the process of co-creation. Perhaps we are not satisfied, at face value, with the concepts we developed in the 'synthesis' phase. Or maybe our prototype tests led to a reframing of the problem, or illustrated the need for further research (Bessant, 2005).

The learning cycle

Learning, in a co-creation context, is the process of assessing whether we are actually getting to the solutions that will effectively address the problem or opportunity at hand. Obviously, learning goes on throughout the process; but at some stage we must reflect more formally and be prepared to chart the direction again. Too often, government projects are pressed for time and resources, and the option of iterating, moving back to one or more of the previous elements of the process, is not available – or is not believed to be available. However, there can be tremendous value in even a quick revisit to the users' context through follow-up interviews, or in refining and retesting a first prototype, improving it further until live test or scaling. The innovation process ends up looking less like a 'knowledge funnel', and more like a 'knowledge cycle'.

Figure 9.2: The iterative cycle of the co-creation process*

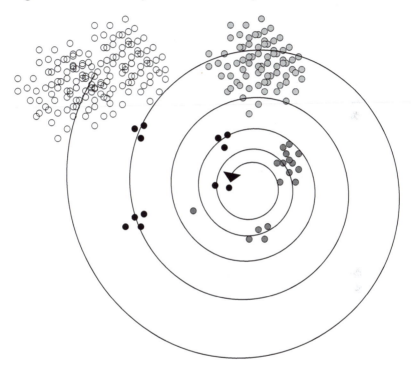

Note: The shadings illustrate the gradual maturation of ideas.

Ultimately, learning is about whether the solution worked as hoped. Once it was implemented and (possibly) scaled, was the desired value created, and can the value be ascribed to the solution to some degree? On the four public sector bottom lines of *productivity*, *service experience*, *results* and *democracy*, how do we fare? Is the solution successful on at least some of the bottom lines without being harmful on others? Before turning to the methods of measuring innovation (Chapter 10), let's briefly consider the potential of co-creation for generating radical new value across these four bottom lines.

Co-creating radical efficiency?

Co-creation is not just about finding solutions that deliver better services or generate intended outcomes. Co-creation is about enabling public organisations to innovate and generate new value for less. A recent study illustrates that this is possible.

Against the backdrop of the financial crisis, the budget crunch and mounting calls for radical reform of government, the UK-based Innovation Unit asked: what are the most convincing global examples of public service organisations achieving radical productivity gains while maintaining or enhancing services and dramatically improving results and outcomes? If they can be found, what might we learn from such examples, and are there lessons that are more or less universal? In early 2010, the results were ready. From South Africa to India to the United States, the more than 120 case examples showed that it is in fact possible to have a rather large piece of cake and eat it too. There were four key components that generated radical efficiency solutions in public services (Gillinson et al, 2010):

- *New insights*, for instance from collecting new data, from involving citizens, from getting a new colleague, from other sectors, from mining data or simply from uncovering old ideas in new places.
- *New customers*, which implies reconceptualising who the organisation is truly serving. It might for instance involve shifting an understanding of users as 'partners', rather than as 'recipients', such as in the case of the Danish enterprise agency mentioned earlier, which harvested massive productivity and service gains by reconceptualising 'clients' into 'customers'.
- *New suppliers*, which could entail finding service providers in entirely different fields, such as when a Swedish hospital partnered with a hotel chain to run patient hotels, or it could entail engaging citizens as co-producers.
- *New resources*, which are assets or tools like people, buildings and technology, such as a new virtual crime-mapping tool applied by the Chicago police.

The authors point out that what can really deliver 'radical efficiency' are new perspectives on the challenges (upper part of Figure 9.3). It is new insights and new resources that, when combined with the latter two dimensions, are catalysts for different, lower-cost and better outcomes. From the Restorative Circles in Brazil, which introduced conflict resolution in schools and poor neighbourhoods, to the US Chicago police's CLEAR programme, it was by connecting in entirely new ways to stakeholders and users that radical new solutions were shaped.

Figure 9.3: The radical efficiency model

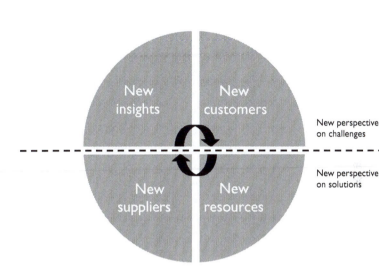

New perspective on challenges

New perspective on solutions

Source: Gillinson et al (2010)

These insights are important in the context of co-creation because they show that it is only by placing *people* – citizens, communities, businesses, families – and their relationships at the very centre of our thinking that we can radically re-imagine and redesign public services. Co-creation offers a set of approaches that can help us not only recognise when we've succeeded in reaching surprisingly radical new solutions – but actively work to create more of them. It is by understanding people, and by 'rehearsing the future' with them, that we can make a serious stab at achieving the better society that we strive for.

How to do it

This chapter has provided a comprehensive guide to the co-creation process from framing to scaling and learning. A common thread has been how to get people – colleagues, citizens, experts – involved in meaningful and effective ways throughout the different dimensions of the process. There is no 'right' model for orchestrating co-creation, or for who to involve, how and when. However, it has been the ambition to give a concrete sense of the activities involved.

The barriers to orchestrating the process are mainly questions of *lacking consciousness* (public servants are not even aware that there is a different way to develop new solutions), lack of *tools* (people are not trained in how to conduct co-creation in practice) and lack of *enabling resources* or platforms (there's no one to help overcome the barrier of trying it for the first time). How do we get traction with your process of co-creation? Some of the key points are as follows.

Apply methods that leverage design thinking and ethnographic skills

Because co-creation and, in the end, innovation, are about *doing*, the process I've described in this chapter is quite method-heavy. Either key project developers within the organisation have to learn a number of the approaches, methods and tools I've reviewed, or outside expertise must be brought in. Often, a combination of in-house 'innovation experts' and some degree of external support from designers, management consultants, academics and others can work well. What is crucial, though, is to *never* subcontract the entire process to someone outside the organisation, depositing key experiences, insights and learning to people who will never have to live with the outcomes of the process. There should be a very hands-on, engaged and proactive nature to the way the public organisation's own staff are involved; and there must be clear accountability and engagement at leadership level, ensuring access to the relevant hierarchies and an ongoing connection to other activities and innovation processes in the organisation. The public manager must therefore ask:

- *Who are our innovation experts that we could put in charge of orchestrating co-creation?*
- *If we have no design or ethnographic competencies in the organisation, how could we get some?*

Create platforms for support

Because co-creation processes are complex, in that they take account of a range of stakeholders and introduce new modes of knowledge, support platforms are necessary. They can take the form of guides or toolboxes that make access to specific approaches and methods easy. They can take the place of innovation labs that can support and ensure a professional and nurturing environment for the process may be relevant. As a very minimum, a professional project organisation is needed:

- *Do we have sufficient enabling resources that can make it easier for people to succeed with co-creation, lowering the barriers to get started and run the process successfully?*

Obtain permission

Co-creation involves using tools and methods that are foreign to many public sector organisations. Gaining 'permission' from the next level or two in the internal hierarchy to run projects as open co-creation processes rather than traditional, internally oriented stage-gate models or committee meetings can be a challenge in itself. Even the workshop format is still unfamiliar to many, and it may require a bit of managerial massaging to be allowed to run things this way, rather than as traditional meetings:

- *Who needs to give permission to run co-creation processes (or who should we be prepared to convince)?*
- *What would be the best way to get buy-in from those we need it from?*

Lead the process

Orchestrating co-creation is a leadership task. In my experience, only where a responsible manager has 'got it' and really embraced the co-creation process is it likely that benefit will be harvested. 'Getting it' includes facing the pain of *really* seeing what doesn't work today, and having the courage to embrace divergence, envisaging how different the future could be, and motivating the staff to stick to the process, even if the findings may be unpleasant. It is challenging to the ways of working in government to recognise that by letting go of much of the process, more can achieved:

- *Are the managers involved in the co-creation process prepared to contribute actively, and are they prepared to take the consequences of the insights and new solutions that are likely to emerge from it?*

The last chapter in this book addresses the question of leadership and how it is fundamental to realising public sector innovation. Before that, however, we will consider how we can drive innovation by measuring to learn.

10

Measuring to learn

'Productive societies, to sustain themselves, must be both efficient and creative.' (Professors Richard K. Lester and Michael J. Piore, 2006)

Youth Villages is a non-profit organisation, headquartered in the state of Tennessee, that works on behalf of government agencies to serve emotionally and behaviourally troubled youth between the ages of six and 22. The organisation provides in-home and residential programmes that help children and young people improve academic achievement, make a successful transition to employment and avoid criminal activity. Most of the youth they serve have cycled in and out of foster care or are involved in the juvenile justice system. The results of Youth Villages' efforts are remarkable: compared with traditional US child-welfare services, Youth Villages' in-home programme has a 38% lower average monthly cost, a 71% shorter average length of stay and a long-term success rate of 80%. That is twice the national average (Edna McConnell Clark Foundation, 2010). And from being a small Tennessee-based organisation at its foundation in 1986, Youth Villages today has 11 offices in as many states – a successful example of scaling innovation. Youth Villages has been widely recognised for its success: by academia in the form of a *Harvard Business School* case study, praising it as a national leader in the field of children's behavioural health; and by policymakers, earning recognition from the Obama administration's new Social Innovation Fund.

How did the story of Youth Villages unfold to become such a success? By allowing measurement to drive learning, which in turn improved organisational performance. Continuous innovation and experimentation was at the heart of their growth from a single-site NGO to a national organisation. 'It's like a science project every day', said Patrick Lawler, founder and Executive Director of Youth Villages, at a conference. He also highlighted how a key turning point in the performance of Youth Villages was the result of his decision to have key staff spend a year studying evidence-based youth services. Their new insights resulted in the recognition in 1993–94 that Youth Villages' effectiveness would be far greater if it used research-validated in-home services (specifically, Multisystemic Family Therapy, MST). This entailed working with families, rather than continuing to work with individual youths in residential and hospital-based treatment approaches away from home. The reason? Because, as Youth Villages learned, the systemic causes of the problem were with families, not with the individual youths. From the moment the organisation acted on that research-based insight, by redefining how they related to their users and then redesigning their core services, they started their remarkable path to success. The key to Youth Villages' subsequent growth was the organisation's ability to convince government offices that Youth Villages not only could provide less expensive services than those provided by government programmes, but also, that the organisation could get far better outcomes – as demonstrated by its outcome tracking data. One might say, with Roger Martin's terms, that Youth Villages, once having solved the 'mystery' of the most effective approach to its core mission, had successfully leveraged an 'algorithm' that could take its efforts to scale.

With limited resources and rapidly growing needs, public organisations must invest in activities that create the desired value for society. To that end, organisations must measure whether they contribute positively to that change, or whether they are simply keeping themselves busy. Because innovation is the link between strategic intentions on the one hand, and the creation of more value on the other, it is natural to view measurement in that context. We have to understand whether we are working hard enough to be creative – and yet we must also understand whether in fact that creativity and innovation lead us in the direction we want to go.

In considering *value*, public organisations must have some sense of their performance on the four bottom lines I introduced in Chapter 2. With regard to *innovation*, it is relevant to generate at least some level of data about the organisation's capacity to innovate and about the kind of innovation activities that are undertaken, to better understand the degree to which those activities lead to the desired outcomes. It sounds simple on paper. But measuring to manage performance is a difficult discipline; unlike Youth Villages, few get it right. And it took them over 30 years to get to where they are today.

This chapter discusses innovation measurement in the context of the wider question of 'public value', and how to learn from it:

- The measurement challenge and the 80/20 rule.
- How can one assess an organisation's innovation *potential*?
- How can the *process* of innovation be measured?

- How can one measure the ultimate *value* of innovation?
- Can performance management catalyse innovation?

What you measure ...

It has become conventional wisdom that 'what you measure, you can manage' (Cole and Parston, 2006; Pfeffer and Sutton, 2006). In the best of worlds, relevant, meaningful and timely measurement is used proactively in an ongoing dialogue to power learning and drive increased performance, enhancing productivity and delivering more and better outcomes.

However, the opposite also holds true: *what* gets measured is potentially subject to human decisions, actions and even manipulation, and so there's no guarantee that you end up getting the behaviour you wanted, just because you measured it. Austin (1996) points out that 'measurement dysfunction' can be a significant trap in organisations, with the implication that staff behaviour and organisational performance doesn't improve at all, perhaps even to the contrary. In their work on public service innovation, Parker and Heapy (2006, p 65) similarly point out that the right balance has to be struck between the 'productivity' bottom line and the 'service' and 'results' bottom lines, arguing that in the UK, 'Existing targets have tended to focus energy on underperformance in operational excellence, at the expense of underperformance in the transformation of people's lives'. As the case of Youth Villages illustrates, the relevant use of performance measurement and management can lead to significant improvements in *both* organisational performance *and* the transformation of people's lives.

Why do we want to measure? Answer: to understand the value of our work so we can improve upon it, and to be accountable, informing public policymaking and funding priorities. The challenge, however, is to ensure that measurement in fact benefits these two key intended purposes, which can be characterised as *informational* and *motivational* (Austin, 1996):

- *Informational.* Measurements that are valued primarily for the logistical, status and research information they convey, which provide insights and allow better short-term management and long-term improvement of organisational processes. In the public sector, informational types of measurements have the additional (and often overarching) objective of enhancing accountability, making the operations and results of public bodies transparent to taxpayers, the

media and politicians alike, ultimately making it possible to hold administrative and political leaders responsible.
- *Motivational.* Measurement that is intended explicitly to affect the people who are being measured, to promote greater efforts in pursuit of the organisation's goals and drive performance.

Austin emphasises that while motivational measurement seeks to alter behaviour positively, informational measurement is, as a point of departure, not intended to influence behaviour, because it seeks to capture events as they take place as if people didn't know the measurement system existed. Thus, to the degree that measurement is only used for informational purposes – for accountability – it won't have much impact on performance. As Mulgan (2009, p 228) has stated rather succinctly, 'you can't fatten a pig by weighing it'. In fact informational measurement may have unintended negative impacts, because people tend to know they are being measured and behave accordingly, even if they aren't supposed to (Austin, 1996).

Unfortunately, many public sector organisations place a greater emphasis on measurements of informational value, and thus we keep ourselves busy measuring, using more of our resources on documenting the past and monitoring the present, rather than learning from it and creating the future. Such 'metrics mania' is dangerous (Cole and Parston, 2006). This is the 80/20 rule that I introduced at the beginning of the book. It is no coincidence, therefore, that I call this chapter 'Measuring to learn', even though it will focus quite a bit on how to measure (in order to learn how to drive performance). The point is that we should be careful about which measurements, and how many, we put in place.

Measuring innovation

To many, 'measuring innovation' is as much an oxymoron as is 'innovation in the public sector'. However, as I have attempted to show throughout this book, innovation isn't a random, one-off event, impossible to capture, but is rather a systematic process, a discipline that focuses on achieving desired strategic objectives. Because innovation is at the heart of what government can do to become more successful, of course the process can also be captured, understood and improved.

What often confuses people, however, is the question: in what sense are we speaking of measuring innovation? In this chapter I will consider three distinct perspectives on measuring and learning in the context of public sector innovation:

- *Assessing the organisation's potential to innovate.* This addresses all the four Cs of the innovation ecosystem. This is a snapshot or 'static' type of measurement that can inform us about the status quo: how do we strengthen the organisation's efforts across the four dimensions of the system?
- *Learning from the individual innovation processes.* This picks up on the previous chapter and concerns how some organisations are trying to measure and improve how they innovate. This is a dynamic measurement that allows us to learn immediately from doing, and to adjust and change our ongoing innovation efforts.
- *Measuring the value of innovation.* This addresses how to measure the four ultimate bottom lines of innovation that I introduced in Chapter 2. This is more of a systems-level measurement that requires some time-lag before we can learn from it. However, once we begin to harvest feedback on the ultimate 'real-world' impact of innovation efforts, we have established a tremendous learning environment.

The logic of these three types of innovation measurements is, essentially, a theory of change that reflects the following logic:

- IF we build an innovation ecosystem;
- AND we continuously learn from our innovation processes;
- THEN we can create more and better value.

A truly innovative public sector organisation would be one that in fact measures and learns from its performance on all of the three dimensions described here. I am currently not aware of any organisation that does this systematically, although some are certainly trying.

Assessing innovation potential

When the Danish Ministry of Integration chose to create an innovation strategy, they first conducted a thorough review of the organisation's current practices, with the assistance of external consultants. They asked: 'What is our innovation potential?', 'Are we doing enough at all levels to create an environment that increases the likelihood that we will get more and better ideas, and that our organisation is able to implement them?'.

To assess an organisation's total innovation potential is to analyse how it is faring on each of the four Cs, or dimensions of the innovation ecosystem, that make up the framework for this book. In this sense it is a total baseline for the level of innovation potential embedded in the organisation, its people and its processes.

Although we haven't yet discussed the Courage, or leadership, dimension (that is the final section of the book), this would be included as well. Examples of the key elements needed to assess a public sector organisation's innovation potential are:

- *Consciousness*
  - We have a common **language** of innovation and our people are able to reflect independently on their own innovation practices.
  - Managers and staff across our organisation see the same innovation landscape.
- *Capacity*
  - Our organisation's political and legal **context** allows freedoms to innovate; for instance, are there exemptions from legislation that we can access?
  - We have a clear **strategy** stating our organisation's long-term objectives, the means with which to reach them and how the objectives and means are related in a theory of change.
  - We have a strategy for how we will work in practice with innovation.
  - We have an innovation portfolio that we actively manage.
  - We are **organised** in such a way that we allow for open, systems-level collaboration with other actors in government, business and the third sector.
  - We are wired to the opportunities in e-government.
  - We have an environment to support innovation, for instance a project organisation or an innovation lab.
  - We actively manage our **people and culture** to be a modern work organisation on dimensions such as values, involvement, diversity and incentives.
  - We have a pro-innovation culture, both when it comes to embracing ideation and experimentation, and when it comes to executing the new solutions.
- *Co-creation*
  - We have the necessary **competencies** in fields such as design thinking and citizen-centred (ethnographic) research.
  - We have an explicit **process** for co-creation in place, and the **methods** and the process itself is codified so everyone in our organisation can know and use it.

- We have the appropriate **measurement and learning processes** in place, so that we are able to discern when our innovation efforts succeed, and learn from them when they fail.
- *Courage*
  - Our managers, from the top executive to institution heads, embody the **leadership** values and skills that we believe are essential for our organisation's future.
  - Our managers have the courage to lead innovation processes from their respective levels.

As I have presented these topics they could be answered like a loose type of self-assessment (say, on a scale from 1 to 5); however, they might also be assessed more thoroughly, underpinning them with quantitative and qualitative data where possible, perhaps engaging external consultants as the Danish integration ministry did. Measuring innovation potential is, in itself, a static exercise. But it could be the beginning of a change process. Taking a snapshot of how mature the organisation is when it comes to nurturing and conducting innovation processes, is also to identify spots of weakness that should be addressed, or potentials that should be released.

Learning from the innovation process

How good is our innovation process? Are we always able to generate as many high-quality ideas as we need? Is our level of ambition always high enough? Are our ideas radical enough (or, are we allowing for sufficient divergence, at least in the early stages of ideation)? What about engagement and learning – are we truly running co-creation processes or are we treating innovation as something that can be outsourced to someone else?

If an organisation wants to improve a process, it needs a vehicle to allow it to reflect on it. That vehicle needs to give some type of feedback on the quality of the process, based on the perceptions and experience of the key people involved in it. At MindLab, when we reformulated our strategy in early 2007, we realised that something as fluffy-sounding as a public sector innovation lab needed some hard-core measurement. So we institutionalised a mandatory questionnaire, or rather two questionnaires, to be filled out by the government officials we collaborate with. One questionnaire is to be answered immediately after the end of an innovation project, typically at the conclusion of the testing phase; the other is to be answered three to six months later, typically after the implementation phase (but often before any significant scaling). Both questionnaires include closed (quantifiable) questions as well as open-ended questions. The first (immediate) questionnaire obtains feedback on questions such as:

- Did we generate the right input (knowledge, competencies, skill mix)?
- Did we manage the innovation process professionally?
- Were the co-creation methods, and their combination, appropriate?
- How did the involvement of citizens and other key people work?
- Did the output (ideas, concepts) live up to or exceed expectations?
- Is it likely that the solutions we helped generate will enable realisation of the defined strategic objectives?

There are obvious learning points associated with each of these dimensions. For instance, if it turns out that some of the methods were not experienced by our partners as appropriate to the task at hand, that could challenge the legitimacy of the innovation process. Perhaps we should apply different methods the next time we encounter a somewhat similar project, or we should clarify expectations better.

The follow-up questionnaire is submitted from one to six months later. We ask questions such as:

- To what extent were the ideas or concepts taken up and implemented?
- Were there challenges or barriers to implementation? If so, what were they and how were they addressed?
- Has any kind of value following implementation been generated, and, if yes, what type – productivity, service experience, results and/ or democracy? What evidence do you have that this is the case?
- Is there something we could have done differently?
- Is there something that we could do now to move the project further along?

Often, the most significant learning about the innovation process is harvested from the follow-up questionnaires. At that point it is possible to view the process a bit from the distance. It is also possible (and a very good idea) to not just ask, but go and see for yourself how the project turned out. If the project has been implemented you can venture into the field and observe the new activities as they happen. In one project, when a project manager from MindLab ventured out to observe the results of our contribution in a project for which he had been responsible, he could see that much had changed as intended, but also that there were a few points that could still be improved. Our project manager then took the opportunity to provide instant suggestions to the responsible manager – and the new changes could be implemented immediately. This learning helped us at MindLab reach the decision that we should extend our work further into implementation, in order to help ensure maximum impact of our efforts.

Measuring the value of innovation

Ultimately, innovation is about creating value. In Chapter 2, I highlighted the four 'bottom lines' of public sector innovation: productivity, service experience, results and democracy. Throughout the chapters of the book we have witnessed numerous innovations that have made a real difference across these dimensions. We've seen radical productivity gains through the application of new technology and new work processes; increased service experience through redesign of the service interactions with citizens and communities; stronger results through new methods that engage citizens in co-production; and we've even witnessed innovations that utilise new web technologies to enhance the transparency of the public sector.

The four innovation bottom lines

To document that our innovation activities work, and to learn from how they impact the real world, we need to measure the organisation's performance on all the four bottom lines I introduced in Chapter 2.

Figure 10.1: The four bottom lines of public sector innovation

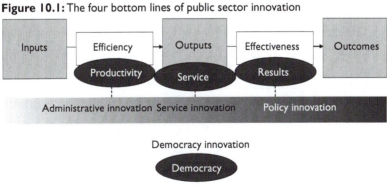

Source: Inspired by National Audit Office (NAO, 2006)

As I discussed in the book's introduction, however, many public managers essentially lead into a vacuum: they do not receive sufficient meaningful, ongoing feedback on whether new process changes (which might lead to increased productivity), service programmes (which are intended to increase citizens' service experience) or policy initiatives (which are supposed to generate short-, medium- or long-term results) produce the intended value. And usually, we have only a very vague sense of whether citizens' empowerment, participation and rights are impacted positively or negatively (even though such democratic principles are at the heart of governing).

This doesn't mean that public organisations don't manage anyway. Only a minor proportion of what takes place in government can be truly ascribed to strategy; much of what happens is the reactive, day-to-day decision-making that is part and parcel of politics (Mulgan, 2009). Measurable 'evidence' is only one of many parameters that public managers rely on for decision-making. Other parameters include the values, decision-making context, experience and expertise of the staff, individual judgement, available resources, habits and lobbyist pressures. A significant parameter will also be the accountability system within which the managers work.

Sometimes we just keep on doing what we've always done, perhaps because that is the easiest. In fact, it is often much less controversial to throw additional cash at existing public organisations and initiatives even though no one really knows whether they work or not. At Dance United, the dance company that helps ex-convicts increase their prospects, director Andrew Coggins finds this extremely frustrating; at a 2009 seminar he said, 'The challenge is to get government sponsors simply to invest in what actually works. Formidable sums of money are thrown at projects that patently do not work but are protected by their commissioners. The problem is to break into that circle whilst at the same time maintaining the integrity of the work.' We saw earlier that Youth Villages achieved exactly that – to break the circle and find an 'algorithm' that works, sustaining significantly better results, and making growth and scaling possible.

The challenge is, therefore, to place meaningful, ongoing measurement and learning more squarely at the centre of public decision-making and innovation. For citizens to trust government, we must make a concerted effort to understand the impact our efforts have on the world; to learn and improve our efforts, we must also make our efforts transparent to politicians, the media, other decision-makers and stakeholders alike.

The performance management paradigm

Results-based management, or *performance management*, has received wide interest across modern economies over the last few decades. According to the OECD (2005, p 59), the term characterises 'A management cycle under which programme performance objectives and targets are determined, managers have flexibility to achieve them, actual performance is measured and reported, and this information feeds into decisions about programme funding, design, operations and rewards or penalties'. More than three quarters of OECD Member States have taken up performance management to some degree. Countries like the US, Canada, the UK and New Zealand have gone relatively far, and have to varying degrees placed performance management requirements into law. Others have taken a more limited approach, in particular in Continental and Southern Europe, using only a few non-financial indicators as part of the budgeting process; finally, some are addressing performance management pragmatically – on a sector-by-sector basis – including the Scandinavian countries and the Netherlands.

Performance management has sometimes proved controversial. For instance in the UK, the Labour government's Public Service Agreements were criticised for, amongst other things, being over-centralistic, over-managed and introducing too many targets at too high a level of detail, creating a lack of ownership at local level (Parker and Heapy, 2006; Mulgan, 2009). (The programme has since been adjusted in a number of ways.) In the US, after a relatively long period of phasing in, the 1993 Government Performance and Results Act seems to have been relatively successful in strengthening an emphasis on outcomes in federal policymaking. As with any other social technology, performance management can be applied in ways that are more sensible and helpful than others.

As I discussed in Chapter 4, strategic innovation is to couple the management cycles of strategy, innovation portfolio, measurement and budgeting in a coordinated way. The portfolio of innovation activities determines *how* the strategic goals should be reached, while the measurement process tells us *if* they were reached or not. The budgetary process allocates resources not only to ongoing business, but also to the strategic innovation efforts. In high-performing public sector organisations, there should be a coherent, systematic cycle of measurement attached to all innovation efforts; a share of the budget is also allocated to ensure sound measurement and subsequent learning.

Let us consider in a bit more detail how each of the four types of value, or bottom lines, of public sector innovation can be measured.

Figure 10.2: Innovation and measurement process

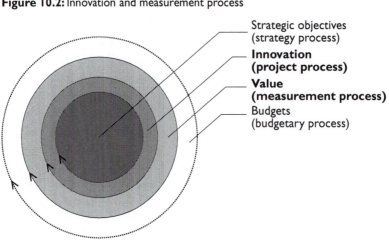

Strategic objectives
(strategy process)

**Innovation
(project process)**

**Value
(measurement process)**

Budgets
(budgetary process)

Productivity

Public sector productivity is a much-debated matter; part of the debate has to do with whether it can be measured at all; part of the debate is about why it isn't any higher and why it always seems to be lagging the private sector; and, finally, part of the debate is about how to improve it. I won't go into the first two debates in any detail; in the context of innovation, what is interesting to consider is how we might measure a (positive) change in public sector productivity. According to Mulgan (2009), until the 1990s it was widely considered in the international accounting community that public sector productivity never improved. Contrary to what is apparently conventional wisdom, many public sector organisations are acutely aware of their productivity. Most organisations that do any significant volume of case management know pretty much how long the average case takes, how much manpower each case consumes, and it has the measures to register an improvement in cases handled per worker, other things being equal. Now, case output per staff input is only one measure of productivity, but it is one that is common and widely used. Innovating the case process would imply improving on the productivity ratio, as many organisations have done in recent years, applying the principles of lean management. Productivity improvements in the range of 20–30% aren't unusual. The UK NHS, for instance, has harvested that type of productivity gains in enhancing patient flows in a number of fields. In Denmark, hospitals employing the *joint care* methodology for knee and hip patients have similarly gained, as hospital stays have been shortened from an average of six and a half days to an average of four (Bason, 2007; Cabinet Office, 2009).

Innovations that not only apply new processes, but also new technology, often lead to productivity gains. As mentioned in Chapter 4, the Danish tax authority has been able to reduce its workforce by around 25%, while upholding service levels and legal obligations, by employing advanced digital services and integrating public tax systems with private databases, drawing data directly from the payroll systems of companies.

Sometimes registering productivity gains from new innovations is extremely simple. When the *Growth House*, a regional public business advisory body in South Denmark, employed a new service strategy designed by MindLab, Henrik Jacobsen, the director, could quickly discern one thing: his advisors held fewer meetings. Because the service process had been redesigned to better clarify expectations with the organisation's clients, the staff were less likely to engage in unnecessary meetings and they could hold shorter, more productive, sessions with businesses instead. Just cutting one or two meetings per client represented a substantial productivity improvement, even though Mr Jacobsen couldn't place an exact percentage figure on it. (One notes, however, that such a measurement wouldn't be very difficult to do, and that generating this kind of productivity data might in fact be a relevant metric for the *Growth House* to work with.)

Service experience

Measuring citizens' subjective service experience can help turn the organisation's focus outside-in and place citizens more at the heart of government. As Sophia Parker and Joe Heapy (2006, p 67) state in their work on the citizen–government interface, performance must be measured in ways that illuminate the subjective quality of the experience, not just operational performance: 'Organisations need to measure what users value, as well as what organisations and service systems value.' This is important not just to achieve a desired level of user satisfaction, but also because understanding what users value may be an important key to identifying the kinds of interventions that will lead, ultimately, to better outcomes. For instance, if users in employment centres are treated with dignity, respect and professionalism, might they be more active participants in job services and hence helped faster into steady employment?

In many public organisations, there is no lack of citizen satisfaction surveys. For instance, every three years, the Canadian government systematically measures its public service satisfaction levels across three levels of government. Similar large-scale national measurements are in place in Norway. In Denmark, they are currently being planned. The problem isn't that user satisfaction isn't measured, it's that it may not be measured in a meaningful way and/or the results aren't used to drive performance. In order for service measures to be useful, they must:

- Measure service outcomes at the individual level. Absent this information, it is impossible even to begin to understand the social value of a public programme. And while this may seem like a cumbersome 'add-on' to the work of service delivery, it is no less essential a 'cost of doing business' than staff training, ongoing professional development and the rigorous tracking of process costs – none of which are controversial.
- Measure both overall (end-)user satisfaction with the service experience as well as the satisfaction with the individual key elements or steps of the service process. For instance, a hospital ward should not only measure overall patient satisfaction, but elements like information prior to arrival, parking, quality of the reception, face-to-face information and so on.
- Be conducted regularly so there is a time-series dataset that can be tracked on an ongoing basis. Otherwise it is impossible to ascribe a change in service experience to any particular service innovation.
- Where relevant, be possible to benchmark externally against similar service activities and results in other sectors and/or organisations. Most public sector organisations could, if they wanted to, also compare themselves to private or non-governmental organisations, or they could benchmark against sister organisations in other countries.
- Be possible to ascribe to the individual unit or team in the organisation responsible for providing the service, and to individual managers' areas of responsibility.
- Be discussed openly by staff and management on an ongoing basis; management must create opportunities for a conversation about service experience, asking questions and holding staff accountable for service results.

There is, however, a dilemma about measuring citizens' service experiences and outcomes. By asking, for instance, about the 'quality of your service experience' on a scale of 1–5, are we measuring what citizens experience, or are we measuring how well the experience matched their expectations? In the public sector, expectations are shaped not just by whatever communications the public organisation might be putting out, or by what citizens hear through word-of-mouth. Expectations of the quality of public services are often hugely impacted by media stories, good or bad, and by the politicians who want to display a certain picture about the state of the public sector. Usually this means that roughly half the stories will be spun positively, while roughly another half will be spun more negatively. How do we deal with service experience in an environment where expectations are framed with such variance? And how do we tease apart citizens' reports about their ultimate service outcomes (results) from their level of (dis)satisfaction with how they were treated?

In the Netherlands, employment policy officials have developed a measurement tool that they feel addresses this issue. It is what they call the 'balance model', which measures the balance between expectations and experience, through two different sets of questions directed at citizens before and after they are engaged in a particular employment service. The challenge with such a method may be, however, that the expectations–experience gap, by nature, changes once the service has been used the first time. The citizen's ability to tune expectations to actual experience changes dramatically. In Denmark, surveys have shown very significant differences between what non-users of health care think about the quality of hospitals (they don't think much of it) and what citizens think once they have in fact used one (they are generally quite satisfied). So it really only makes sense to measure the expectations–experience gap for first-time users, while experienced users can be asked the more straightforward question 'So, how was it this time?'.

The real challenge is to understand what is behind the rather superficial data that is generated by user surveys: what kind of context was the survey delivered in? What was it exactly that triggered the particular experience? And *how might it be improved?* To learn the answers to these kinds of questions, surveys are vastly inadequate. We must return to ethnographic research, applying qualitative methods and getting a much more tangible sense of how the service plays out in practice. We must turn to co-creation.

Finally, a note of caution concerning service experience: how citizens experience a public service should never be considered as an end goal in itself, just as customer satisfaction for a private enterprise is only a means to an end (profits usually being the end). Some public organisations believe that because they focus on 'customer satisfaction', they have identified how to measure their outcomes. That is not the case. Service experience is an important, but not sufficient, parameter for public performance. The most important performance dimension of any public service organisation should be *results*.

Results

I introduced this book by claiming that public organisations are established with some kind of 'good' in mind. Results are, in essence, about the ultimate good that an organisation is put into the world to produce. Results are about creating a better society. When Youth Villages demonstrates a consistent success rate of 80% of creating better outcomes for troubled youth, far distancing other organisations in their field, this is what it is about.

Once, at a presentation I gave to the library association of Northern Zealand in Denmark, I asked the library managers what the ultimate good was of the library as an institution. 'A democratic society' was the swift answer. 'Of course', I thought to myself. The purpose of a library is not to lend out books (that's an output). The purpose of a library is to build a democratic infrastructure of openness, knowledge and learning. Not a small ambition, but certainly one that could motivate you to get up in the morning and go to work every day.

Results concern the goals of public organisations, and measuring them helps us understand whether they are being achieved or not (Rist and Kusek, 2004). Results are the short-, medium- and long-term societal outcomes that public sector organisations strive to achieve. Jobs, security, health, education, sustainability and growth are among the kinds of ultimate objectives that the public sector is charged with achieving. Often, the challenges and problems involved are 'wicked', without hope of ultimate success ('When is a democracy strong enough?', 'When have we created enough jobs?'), but with hope of making progress (Rittel and Webber, 1973). And how do we know we are making any kind of progress? We must measure our results.

What constitutes good measurement of results – what are the quality criteria? The sound measurement of results must be undertaken within a frame of reference – namely the organisation's strategy and more specifically *the theory of change*, which is the blueprint for making something about the world better. As discussed briefly in Chapter 4, the theory of change is a clear description of the causal links between the organisation's efforts and the outcomes it seeks to produce. The theory of change should guide the action that the organisation takes, and it is therefore the theory of change that should be measured in order to drive higher organisational performance. This is exactly the framework that an organisation such as Youth Villages has been pursuing in order to achieve their remarkable successes.

According to David Hunter (2010), a performance management expert and former Director of Evaluation at the US-based Edna

McConnell-Clark Foundation (who helped Youth Villages clarify its theory of change), such a theory of change must be:

- *Meaningful* to key constituencies.
- *Plausible* in that they conform to informed critical analysis.
- *Possible* within resource and other constraints.
- *Testable* through agreed-upon measurements.
- *Monitorable*, that is, able to provide reliable data for managing performance.

The first point is, I believe, the most important. If, ultimately, the indicators that are measured are not considered meaningful and helpful to those who are responsible for measuring them, the data will not be of sufficient quality. And worse, people will lose motivation and there will be no incentive to use the data actively and to learn anything from them. This implies that there must be a *line of sight* from the everyday work to the overall strategy and mission the organisation is pursuing: employees must be able to see the connection between their efforts and the organisation's success; if not, they aren't motivated to innovate to improve their performance (Behn, 1995).

There is both an art and a practice to establishing good results-based management systems. Here, the principles of co-creation also apply: the best, if not the only, way of building a results-based management system for an organisation is through a workshop format, involving representatives of all levels and areas of the organisation in a common process, establishing the theory of change, defining what results are and mean to the organisation, how they are brought about, for whom, and how they can be measured. At MindLab, for instance, when we created our most recent strategy, we did it through a workshop that included all staff and our key stakeholders. We started by defining our innovation objectives, and worked our way backwards (in terms of causality) to define outputs, activities and inputs. I will discuss this process of crafting strategy through an outcome-based process towards the end of this chapter.

Without a clear picture of the results it is put into the world to create, and without the methods of measuring them, how can an organisation know whether its innovation efforts ultimately make a difference or not? Perhaps it is even doing more harm than good? As Osborne and Gaebler (1992) have pointed out: 'If you do not measure results, you cannot tell success from failure; if you cannot see success, you cannot reward it; and if you cannot reward success, you are probably rewarding failure' (quoted in Rist and Kusek, 2004). While the four innovation bottom lines should be balanced against each other, results play a special role and should really be squarely at the centre of any measurement effort undertaken by a public body.

Democracy

Strengthening democracy can be a result, as in the case of the library; but it is also an end, or an innovation bottom line, in itself. However, it is often perceived as secondary, as organisations pursue objectives of productivity gains or service improvements. When creating new public sector solutions, we must of course consider questions such as:

- Are we protecting or even increasing citizens' equality before the law?
- Are we increasing public transparency?
- Are we improving accountability?
- Are we changing citizens' channels of democratic participation and influence?

Achieving high productivity gains would be pretty easy if we didn't have to care about equality before the law (*creaming* is a powerful way of creating better results across a wide range of public services). We would probably also achieve efficiency gains by reducing transparency, limiting documentation or making it exceedingly hard to come by (but that may be politically unacceptable). We could maybe make a government form much simpler and easier to read (but perhaps we must inform citizens of their rights, even if it takes up space we'd like to use for something else).

Democracy is, however, not a bottom line that should be viewed as a barrier to productivity or service improvement. In politically governed organisations, and in a democratic society, equality, transparency, accountability and participation are dimensions that can be innovated upon. When the Swedish government chose to post performance data of health care services on a transparent, online platform, it was clearly not only a service innovation, but also a democracy innovation. When the US government posts the performance data and rankings of all federal programmes on expectmore.gov, it is not just of interest to policymakers and technocrats, but to citizens. As discussed in Chapter 4, through digital government, citizens are gaining unprecedented access to government data (such as US initiatives like recovery.gov and data. gov) and to their own case files. In some countries, such as Denmark, citizens can now proactively give government permission to share their personal data across agencies, where it is helpful to them. New forms of democratic participation have been made possible through the internet, allowing for electronic town hall meetings and 'crowdsourcing' such as online idea generation as inputs to government. In health care, as in the *joint care* case example, empowering citizens to be a more active part of the treatment process can deliver productivity gains as well.

Public sector innovation is as much about transforming democracy, as it is about transforming public policies and services. Perhaps we can't even have the one without the other.

Innovating the bottom lines

The earlier discussion highlights the question of the interrelatedness of the different types of value of public sector innovation: what are our key productivity indicators, and how do they relate to the level of service we are able to deliver? What constitutes our measures of service experience, and to what extent does user satisfaction contribute positively or negatively to the results we are trying to achieve? Given the results we ultimately exist to produce, how can we deliver them with the highest level of productivity? How are we doing on 'democracy'; are we damaging this bottom line in order to get more on the others?

Recognising that the kinds of value a public organisation can create through innovation are multiple and intertwined is important. It is also important to seek radically new ways of getting more of everything. Throughout this book, and in particular in Chapter 9, I have highlighted the concept of 'radical efficiency', which emphasises how innovation can lead to different, better and lower-cost outcomes. The notion of radical efficiency highlights the potential of creating significant value on more than a single bottom line.

One can thus view the four bottom lines as a two-dimensional plane or square, which can be expanded in all four directions. It is a 'balanced scorecard' for the public sector (Kaplan and Norton, 1996). How do we identify the innovative solutions that, in these times of economic uncertainty and budgetary cutbacks, can not only improve service experience, results or democracy, but also, as a minimum, increase productivity?

Public managers and staff must engage with people in the process of co-creation to radically improve two, three or even four of the bottom lines – simultaneously.

Figure 10.3: Navigating the four bottom lines

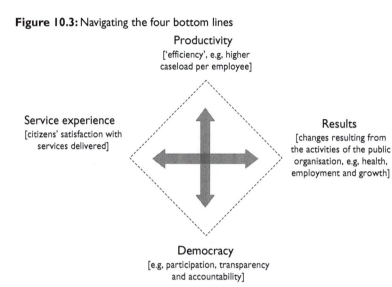

Productivity
['efficiency', e.g, higher
caseload per employee]

Service experience
[citizens' satisfaction with
services delivered]

Results
[changes resulting from
the activities of the public
organisation, e.g, health,
employment and growth]

Democracy
[e.g, participation, transparency
and accountability]

Performance leadership

Bureaucracies, once they make up their mind, are pretty good at creating new systems. Measurement systems and processes are no exception. But once the system is in place, and the organisation regularly harvests knowledge about its performance, what then?

The key challenge, of course, is to utilise data about performance as part of an ongoing leadership practice. Managers must not only ensure that the performance data that is registered is accurate and timely. It is a leadership role to communicate why measurement is meaningful to do, and to create a systematic dialogue with staff about the organisation's performance on the basis of the data (Behn, 1995). Again, meaningfulness must be at the centre of the dialogue. As Stanford professors and authors of *Hard Facts, Dangerous Half-truths and Total Nonsense: Profiting from Evidence-based Management* (2006), Jeffrey Pfeffer and Robert I. Sutton, emphasise, it is one thing to believe that organisations would perform better if leaders knew and applied the best evidence; but quite another to put that belief into practice.

Carried out sensibly, the potential of performance management is to enable continuous real-time learning to help improve existing practices *and* to get feedback on more radical changes to policies or programmes (Rist and Kusek, 2004). This was the case, for instance, for Youth Villages, when they recognised that home-based programmes would be much more effective than the residential services they had been providing, and consequently made the shift to home-based services in their core programming. Pfeffer and Sutton (2006) recognise that performance data will never be perfect. But they firmly believe that managers should employ a practice where they:

- demand documentation from colleagues and staff;
- discuss and challenge the logic behind the data employed by the organisation;
- view the organisation as a prototype, where tests, experiments and pilots are encouraged; and
- reward learning from experimental activities, perhaps especially when they fail.

These are essential practices in an organisation that wants to learn from innovation, and to improve its performance, every day.

Outcome focus as an innovation driver?

Focusing on results – the outcomes of the organisation's efforts – is not only at the heart of learning whether innovation is successful or not. Focusing on results can also be the starting point of transforming the organisation itself (Rist and Kusek, 2004; Ulwick, 2005; Cole and Parston, 2006).

By taking a results-based view of the organisation, ultimate *value* is given a central role. What if a library manager and his staff asked themselves the following question: 'What would be the most effective way of achieving a more democratic society?'. They would be forced to rethink the activities and role of the library in the local community; perhaps challenging conventional thinking about what a library should be, which skills its staff should have and what kind of activities should take place there. By starting with outcomes, the organisation opens up for a much broader range of possibilities; that doesn't mean it has to embrace them all, but it has the choice. Mulgan and Albury (2003, p 15) have stated this point rather succinctly, emphasising that, 'Methods which work backwards from outcomes rather than forwards from existing policies, practices and institutions often generate a much wider range of potential options.'

The innovation potential is, in other words, inherent in the (re)formulation of the organisation's strategy from focusing on activities or processes, to focusing on results. The question becomes: with which inputs, tools, methods and activities would we most effectively achieve the results we want? The key is to build such a *theory of change* backwards, from end to beginning: establishing the causal links between results, outputs, processes and inputs. As mentioned, this was how we created MindLab's most recent strategy.

Sometimes the result can be revolutionising. David Hunter, who helped transform dozens of social organisations through the lens of results-based management, has pointed out that there is nothing more powerful for an organisation than 'holding up a mirror for them and showing them the implication of outcomes for what they are doing' (quoted in Bason, 2007, p 302). As I discussed in Chapter 9, creating a theory of change, or at least checking what the existing theory is, is often a very helpful starting point for the co-creation process.

How to do it

This chapter has provided three perspectives on measuring innovation, from measuring capacity and potential, over processes, to measuring the four 'bottom lines' of public sector innovation, including ultimate results of the organisation's efforts. The barriers facing the measurement of innovation and value are significant; few public managers have a thorough understanding of what constitutes the types of value that innovation in government can result in; and they usually have few if any systematic measurements in place that can help them obtain feedback on the quality of innovation processes. In spite of increased efforts in recent years to put in place monitoring and performance management systems, managers still risk leading into a vacuum, causing them to spend too much time looking back, and too little looking forward. They are not getting timely and sufficiently meaningful data on the four types of value that may be created through the efforts of their staff. The most significant challenge is lack of learning: without trusted data, and without a sound management process to establish conversations about ongoing measurement findings, how can behaviour change accordingly to improve performance?

Leaders must be fearless in learning from experience. High-performing, innovative organisations are able to reflect, at all levels, on their own practices, learn from their successes and failures, and achieve their results through intentional action. Public leaders should consider the following:

Know the innovation metrics

Measuring the organisation's innovation potential across the four Cs of consciousness, capacity, co-creation and courage can be helpful as a reference point for improving the organisation's innovation ecosystem.

By establishing a baseline, it becomes possible to see how and where to invest to increase the organisation's ability to create and implement more and better ideas. In addition, measuring the quality and impact of individual innovation processes can pinpoint how to improve the way innovation is carried out. Such measurements should, however, not be done very often, and they should certainly be done in a way that is as non-intrusive as possible. Perhaps a comprehensive, quantitative innovation survey could be carried out to establish a first baseline; but conducting massive surveys regularly to assess innovation potential is not advisable; creating more bureaucracy is not in the spirit of innovation. Following a baseline survey, one could for instance pick highly focused questions that reflect what are considered to be the most important 5–10 metrics, and include them as part of ongoing employee satisfaction surveys, management surveys or similar data-gathering activities – embedding them in the existing data-collection infrastructure:

- *How might we capture essential insight concerning our innovation potential in an effective manner?*
- *Are there existing surveys where we might add a few key questions?*

Improve innovation processes continually

This concerns learning from experience from internally run projects and investing in building the ability to orchestrate co-creation effectively:

- *What kind of learning processes do we have in place at project, unit and organisational levels in order to learn from the individual innovation project processes?*

Measure performance on the four bottom lines

To learn from the innovation efforts, organisations must measure systematically how their initiatives impact productivity, service experience, results and democracy. It is not difficult to create an impact on just one of these bottom lines; the real paradigm-changing innovations shift two, three or all four bottom lines positively, at the same time:

- *Do we have good measurement processes in place to measure the four types of value?*

- *To what extent are results and outcomes placed centrally in our measurement system?*

Sustain a dialogue about performance

Measurement in itself does not create value. The smart use of documentation for *motivation* and learning, or for *information* and accountability, creates value. To use measurement to drive organisational performance, managers must lead by example, making a habit of engaging directly with their staff in an honest conversation about what seems to work, and what doesn't. They must display curiosity, interest and willingness to act on the findings. In the context of innovation the key question is:

- *Now, we tried this because we thought it would lead to these results. What in fact happened, and what can we learn from it?*

Part Four
Courage

FOUR LEADERSHIP
ROLES

11

Four leadership roles

'Courage comes from the willingness to "die," to go forth into an unknown territory that begins to manifest only after you dare to step into that void. That is the essence of leadership.' (C. Otto Scharmer, Senior Lecturer, MIT, 2007, p 401)

The New York State Associate Commissioner of Education, Sheila Evans-Tranum, is among the highest-ranking African-American women in US state government. As the first academic in her family (she has a double major in English and mathematics), she represents a remarkable story of overcoming enormous challenges to achieve a stellar career in public service. She also embodies a philosophy that speaks very strongly to innovation, for instance having emphasised accountability at all levels of the New York state school system as a key driver of positive change in the public school system. She firmly believes that what she tries to accomplish is more important than her personal position. At a recent conference on performance management practices she said, 'You can achieve nearly anything in government if you don't care about losing your job'.

Leading public sector innovation shouldn't be about risking your job. But to lead innovation, and in particular co-creation, is also to be courageous. If we as public managers don't strive, every day, to do better than yesterday, why should politicians and taxpayers endow us with their money and their trust? For innovation activities to become strategic and systematic, they must be considered the public manager's personal responsibility: part of the professional ethic, of the essence of public service. Public managers must be held just as accountable for their innovation efforts as for meeting the budget. Sometimes that means mustering the courage to challenge the very system that holds one accountable.

As Professor Jean Hartley of Warwick Business School has pointed out, 'Innovation under networked governance revitalises the leadership role of policy-makers in translating new ideas into new forms of action' (2005, p 30). This revitalisation comes at a price, however. Leading public organisations in a more collaborative, open and inclusive way – to orchestrate co-creation – makes significant demands on the confidence and courage of leaders.

The idea that 'courage' is necessary for managers to drive innovation is widely accepted, not least due to the sense that innovation involves some degree of risk (Bossidy and Charan, 2002; Attwood et al, 2003; Dyer et al, 2009; Eggers and O'Leary, 2009). Hamel (2000) even highlights courage as the most important innovation leadership attribute of all. The challenge is to consider how 'courage' can play out in practice in a public sector context. For instance, in 2009 the UK Cabinet Office took the initiative of establishing the Innovators Council of leading figures from business, public services and the third sector in order to help think more radically about innovation in the public sector (Cabinet Office, 2010). The officials quickly nicknamed the group the 'Heretics Council', because the ambition was to truly challenge how government tackled innovation. The establishment of the council was, in this perspective, a reflection on how central government is recognising that innovation is about personal responsibility and about testing the perceived boundaries of current practice and thinking.

As I've discussed throughout this book, by applying the theory and practice of design thinking and co-creation, public managers can essentially take a significant part of the risk out of the public sector innovation process: running projects in a more iterative mode, developing solutions with people, not for them, and rapidly creating and testing prototypes are all tools which maximise learning and often minimise risk. However, no matter how strategic, systematic, reflexive and co-created the process becomes, there will obviously never be such a thing as entirely 'risk-free innovation'. Faced with the current challenges, public managers must be better prepared to embrace divergence, to act without complete knowledge, to face their fears, and to challenge the system they are part of, in order to help change it. This has implications for leadership roles at all levels of government.

This chapter presents a framework for thinking about the new role of public managers in leading innovation across different levels of the organisation – and beyond it. Already, we have seen a broad range of leadership challenges across the three Cs of consciousness, capacity and co-creation. This chapter asks:

- What is the essence of the challenge of leading innovation in the public sector?
- What are the distinct public leadership roles required to drive innovation at different levels of government?
- Which competencies are required?

Between inspiration and execution

If innovation is new ideas that work, then leading innovation is to straddle that great divide between getting the idea and making it part of the organisation's everyday practice. To be courageous is, in this context, the ability to act in the face of opposition or discouragement. As Dyer et al (2009) emphasise, innovative entrepreneurship is not a genetic disposition; rather, it is an active endeavour. In this sense, innovation leadership is played out in a forcefield between inspiration on the one hand, and execution on the other. Inspiration thrives on openness, divergence, motivation and creativity. Execution is the art and practice of getting things done (Bossidy and Charan, 2002). It thrives on traits such as structure, discipline, focus and stamina. One might also think of the difference between inspiration and execution as the often-evoked difference between leadership and management: leadership is doing the right thing; management is doing things right. Or even better, as Henry Mintzberg (2009) says, pinpointing the nexus of management and leadership: leadership is management done well.

Table 11.1: Between inspiration and execution

	Low execution ability	**High execution ability**
Inspired	Creativity *All talk, no action*	Innovation *Change and value*
Not inspired	Weak operations *Downhill*	Stable operations *Status quo*

Source: Inspired by Kollerup and Thorball (2005)

This book has emphasised the process of co-creation as a key approach to gaining the inspiration needed for identifying, developing and implementing new ideas that work in government. However, in many public organisations, co-creation will represent a significant departure from 'how we work here'. Part of the courage needed to drive public sector innovation is therefore, simply put, about daring to embrace co-creation. For public managers, working in a different way, involving a wider scope of people, utilising deep qualitative knowledge, and running a more open, experimental and collaborative process, will require a significant measure of courage. Likewise, actually realising the change needed for new ideas to generate value can imply facing significant resistance. From a leadership perspective, courage thus involves both the boldness to really allow new ideas to flourish, and the determination to make them happen.

People who do not provide inspiration, and who cannot execute decisions, are really just managing a dying organisation. Operations become weak and unstable, and nothing new is ever attempted with any degree of success. Dying organisations can exist for years – at least in the public sector. But no one wants to work for one, and sooner or later others will be able to solve its tasks better and more efficiently. Even in government, dysfunctional organisations (usually) don't last forever.

Focusing overly on creativity without considering implementation leads to an organisation that constantly talks about the next great thing, but never gets around to choosing what to do, and doing it. The result is an abundance of creative ideas, but also frustration and waste. When I was head of a consultancy business unit, one of our project managers interviewed hospital staff about their ideas for organisational change. An administrative assistant said that she'd been systematically collecting all her ideas for the past five years or so. 'What happened to them?', the project manager asked. The assistant pulled out her drawer. 'They're all right here', she said, pointing to bundles of post-its and notes that she'd written down over the years. 'But why didn't you share your ideas with management?', asked the consultant. 'Oh, but I did', said the nurse. 'I've been bringing these suggestions up at our weekly department meetings, and we've had some very nice conversations about them.' 'And then what happened?', asked the consultant. 'Nothing', said the assistant.

Public managers are often relatively good at execution – they just aren't very inspired. Managing the status quo, carrying out decisions, going about day-to-day business is all well enough. That is how many (some would say the majority) of public sector organisations are run. However, if we believe that the key challenges facing the public sector are real – scarcer resources, ageing, chronic health problems, increased citizen expectations – then sound management alone is not an option. The organisation that excels at operations excels at doing things right. But what if it is no longer doing the right thing?

The only true leadership option is, of course, to strike an effective balance between inspiration and execution. Martin (2009) would characterise the two traits as the ability to deal with validity and the exploration of mystery versus the ability to deal with reliability and harnessing the optimal algorithm of stable operations. For some leaders, this means moving out of their comfort zone, embracing divergence and change to a much larger extent than today. Martin (2009, p 160) characterises this as attaining 'a design thinker's stance', shifting to a better balance between reliability and validity. For some, this might mean talking a bit less, and getting a bit more done.

There are many ways of leading within the twin dynamic of inspiration and execution, however. The leadership role in innovation depends on the type of organisation and function. Another dimension that certainly plays a key role is where in the government hierarchy the leader is positioned. Let's explore four distinct leadership roles that relate to different levels of government.

A typology of innovation leadership

It should be more than clear by now that innovation in government is everybody's job (Kanter, 2006; LO, 2006; Patterson et al, 2009). That goes for employees, and it goes for different leadership positions – from the political level to front-line managers (Behn, 1995). Innovation leadership can arise from anywhere in the organisation (Gillinson et al, 2010). Each position of leadership holds distinctive characteristics that can help drive innovation across the first three dimensions of the innovation ecosystem: consciousness, capacity and co-creation. I have chosen to take a closer look at four particular leadership positions, and have given them each a label.

Table 11.2: Summary of innovation leadership roles

Courage	Consciousness	Capacity	Co-creation
THE VISIONARY [Politician]	Formulating a vision that demands innovation	Investing in innovation capacity	Expecting administrators to be professional innovators
THE ENABLER [Top executive]	Engaging managers in a dialogue about innovation	Crafting and implementing strategies for innovation	Extending a licence to innovate
360 DEGREE INNOVATOR [Mid-level manager]	Applying language of innovation to problem-solving	Creating innovation space	Embracing divergence
KNOWLEDGE ENGINEER [Institution head]	Empowering staff to reflect on own practices	Recruiting and developing a diversity of talent	Encouraging small-scale experimentation and learning

The characteristics associated with each role are obviously not as distinct as they are presented here; however, I have attempted to highlight key aspects of the unique contribution that each level of leadership might bring to the innovation process. Applied to the four leadership roles, the implication of 'courage' is that they must act beyond and above the confines of their prescribed role.

The visionary: the political leader

What is the role of politicians in public sector innovation? Some would say it is to 'stay away', interfering as little as possible with the organisation, but expecting loyal, dedicated efforts and clear results against whatever political agenda and outcomes he or she is pursuing. Others might say that politicians are the only true public sector innovators: if, at the end of the day, they don't approve of a new idea, it won't have a chance of being realised anyway. As Eggers and O'Leary (2009) stress, political decision-making is the 'stargate' that any new public policy must enter through. In this view, politicians thus have the legitimate right, and expectation, of being directly involved in the creative thinking going on in the organisation.

The truth may lie somewhere in between. Often, there is a relatively clear divide between the bureaucratic-administrative domain of the public sector organisation, and the more ideological-political domain of elected ministers and mayors. However, the divide may blur, depending on national tradition, administrative and political cultures, and on the particular organisation. In countries such as the US, where the first couple of tiers of top government officials are politically appointed, the relationship between officials and politicians may become more intimate; the same is often the case in small government departments, where the politician by nature is closer and more involved with the day-to-day running of the organisation. The consequences for the conduct and effectiveness of policymaking may be significant (Mulgan, 2009).

In an innovation perspective, what is central is the extent to which the politician is able to formulate a compelling (political) vision, from which the organisation can draw its strategic ambitions. Politicians must formulate the 'why' of innovation, leaving (most of) the 'how' to the administration. The political vision should make the innovation imperative obvious. A classic example, of course, is President John F. Kennedy's ambitious vision of bringing a man to the moon and returning him safely to Earth, which essentially was an extension of a licence to innovate. Allegedly, immediately after the President's 25 May 1961 speech announcing the venture to the moon, the NASA administrator James Webb met with him in the Oval Office. Webb bluntly said, 'But I don't know if we can, sir'. Without looking up from his desk, Kennedy replied, 'You can now' (Nesta Public Services Lab, 2009). With the ability to formulate an ambitious vision comes also an expectation that government officials can be professional innovators. John F. Kennedy certainly expected this of NASA; why don't politicians more often expect that of less prestigious government organisations too?

Finally, with ambition and expectation comes commitment. The role of the politician is also to be the organisation's sponsor and ambassador, and to seek to secure the resources necessary to innovate. Politicians (like everyone else) must view innovation as an investment. Ensuring that government organisations possess the skills, technology and budgets necessary to develop first-rate solutions is a task for the politician.

Co-creation as an innovation approach could hold particular promise to politicians. Often, politicians live in a world where real-life stories, usually as portrayed by the media, dominate their agendas. Meanwhile, bureaucrats live in a world full of statistics and quantitative documentation. Politicians often care about the individual case; civil servants often care about scale and representativeness. Politicians sometimes get emotional; officials are usually detached. By bringing more citizen-centric, qualitative, emotional and intuitive types of knowledge to the table, the co-creation process might in fact be perceived as even more relevant and helpful to the themes and agendas many politicians are trying to pursue. Certainly, the communication style of individual, personal stories is much more natural to politicians than what they are usually presented with by their servants.

The enabler: the top executive

No one should expect top managers to also be their organisation's foremost innovators. Others in their organisation may have better ideas (van Wart, 2008; Patterson et al, 2009). But it is reasonable to expect that the top manager has an ambition when it comes to innovation. Without ownership and a will to innovate at the highest level, initiatives lose steam, resources aren't made available and potential successes are never realised. The day-to-day action of the staff is how innovation is expressed in practice, but top management commitment is a prerequisite for that action to take place. The top manager must be the foremost champion and enabler of the innovative organisation. Like a gardener who tends to the living organisms in his garden, so must a top executive nurture the organisation's innovation ecosystem.

A way to do this is to engage the next tiers of management in an ongoing dialogue about innovation, shaping a common language and a consciousness of what innovation means to the organisation. Such a conversation can be an integrated part of strategy deliberations; the top executive should ask whether the organisation is doing enough to ensure that it has the strategies, organisational design, digitisation, people, culture, methods and tools to deliver what is expected. Through extensive research, Professors Dyer, Gregersen and Christensen have found that the most innovative top executives are particularly adept at questioning, observing, experimenting and networking to power their own thinking and inspiration. Through these patterns of action, they are able to better associate, successfully connecting seemingly unrelated questions, problems or ideas from different fields (Dyer et al, 2009).

At the core is dialogue. However, as discussed in Chapter 4, the challenge is whether the organisation has sufficiently clear, results-based strategic objectives to frame such a conversation against. Most organisations merely describe their role, tasks and possibly their mission. But if the top executive does not communicate to everyone where the organisation wants to go, then what is the chance of getting there? This conversation becomes all the more relevant, and difficult, due to the complexities of the public sector context. Politicians and top executives often don't know the path ahead. In an op-ed piece, *New York Times* commentator David Brooks points out that public leaders 'have general goals, but the way ahead is pathless and everything is shrouded by uncertainty' (*New York Times*, 2009).

Finally, there is a crucial task for the public sector top executive to say out loud that innovation is an essential part of the business of government. When the Permanent Secretary of the Danish Ministry of Economic and Business Affairs hosted a reception for MindLab on a warm June day in 2008, he extended a licence to innovate. He invited MindLab's staff to be challengers of the system: internal critics and a 'loyal opposition' to their colleagues. That is not just an opportunity; it is an obligation. It is the kind of challenge that any top public executive should endow his or her institution with, just like JFK did in 1961: 'I expect you to create bold, new ideas. In fact, I demand it.'

Top managers play other roles as well. In a country such as Denmark, the number of public managers who run the state, regional and local administrations is so low (around 120) that they can be expected to know each other. Certainly, they would all fit into a medium-sized conference room. These top managers have a particular role to play in powering collaboration across government, encouraging their staff to work effectively together – and even to generate new ideas and solutions through co-creation processes. In the UK, the role of top executives in central government is considered so essential that they meet twice a year, bringing the key decision-makers together at the so-called Top 200 events. Their responsibility for driving innovation is also recognised; at their autumn session of 2009, for instance, the theme was innovation in government. The hope with such events is probably not so much that top executives can harness their innovation skills, but more that they can network, build a common language and understanding, build relations and trust, and perhaps even inspire each other.

Whether the most relevant source of new inspiration is other agency heads or permanent secretaries is, however, an open question. Research does show that public top executives obtain new ideas from a variety of sources. In a study conducted by Rambøll Management, a consultancy, the top three sources of inspiration for top public executives across Danish public organisations were: managers in their own organisation, their personal professional network and internal projects and research. The three least-mentioned sources of inspiration were, interestingly: politicians, academic research and first-hand input from citizens or businesses (Rambøll Management, 2006). This highlights the challenge of helping decision-makers see how citizens experience their services for themselves, as discussed in Chapter 8.

Of course, the use of these various sources of inspiration varies tremendously from person to person; and only very few, if any, are able to draw from all potential sources in a systematic way. The Rambøll study indicates that there seems to be very little explicit 'horizon scanning' going on, where opportunities and challenges are identified, and where potential ideas and solutions are examined on an ongoing basis (Day and Schoemaker, 2006). The key executive 'innovation skills' mentioned by Dyer et al (2009) don't get honed. Often, the day-to-day running of the (often quite large) public organisation gets in the way.

What is perhaps more remarkable is that politicians do not seem to be a major source of inspiration. One explanation for this divide could be that in the view of (non-politically appointed) top executives, there is and should be a clear dividing line between the ideology of politics and the pragmatic solutions of bureaucracy.

Academia – universities and research institutions – are also not very strongly represented as sources of inspiration for top public executives. There might be a more universal point here about the relationship between academia and decision-makers: 'More knowledge doesn't make decision-making simpler, and in any case it is often ignored, suppressed, or simply mis-interpreted' (Mulgan, 2009, p 134). The challenge may not so much be that the research community doesn't produce concrete, ready-to-apply solutions to the public sector. There are other actors, including management consultants, who are often better at that. The challenge may be that there isn't sufficient strategic, scenario-based social research being produced that can help public managers see the consequences of their decisions in a long-term perspective. In an ever-more complex and changing world, public managers need less strategic planning and more strategic foresight (Kao, 2002; Drejer et al, 2005).

Finally, hardly any top executives seem to have the opportunity to be inspired by the end-users of the efforts of the organisations they lead. That is not surprising, given that leaders of large organisations have much other business to attend to than to meet citizens first-hand. However, if top executives never see and experience for themselves the reality they are working so hard to make an impact on, how can they tap into the entire emotional, intuitive mode of knowledge so necessary for co-creation and innovation?

The 360 degree innovator: the middle manager

In *Myself and Other More Important Matters* (2006), Charles Handy, the Irish management thinker, tells a story about one of his first personal management experiences as a young oil executive with Royal Dutch Shell. As a young manager in such a large organisation, one has virtually no discretionary spending budget. So you can't get much done. At Shell, however, the young Handy discovered that even though he couldn't contribute to positive change, he could prevent changes from happening: bored out of his mind in his posh London job, he single-handedly managed to stall for several months the building of a new Shell refinery in Napoli Bay by throwing the Italian contractor's application letter in the trash. (He had been to the bay himself on vacation and thought it was too beautiful to tarnish with an oil refinery.) Eventually, the contractor sent letters to everyone at the London headquarters, and the refinery was built. Although he wasn't happy about what he'd done, Charles Handy recognised that there can be quite some satisfaction in exerting one's power to hinder everyone else from getting anything done. In fact, according to Handy, up to 10% of employees are so dissatisfied with their organisations that they are prepared to do something actively to sabotage it (Handy, 2006).

In more modern, 'flat' project organisations, such as professional service firms, the lower ranks, such as project managers, hold the keys to performance: he or she oversees the application of resources and expertise on client projects, and is often directly responsible for quality. In *Aligning the Stars* (2002), Thomas Tierney and Jay Lorsch show how the leading consultants or lawyers become the organisation's stars, essentially driving strategy – not the management. In these kinds of organisations, power is (relatively) evenly distributed (Tierney and Lorsch, 2002).

Mid-level managers often wield enormous power to halt the decision-making process, since, in bureaucracies, decisions must move up and down through the organisational hierarchy. As a consequence, mid-level managers are able to stop the process of innovation dead in its tracks. The flip side of this is that mid-level management is seldom recognised sufficiently as a key to achieving innovation, in particular in hierarchical organisations.

Although there may be some element of project management, hierarchical bureaucracies place much more emphasis on formal position, and decision-making power is not delegated to nearly the same extent. Middle managers are in a position where they are formally charged with generating performance within the unit for which they are responsible. However, their real role is broader than that. Although power (in particular of the decision-making sort) is concentrated at the top of the career ladder, innovation power rests to a high degree in the middle steps of advancement. Unpublished research we did at MindLab in 2009 among more than half a dozen mid-level managers in three government departments and associated agencies, showed a multitude of roles in creating opportunities for innovation. These men and women manage 'down' towards their staff, 'up' towards their own boss and 'out' towards colleagues across their organisation and towards external contacts within and outside the public sector. In each of these four management directions, middle managers can drive or limit innovation. They are potentially 360 degree innovators, creating links between their units' (and their own) insights, resources and capabilities with the people and organisations surrounding them.

While they may not be the ultimate decision-makers, they are, usually, the ultimate executioners. Mid-level managers can not only connect with different resources, innovate through new combinations or adopt practices from elsewhere; they also ensure that things actually get done. As management gurus Bossidy and Charan point out in *Execution*, strategies most often fail because they aren't executed well' (Bossidy and Charan, 2002). The obvious risk for the mid-level manager is perhaps not that he or she doesn't innovate, but that he or she doesn't facilitate and execute the activities necessary for other people's innovations to succeed in the organisation throughout a co-creation process. Whether 'other people' are users (as in citizen-centred innovation), staff (as in employee-driven innovation) or external contacts and organisations (as in open innovation), is less important.

The challenge for the public mid-level manager, then, becomes to create a strategic innovation space that allows for the adoption of innovative approaches and practices, shape strong collaboration with internal and external partners, and contribute to and empower the staff's innovation capacity (Behn, 1995):

Figure 11.1: The 360 degree innovation manager

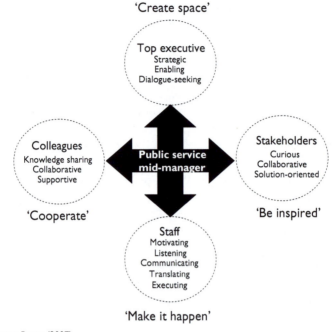

Source: Bason (2007)

- Up, towards top management. Creating 'innovation space' upwards in the organisation through strategic dialogue with top management, exploring possibilities for innovation, challenging the political and structural context and identifying resources (including funding opportunities).
- Sideways, towards management colleagues. Creating cooperation through sharing knowledge and mutual support, building internal coalitions and thus expanding the innovation space further.
- Sideways, towards external stakeholders. Searching for inspiration and ideas through approaches such as open and citizen-centred innovation, developing partnerships to implement innovative solutions. The challenge for mid-level managers is to really embrace the diversity of ideas that can come from the outside.
- Down, towards employees. Supporting innovation capacity, building a culture of innovation, listening to staff and allowing time and resources for entrepreneurial ideas, allowing for a significant divergence of ideas and ensuring that solutions are followed through, activities are carried out and generate intended results.

Like the other leadership roles, mid-level managers must nurture the ability to inspire while overseeing that concrete, positive change takes place in practice. However, their particular 360 dregree position is unique. Any public sector organisation looking to strengthen the four Cs of the innovation ecosystem had better start by taking a hard look at the role of middle management. The language used, the capacity being built, the concrete projects and processes undertaken all depend on middle managers stepping up to the challenge, lifting their perspective from everyday operations to becoming a driver for desired change.

The knowledge engineer: the institution head

When a Copenhagen public day-care institution considered letting parents conduct their own field research within the institution to explore how pre-school children experienced their daily 'work environment', the staff had significant reservations. Letting a couple of parents on the institution's governance board explore the children's social, physical and aesthetic environment could be a challenge to their own pedagogical principles and practice. Further, would such a 'kids-centred' piece of qualitative research in any way be representative of the whole population of children? The institution head cut through the discussion, saying to her staff: 'If we don't dare do something like this, we die' (Bason et al, 2009).

What this manager did was not only to allow user representatives (parents) and, indirectly, users (kids) to become part of the institution's innovation process; she also shared with her staff how passionately she felt about trying something new that could strengthen their own reflection and improve their practices. She showed the courage to experiment in a small scale, leveraging an under-utilised resource such as the parents' board. As Boyett (1996) has pointed out, with devolution of competencies and budgets, the potential of heads of public institutions to essentially become entrepreneurs increases. The project turned out to be a success, the parents sharing qualitative insights from their personal field research into two selected children's 'day in the institution', and everyone on the staff and in the parents' board getting involved in a process of co-creating ideas for developing an even better institution.

The individuals who run schools, day-care institutions, care homes and hospitals are, in most welfare states, the backbone of front-line service provision. This is the group that recruits and retains the professional staff that care for children, patients and senior citizens – every day. As this book has shown again and again, it is the interactions that offer opportunities for creating value: co-creation processes are usually most successful when they are aimed at transforming the public sector's relationship with citizens in one way or another. As a knowledge engineer, the role of the institution head is to connect the abstract, administrative world of governance, budgets and targets with the world of daily service provision, empathy, professionalism and respect (Nonaka and Takeuchi, 1995; Mulgan and Albury, 2003). No matter how innovative politicians, top management or middle management are, if institution heads and their staff do not transform ideas into daily practice, citizens won't notice any difference (Gillinson et al, 2010).

However, very few institution heads possess the resources, methods or tools to engage staff, citizens, user representatives and other participants in a process of co-creation. Also, they aren't always able to recruit and develop staff that can encompass both the more closed mode of daily operations, and the open-ended nature of innovation processes. The challenge for institution heads, therefore, is to build their own competencies in co-creation, as well as those of their staff, and to encourage the kind of experimentation that took place at the Copenhagen day-care facility. Perhaps policymakers at central level should recognise that to truly scale innovation, this is the place to invest.

About civil disobedience

Sometimes, when it comes to innovation, the best leadership practice is breaking the rules. Not long ago I conducted a workshop for public managers in Wellington, New Zealand. Towards the end of the session, the participants presented the ideas and concepts they had developed – many of which were quite inspired and clearly represented bold thinking. One of the presentations prompted me to say that sometimes, to innovate, we need a good dose of civil disobedience. Everyone in the room giggled. Coming from Denmark, where the 'power distance' in most workplaces is quite short, and there is arguably a high degree of pragmatism about rules and regulations, I didn't quite get what the fuss was about; but someone later that day explained to me that the very notion of 'civil disobedience' was rather unthinkable in a New Zealand government context (but, she added, it probably was exactly what the country needed).

This experience has made me think about the role of breaking rules in innovation – and in particular the role for managers in breaking the rules. There certainly is something to the idea of asking for forgiveness, rather than permission. It is sometimes necessary to stretch the rules or interpret a directive rather loosely to do something different. If that kind of flexibility isn't there, if it isn't taken, we'd have a lot less innovation in the public sector. Obviously, it is also the kind of action that can get you fired. But as New York State Assistant Education Commissioner Sheila Evans-Tranum has pointed out, perhaps you really do need to be willing to walk away from your job in order to achieve great things in government.

How to do it

Leading public sector innovation is the art and practice of balancing between inspiration and execution, between exploring mysteries and exploiting resources to generate results. This book has suggested that public organisations must build an ecosystem of innovation across the four Cs of consciousness, capacity, co-creation and courage. Without the courage to lead innovation at all levels of government organisations, the transformative potential of co-creation will not be realised. Visionary leadership – the ability to formulate a compelling future and show in practice how it might be created – is at the core of leading innovation. Barriers abound: internal recruiting of managers; the complexities of the tasks leading public organisations; the sometimes diffuse relationship between public administrators and politicians; and lack of tolerance for a diversity of people, ideas and solutions at all levels are among them.

Especially in the public sector, 'challenging the innovation space' seems crucial. This entails taking a broader view of one's own role than simply 'managing' a department, a unit or an institution. It entails taking a more systemic view. Public managers must step into the role of leaders, shaping the arena for innovation through their interactions with the political leadership, with each other across government and with citizens, businesses and other stakeholders. Formal position is, in most public organisations, important. Each holds particular innovation opportunities. To lead public sector innovation is to embrace four different archetypes of public sector innovation leaders:

The Visionary

The political leader who is able to formulate an ambitious, even audacious vision, give the organisation direction and ignite the energy and motivation of the employees. The Visionary must ask:

- *Have I formulated a sufficiently clear, ambitious and long-term vision that will energise the public organisation(s) for which I am accountable, so they dare to innovate?*

- *Have I articulated clearly the outcomes I consider as concrete expressions of success?*
- *Am I ensuring that the organisation(s) I am accountable for have sufficient political support and resources to achieve the objectives I expect of them?*

The Enabler

The top executive of a government department or agency. The Enabler's unique contribution is to create optimal framework conditions for the innovative organisation. At the best of times, the Visionary and the Enabler work in tandem, ensuring that the political vision can be realised through an innovative public organisation. The Enabler faces the following questions:

- *Have I clearly extended a 'licence to innovate' to the organisation I am heading, and do my actions show in practice that I mean it?*
- *Do we as an organisation have a clear strategy, do we have strategies for how we want to innovate, and do we manage our innovation portfolio?*
- *Am I sufficiently actively investing in building my organisation's innovation ecosystem from top to bottom?*
- *Am I engaging my staff in an ongoing dialogue about what innovation means to us, and how we get more of it?*

The 360 Degree Innovator

Perhaps surprisingly, is the middle manager in a department or agency. Often the middle manager is in practice one of the most powerful positions in the organisation. Middle managers may have very limited discretionary budgets; but they may also be able to stop any development effort dead in its tracks, if they choose to do so. For the same reason, they are in a position to let loose the innovation potential in the organisation, letting go, embracing co-creation and helping drive a greater diversity of solutions. As a 360 Degree Innovator in government, the questions to ask are:

- *Am I aware of the position I have in the organisation, and how I may contribute in a much wider sense to help address the opportunities we face and tackle our most pressing challenges?*
- *Who are my 360 degree constituents that I should be collaborating with – up, across and down?*

- *Am I recognising that I can achieve more by letting go, allowing a process of co-creation to unfold through active involvement of all constituents surrounding a particular problem, rather than through control?*

The Knowledge Engineer

The institution head – leader of a school, a hospital, day-care institution, care home – who encounters citizens and their challenges, problems, fears, resources and hopes every day. Borrowing again from Ikujiro Nonakas's concept, the institution head must play the role of transforming innovations elsewhere into workable solutions in his or her own institution. Only institution heads and their staff understand exactly what it would take in terms of new skills, processes and organisational changes, and communication to implement a good idea from somewhere else. This requires a proactive emphasis on both employee involvement and innovation. The questions to ask as a Knowledge Engineer are thus:

- *To what degree have we created a modern work environment where everyone can contribute with their ideas, and see them taken seriously?*
- *Are we sufficiently actively seeking for workable, new solutions from sources outside our organisation?*
- *How are we ourselves sharing the solutions we have found to be effective, so our peers may learn from them?*

No matter what position of leadership is in question, leading public sector innovation boils down to courage: the ability to embrace and manage the divergence of new ideas that we so desperately need if we are to tackle tomorrow's problems and capture the opportunities in front of us. To lead innovation is, in the quote that introduced this chapter, to go forth into unknown territory. If it takes a bit of 'civil disobedience' to take the first step, then maybe that is what we need.

References

Ackoff, Russel L., James Magidson and Herbert J. Addison (2006) *Idealized Design: How to Dissolve Tomorrow's Crisis … Today*, Upper Saddle River: Wharton School Publishing.

Aiken, Caroly and Scott Keller (2009) 'The Irrational Side of Change Management', *McKinsey Quarterly*, April, No 2, pp 101-9.

Albury, David (2005) 'Fostering Innovation in Public Services', *Public Money and Management*, January, vol 25, no 1, pp 51–6.

Allison, Graham T. (1971) *Essence of Decision: Explaining the Cuban Missile Crisis*, Boston: Little, Brown and Company.

American Society for Quality (2010) *Great Ormond Street Case*. Available at: http://www.asq.org/healthcare-use/why-quality/great-ormond-street-hospital.html

Attwood, Margaret, Mike Pedler, Sue Pritchard and David Wilkinson (2003) *Leading Change: A Guide to Whole Systems Working*, Bristol: The Policy Press.

Austin, Robert D. (1996) *Measuring and Managing Performance in Organizations*, New York: Dorset House Publishing.

Austin, Robert, Jonathan Wareham and Javier Busquets (2008) *Specialisterne: Sense & Details*, Harvard Business School case 9-608-109

Australian Government (2010) *Empowering Change: Fostering Innovation in the Australian Public Service*, Canberra: Commonwealth of Australia, available at: http://www.apsc.gov.au/mac/empoweringchange.htm

Bannerjee, Banny (2009) Cross-disciplinary approach as a key to successful innovation. Available at: http://copenhagencocreation.com/video/banny-banerjee/

Barosso, Manuel (2009) 'Transforming the EU into an Innovation Society', Speech given 13 October in Brussels. Available at: www.europa.eu/rapid

Bason, Christian (2007) *Velfærdsinnovation: Ledelse af innovation i den offentlige sektor* [*Innovating Welfare: Leading Innovation in the Public Sector*], Copenhagen: Børsens Forlag.

Bason, Christian, Agi Csonka and Nicolaj Ejler (2003) *Arbejdets nye ansigter – ledelse af fremtidens medarbejder* [*New Faces at Work: Leading the Employee of the Future*], Copenhagen: Børsens Forlag.

Bason, Christian, Sune Knudsen and Søren Toft (2009) *Sæt borgeren i spil: Sådan involverer du borgere og virksomheder i offentlig innovation* [*Put the Citizen Into Play: How to Involve Citizens and Businesses in Public Sector Innovation*], Copenhagen: Gyldendal Public.

Bate, Paul and Glenn Robert (2007) *Bringing User Experience to Healthcare Improvement:The Concepts, Methods and Practices of Experience-based Design*, Abingdon: Radcliffe Publishing.

Behn, Robert D. (1995) 'Creating an Innovative Organisation: Ten Hints for Involving Frontline Workers', *State and Local Government Review*, vol 27, no 3, pp 221–34.

Benington, J. and Hartley, J. (2001) 'Pilots, Paradigms and Paradoxes: Changes in Public Sector Governance and Management in the UK', conference proceedings: *International Research Symposium on Public Sector Management*, Barcelona, Spain.

Bernard, H.R. (2006) *Research Methods in Anthropology: Qualitative and Quantitative Approaches*, Oxford: Alta Mira Press.

Bessant, John (2005) 'Enabling Continuous and Discontinuous Innovation: Learning From the Private Sector', *Public Money and Management*, vol 25, no 1, pp 35–42.

Bhatta, Gambhir (2003) 'Don't Just do Something, Stand There! – Revisiting the Issue of Risks in Innovation in the Public Sector', *The Innovation Journal: The Public Sector Innovation Journal*, vol 8, no 2, pp 1–12.

Binder, Thomas and Eva Brandt (2008) 'The Design:Lab as Platform in Participatory Design Research', *CoDesign*, vol 4, no 2, pp 115–29.

Boland, Richard J. and Fred Collopy (2004) *Managing as Designing*, Stanford: Stanford University Press.

Borins, Sandford (2000) 'Loose Cannons and Rule Breakers, or Enterprising Leaders? Some Evidence about Innovative Public Managers', *Public Management Review*, vol 60, no 6, pp 498-507.

Borins, Sandford (2001a) *The Challenge of Innovating in Government*, IBM Centre for the Business of Government, available at: http://www.businessofgovernment.org/report/challenge-innovating-government

Borins, Sandford (2001b) *Innovation, Success and Failure in Public Management Research: Some Methodological Reflections*, Public Management Review, vol 3, no 1, pp 3–18.

Borins, Sandford (2001c) 'Public Management Innovation in Economically Advanced and Developing Countries', *International Review of Administrative Sciences*, vol 67, pp 715–31.

Borins, Sandford (ed) (2008) *Innovations in Government: Research, Recognition and Replication*, Washington, DC: Brookings Institution Press and Ash Institute for Democratic Governance.

Bossidy, Larry and Ram Charan (2002) *Execution: The Discipline of Getting Things Done*, New York: Crown Business.

Boyett, Inger (1996) 'The Public Sector Entrepreneur – A Definition', *International Journal of Public Sector Management*, 9(2), 36–51.

Boyle, David, Julia Slay and Lucie Stephens (2010) *Public Services Inside Out: Putting Co-production into Practice*, London: The Lab, Nesta.

Brandi, Søren & Steen Hildebrandt (2003) *Mangfoldighedsledelse: Om mangfoldighed i virksomheds- og samfundsperspektiv* [*Diversity Management: Diversity in a Business and Societal Perspective*], Copenhagen: Børsens Forlag.

Brown, Tim (2008) 'Design Thinking', *Harvard Business Review*, June 2008.

Brown, Tim (2009) *Change by Design*: *How Design Thinking Transforms Organizations and Inspires Innovation*, New York: HarperCollins.

Business Week (2007) *At 3M, A Struggle Between Efficiency And Creativity*, 11 June.

Cabinet Office (2009) *Power in People's Hands: Learning from the World's Best Public Services*, London: Cabinet Office, available at: http://www.cabinetoffice.gov.uk/media/224869/world-class.pdf

Cabinet Office (2010) *Enabling Innovation: The First Year of the Innovators Council*, London: Cabinet Office, available at: http://www.hmg.gov.uk/media/60278/enabling_innovation.pdf

Chesbrough, Henry (2006a) *Open Innovation: The New Imperative for Creating and Profiting from Technology*, Boston: Harvard Business School Press.

Chesbrough, Henry (2006b) *Open Business Models: How to Thrive in the New Innovation Landscape*, Boston: Harvard Business School Press.

Christensen, Clayton (1997) *The Innovator's Dilemma: When New Technologies Cause Great Companies to Fail*, Boston: Harvard Business School Press.

Climate Consortium (2010) *Climate Consortium Denmark*. Available at: http://www.brandingdanmark.dk/international/en-gb/menu/marketing-of-denmark/climate-conference/climate-consortium/climate-consortium.htm

Cole, Martin and Greg Parston (2006) *Unlocking Public Value: A New Model for Achieving High Performance in Public Service Organizations*, Chichester: John Wiley & Sons, Ltd.

Dance United (2009) 'Dance United Annual Report and Accounts 2008/09'. Available at: www.dance-united.com

Danish Ministry of Finance (2005) *Bedre innovation i den offentlige sector* [*Better Innovation in the Public Sector*], Copenhagen: Ministry of Finance.

Danish Government (2006) *The Danish Globalisation Strategy*. Available at www.globalisation.dk

Danish Ministry of Finance (2006) *Public Governance: Code for Chief Executive Excellence*. Available at: http://www.publicgovernance.dk/resources/File/FFOT_bog_UK.pdf

Danish Ministry of Finance (2010) *National Budget 2010*, Copenhagen: Ministry of Finance.

Danish Ministry of Taxation (2007) *Kunstneriske metoder i Skatteministeriet [Artistic methods in the Danish Ministry of Taxation]*, Copenhagen; Ministry of Taxation, available at: http://www.skm.dk/public/billeder/omministeriet/strategier/kunst/projektessenser.pdf

Danish State Employer's Authority (2006) *Motivationsundersøgelsen [The Employee Motivation Survey]*, Copenhagen: Danish State Employer's Authority.

Darsø, Lotte (2001) *Innovation in the Making*, Copenhagen: Samfundslitteratur.

Day, George S. and Paul J. H. Schoemaker (2006) *Peripheral Vision: Detecting the Weak Signals that Will Make or Break Your Company*, Boston: Harvard Business School Press.

Design Council (2009a) *Public Services by Design: A New Route to Public Sector Innovation*, London: Design Council.

Design Council (2009b) *Design Bugs Out*, London: Design Council.

Digital Health [Digital Sundhed] (2010) *Telemedicin kan effektivisere sårbehandling [Telemedicine can make treatment of wounds more effective]* Available at: http://www.sdsd.dk/Aktuelt/Nyheder/Telemedicin_ansogning_abt.aspx

Digmann, Annemette Kirsten Engholm Jensen, Jens Peter Jensen and Henrik W. Bendix (2008) *Principper for offentlig innovation: Fra best practice til next practice [Principles of Public Sector Innovation: From Best Practice to Next Practice]*, Copenhagen: Børsens Forlag.

Drejer, Anders, Sten Dyrmose and Claus Homann (2005) *Innovation gennem netværk: På vej mod nye ledelsesformer [Innovation through network: The path to new forms of leadership]*, Copenhagen: Børsens Forlag.

Drucker, Peter F. (1985) *Innovation and Entrepreneurship*, Oxford: Elsevier Butterworth-Heinemann.

Dubhthaigh, Ré and Toke Barter (2006) *Food for Thought*, London: RCA.

Dunleavy, Patrick, Helen Margetts, Simon Bastow and Jane Tinkler (2006) *Digital Era Governance*, Oxford: Oxford University Press.

Dyer, Jeffrey H., Hal B. Gregersen and Clayton M. Christensen (2009) 'The Innovator's DNA', *Harvard Business Review*, vol 87, no 12.

Edna McConnell Clark Foundation (2010) *Youth Villages*. Available at: http://www.emcf.org/portfolio/grantees/youthvillages/index.htm

Eggers, William and John O'Leary (2009) *If we Can Put a Man on the Moon … Getting Big Things Done in Government*, Boston: Harvard Business Press.

Eggers, William D. and Shalabh Kumar Singh (2009) *The Public Innovator's Playbook*, Winnipeg: Deloitte Research and Harvard Ash Center for Democratic Governance and Innovation.

Ellis, Tania (2010) *The New Pioneers: Sustainable Business Success Through Social Innovation and Social Entrepreneurship*, Chichester: John Wiley & Sons, Ltd.

Esslinger, Hartmut (2009) *A Fine Line: How Design Strategies are Shaping the Future of Business*, San Francisco: Jossey-Bass.

European Commission (2009) 'Business Panel on Innovation'. Available at: http://ec.europa.eu/enterprise/policies/innovation/

Executive Office of the President (2009) *A Strategy for American Innovation: Driving Towards Sustainable Growth and Quality Jobs*, Washington, DC: National Economic Council, available at: www.whitehouse.gov/administration/eop/nec/StrategyforAmericanInnovation/

Farmakonomen (2006) 'Sydfynske øer får fjernbetjente medicindepoter' ['South Funen Islands receive Remote Controlled Medicine Depots']. Available at: http://www.farmakonomen.dk/Nyt/Nyheder/Arkiv%202006/Sydfynske%20oer%20faar.aspx

Finland Ministry of Employment and the Economy (2008) *Proposal for Finland's National Innovation Strategy*, available at: http://ec.europa.eu/invest-in-research/pdf/download_en/finland_national_innovation_strategy.pdf

Florida, Richard (2002) *The Rise of the Creative Class*, New York: Perseus Books.

FO (2005) *Danish Futures Magazine*, 5.

Fora (2009) *New Nature of Innovation: Understanding Policy Implications of New Forms for Innovation*. Available at: www.newnatureofinnovation.org

Friedman, Thomas (2005) *The World is Flat: A Brief History of the Twenty-First Century*, New York: Farrar, Straus and Giroux.

Friedman, Thomas (2008) *Hot, Flat & Crowded: Why the World Needs A Green Revolution – and How We Can Renew Our Global Future*, New York: Penguin.

FTF (2007) *Medarbejderdreven innovation* [*Employee-driven Innovation*], Copenhagen: FTF, available at: www.ramboll-management.dk/~/media/Images/RM/RM%20DK%20and%20RM%20Group/PDF/Publications/2007/MedarbejderdrevenInnovation.ashx.

Fuglsang, Jakob (2006) 'Commitment to Public Innovation: Frameworks for Innovation and Management in a Copenhagen Health Care Centre', Paper at the conference 'A New Agenda for Leadership?', The Danish Academy of Management, 11–12 December, Copenhagen.

Gillinson, Sarah, Matthew Horne and Peter Baeck (2010) *Radical Efficiency: Better, Different, Lower Cost Public Services*, London: Innovation Unit, The Lab, and Nesta. Available at: www.nesta.org.uk/library/documents/radical-efficiency180610.pdf

Goldsmith, Stephen and William D. Eggers (2004) *Governing by Network: The New Shape of the Public Sector*, Washington, DC: Brookings.

Government 2.0 Taskforce (2009) 'Engage: Getting on with Government 2.0'. Available at: http://gov2.net.au/report/

Gray, V. (1973) 'Innovation in the States: A Diffusion Study', *American Political Science Association*, 67(4), 1174–85.

Halse, Joachim, Eva Brandt, Brendon Clark and Thomas Binder (2010) *Rehearsing the Future*, Copenhagen: the Danish Design School.

Hamel, Gary (2000) *Leading the Revolution*, Boston: Harvard Business School Press.

Hamel, Gary (2007) *The Future of Management*, Boston: Harvard Business Press.

Handy, Charles (2006) *Myself and Other More Important Matters*, London: Random House Business Books.

Hansen, Søren and Henning Sejer Jakobsen (2006) 'Idéudvikling på en kreativ platform' ['Idea development on a Creative Platform'], in Gertsen, Frank, Poul Kyvsgaard Hansen and Harry Boer (eds) *Innovationsledelse*, Aalborg: Center for Industrial Production, Aalborg Universitet. Available at: www.iprod.auc.dk/~fgertsen/innovation-cip-dk.pdf

Harris, Michael and David Albury (2009) *The Innovation Imperative*, London: Nesta.

Hartley, Jean (2005) 'Innovation in Governance and Public Services: Past and Present', *Public Money and Management*, vol 25, no 1, 27–34.

Hasse, C. (2003) 'Mødet: den antropologiske læreproces' ['The meeting: The anthropological learning process'], in Kirsten Hastrup (ed) *Ind i verden: En grundbog i antropologiskmetode* [*Into the world: An introduction to anthropological methods*], Copenhagen: Hans Reitzel.

Hastrup, Kirsten (2003) (ed) *Ind i verden: En grundbog i antropologiskmetode* [*Into the world: An introduction to anthropological methods*], Copenhagen: Hans Reitzel.

Hattori, Ruth Ann and Joyce Wycoff (2002) 'Innovation DNA: A Good Idea is Not Enough. It Has to Create Value', *Training and Development*, 56(2), 25–39.

Heath, Chip and Dan Heath (2007) *Made to Stick: Why Some Ideas Survive and Others Die*, New York: Random House.

Heskett, John (2002) *Toothpicks & Logos: Design in Everyday Life*, New York/Oxford: Oxford University Press.

Hess, Michael and David Adams (2007) 'Innovation in Public Management: The role and Function of Community Knowledge', *The Public Sector Innovation Journal*, 12(1), 1–20.

Hirst, Paul and Graham Thompson (1999) *Globalization in Question: The International Economy and the Possibilities of Governance*, Cambridge: Polity Press.

Hood, Christopher and Helen Margetts (2007) *The Tools of Government in the Digital Age*, Hampshire: Palgrave Macmillan.

Howe, Jeff (2008) *Crowdsourcing: Why the Power of the Crowd is Driving the Future of Business*, New York: Three Rivers Press.

Hunter, David (2010) 'The Hunter System: Performance Management for Strategic Success'. Available at: http://www.dekhconsulting.com/

IBM (2010) *Together, We're Building a Smarter Planet: IBM Public Sector Top Innovators Report*. Available at: ftp://public.dhe.ibm.com/common/ssi/sa/st/n/puz03001usen/PUZ03001USEN.PDF

iLipinar, Gürsel, Jordi Montaña, Oriol Iglesias, Tore Kristensen and Wes Johnston (2009) 'Designer as Midwife: Towards a New State-of-Mind?', paper for the 3rd annual conference of the International Association of Societies of Design Research, Seoul, October 18-22.

Index (2009) 'Index Award Nominees', Copenhagen. Available at: www.indexaward.dk

Jones, Simon (2003) *Making Innovation Work*, Dublin: MIT Media Lab Europe.

Kanter, Rosabeth Moss (2006) 'Innovation: The Classic Traps', *Harvard Business Review*, November, pp 73-83.

Kao, John (2002) *John Kao's Innovation Manifesto: 20 Precepts about Innovation*, Norwalk: John Kao.

Kao. John (2007) *Innovation Nation: How America is Losing its Innovation Edge, Why it Matters, and What We Can Do to Get it Back*, New York: Free Press.

Kaplan, Robert S. and David P. Norton (1996) *The Balanced Scorecard: Translating Strategy into Action*. Boston: Harvard Business School Press.

Kelley, Tom (2001) *The Art of Innovation*, New York: Doubleday.

Kelley, Tom (2005) *The Ten Faces of Innovation*, New York: Doubleday.

Kettl, Donald F. (2009) *The Next Government of the United States*, New York: W. W. Norton.

Kimbell, Lucy (2010) 'Design Practices in Design Thinking', working paper, Oxford University Säid School of Business.

King, David and Barry Welsh (2006) *Knowing the People Planning*, London: The Nuffield Trust.

Kirah, Anna (2009) *From User-driven to People-centric*. Available at: http://copenhagencocreation.com/video/anna-kirah/

KL [Local Government Denmark] (2009) *Vær med i konkurrencen om KLs innovationspris 2010 [Join the competition for the Local Government Innovation Prize 2010].* Available at: http://www.kl.dk/innovationspris

Koch, Per and Johan Hauknes (2005) *On Innovation in the Public Sector,* Publin Report no D20, NIFU STEP. Available at: http://www.step.no/publin/reports/d20-innovation.pdf

Koen, Peter et al (2001) 'Providing Clarity and a Common Language to the "Fuzzy Front End"', *Research Technology Management,* vol 44, no 2, pp 46–55.

Kollerup, Finn and Jørgen Thorball (2005) *God innovationsledelse [Good Innovation Management],* Copenhagen: Børsens forlag.

Kotter, John (1996) *Leading Change,* Boston: Harvard Business School Press.

Kristeligt Dagblad (2009) *Lægen er venner med sine patienter på facebook [Doctor is friends with patients on Facebook],* 23 January.

Leadbeater, Charles (2000) *Living on Thin Air,* London: Viking.

Leadbeater, Charles (2009a) *We-Think: Mass Innovation, Not Mass Production,* London: Profile Books

Leadbeater, Charles (2009b) The Art of With, An Original Essay for Cornerhouse, Manchester, March 2009. Available at: www.charlesleadbeater.net/cms/xstandard/The%20Art%20of%20With%20PDF.pdf

Richard K. Lester and Piore, Michael J. (2006) *Innovation: The Missing Dimension,* Cambridge: Harvard University Press.

Lettl, C., Hienerth, C. and Gemuenden, H.G. (2008) 'Exploring how Lead Users Develop Radical Innovation: Opportunity Recognition and Exploitation in the Field of Medical Equipment Technology', *IEEE Transactions on Engineering Management,* vol 55, no 2, pp 219–33.

Libbey, Meryl (1994) 'Reengineering Public Innovation', *Public Productivity and Management Review,* vol 18, no 2, pp 163-175.

LiveWork (2006) 'Case Study: Sunderland Inactivity to Activity'. Available at: www.livework.co.uk

LO (Landsorganisationen i Danmark) (2006) 'Undersøgelse af medarbejderdreven innovation på private og offentlige arbejdspladser' ['Survey of Employee-driven Innovation in Public and Private Organisations']. Available at: www.lo.dk

Madsen, Sabine and Lene Nielsen (2008) 'Using Storytelling to Identify Requirements – Exploring Persona-Scenarios in Context', Working Paper. Available at: http://personas.dk/wp-content/using-storytelling-to-identify-requirements1.pdf

Marcus, G.E. (1995) *Ethnography in/of the World System: The Emergence of Multi-Sited Ethnography*, Houston: Department of Anthropology, Rice University.

Martin, Roger (2007) *The Opposable Mind*, Cambridge: Harvard Business Press.

Martin, Roger (2009) *The Design of Business: Why Design Thinking is the Next Competitive Advantage*, Cambridge: Harvard Business Press.

McKinsey Quarterly (2008) 'Lessons from Innovation's Front Lines: An Interview with IDEO's CEO', November. Available at: www.ideo. com/images/uploads/thinking/publications/pdfs/Lessons_from_ innovations_front_lines_1.pdf

Mikkelsen, Hans (ed) (2005) *Ledelse af projektmylderet – om virksomhedslederes håndtering af udviklingsaktiviteter* [*Leading the Project Mess*], Copenhagen: Børsens Forlag.

MindLab (2008) 'Burden-Hunting: A Citizen-centric Approach to Cutting Red Tape'. Available at: www.mind-lab.dk

MindLab (2010) *Why is Innovation a Terrible Word?* blog post at http:// mindblog.dk/en/

Ministry of the Interior and Kingdom Relations (2006) 'Nederland Regelland: Nine Routes Along Dutch Bureaucracy'. Available at: www.lastvandeoverheid.nl

Mintzberg, Henry (2009) *Managing*, Harlow: Pearson Education.

Moggridge, Bill (2009) Presentation at MindLab, June. Available at: www.mind-lab.dk

Mohr, L. B. (1969) 'Determinants of Innovation in Organizations', *American Political Science Review*, 63(1), 111–26.

Monday Morning (2010) *Det offentlige skal sætte spørgsmålstegn ved sig selv* [*The public sector must question itself*] no 16, 26 April.

Moore, Mark H. (1995) *Creating Public Value: Strategic Management in Government*, Boston: Harvard University Press.

Moore, Mark H. (2005) 'Break-Through Innovations and Continuous Improvement: Two Different Models of Innovative Processes in the Public Sector', *Public Money & Management*, January, vol 25, no 1, pp 43–9.

Mulgan (2007) *Ready or Not? Taking Innovation in the Public Sector Seriously*, London: Nesta Provocation 03: April. Available at: www. nesta.org.uk/publications/provocations/assets/features/ready_or_ not_taking_innovation_in_the_public_sector_seriously

Mulgan, Geoff (2009) *The Art of Public Strategy*, Oxford: Oxford University Press.

Mulgan, Geoff and David Albury (2003) *Innovation in the Public Sector*, London: Strategy Unit. Available at:www.michaellittle.org/documents/Mulgan%20on%20Innovation.pdf

Mulgan, Geoff and David Albury (2005) 'Innovation in Public Services'. Available at: http://www.idea-knowledge.gov.uk/idk/aio/1118552

Mulgan, Geoff and Nick Wilkie, Simon Tucker, Rushanara Ali, Francis Davis and Tom Liptror (2006) *Social Silicon Valleys*, London: Young Foundation.

Münster, Ole and Sofie Münster (2010) *Når idealer forenes med forretning* [*When Ideals Meet Business*], Copenhagen: Gyldendal Business.

Murray, Robin, Julie Caulier-Rice and Geoff Mulgan (2009) *Social Venturing*, London: Nesta. Available at: www.nesta.org.uk/publications/reports/assets/features/social_venturing

Nachmias, Chava Frankfor and David Nachmias (1992) *Research Methods for the Social Sciences*, 4th edn, London/Melbourne/Auckland: Edward Arnold.

NAO (National Audit Office) (2006) *Achieving innovation in central government organisations*, London: NAO.

NAO (2009) *Achieving innovation in central government organisations*, London: NAO.

NASA (2004) 'Project Apollo: A Retrospective Analysis'. Available at: http://history.nasa.gov/Apollomon/Apollo.html

Nesta Public Services Lab (2009) Speech by PM Gordon Brown. Available at: www.nesta.org.uk/areas_of_work/public_services_lab/assets/features/public_services_innovation_summit

New York Times (2009) *The Analytic Mode*, 3 December.

NNIT and Computerworld (2006) *Digital Public Governance 2006*. Denmark: NNIT. Available at: www.mrlindholm.dk/files/PDG%20rapport%202006.pdf

Nonaka, Ikujiro and Hirotaka Takeuchi (1995) *The Knowledge-creating Company*, Oxford: Oxford University Press.

OECD (2005) *Modernising Government: The Way Forward*, Paris: OECD

Osborne, Stephen P. and Kerry Brown (2005) *Managing Change and Innovation in Public Service Organisations*, New York: Routledge.

Osborne, David and Ted Gaebler (1992) *Reinventing Government: How the Entrepreneurial Spirit is Transforming the Public Sector*, Reading: Addison Wesley.

Parker, Sophia and Joe Heapy (2006) *The Journey to the Interface: How Public Service Design can Connect Users to Reform*, London: Demos.

Parker, Sophia and Simon Parker (eds) (2007) *Unlocking Innovation: Why Citizens Hold the Key to Public Service Reform*, London: Demos.

Patterson, Fiona, Dr Maura Kerrin, Geraldine Gatto-Roissard and Phillipa Coan (2009) *Everyday Innovation: How to Enhance Innovative Working in Employees and Organisations*, London: Nesta. Available at: www.nesta.org.uk/library/documents/Every-day-innovation-report.pdf

Pfeffer, Jeffrey and Robert I. Sutton (2006) *Hard Facts, Dangerous Half-truths and Total Nonsense: Profiting from Evidence-based Management*, Boston: Harvard Business School Press.

Pilloton, Emily (2009) '*Project H Design (Anti)Manifesto: A Call To Action For Humanitarian (Product) Design*'. Available at: http://projecthdesign.org/about/manifesto.html

Pollitt, Christopher (2003) *The Essential Public Manager*, Berkshire: Open University Press.

Prahalad, C. K. and Venkat Ramaswamy (2004) *The Future of Competition: Co-Creating Unique Value with Customers*, Boston: Harvard Business School Publishing.

Prendiville, Alison (2009) 'Love Lewisham: Improving Stakeholder Satisfaction in Local Government Service: A Case Study of Strategic Public Sector Service Innovation', paper to the first Nordic Conference on Service Design and Service Innovation, 24–6 October.

Pruitt, John and Tamara Adlin (2006) *The Persona Lifecycle: Keeping People in Mind Throughout Product Design*, San Francisco: Morgan Kaufmann.

Rambøll Management (2006) 'Innovationskraft' ['Innovation Power']. Available at: http://www.ramboll-management.dk/da/news/publikationer/2006.aspx

Reich, Robert B. (2009) 'Government in Your Business', *Harvard Business Review*, July–August, pp 93–100.

Rijkswaterstaat (2009) 'LEF Future Centre'. Available at: www.rijkswaterstaat.nl/lef

Rist, Ray C. and Jody Zall Kusek (2004) *Ten Steps to a Results-based Monitoring and Evaluation System*, Washington, DC: World Bank.

Rittel, Horst and Melvin Webber (1973) 'Dilemmas in a General Theory of Planning', *Policy Sciences*, Vol. 4, 155–69. Reprinted in Cross, N. (ed) (1984) *Developments in Design Methodology*, Chichester: John Wiley & Sons, pp. 135–44.

Rosenberg, Howard and Charles S. Feldman (2008) *No Time to Think: The Menace of Media Speed and the 24-hour News Cycle*, London: Continuum Books.

Røste, Rannveig (2008) 'Innovation in the Public Sector – Identifying the Concepts and the Systems of Innovations', in Helge Godø, Magnus Gulbrandsen, Sverre Herstad, Åge Mariussen, Rannveig Røste, Olav R. Spilling and Finn Ørstavik (eds) *Innovation Systems, Innovation Modes and Processes of Commercialization*, NIFU STEP report 4, Oslo: NIFU, pp. 153–71. Available at: www.nifustep.no/Norway/Publications/2008/NIFU%20STEP%20Rapport%20%204-2008.pdf

Rubow, Cecilie (2003) 'Samtalen. Interviewet som deltagerobservation' ['The Conversation. The Interview as Participant Observation'], in Hastrup, Kirsten (ed) *Ind i verden* [*Into the world*], Copenhagen: Hans Reitzels Forlag.

Rudd, Kevin (2009) 'Equipping the Australian Public Service for Australia's Future Challenges', Institute of Public Administration Australia, Sir Robert Garran Oration, Brisbane, 20 November.

Sanders, Elizabeth (2006) 'Design Serving People', Copenhagen Cumulus Working Papers, Helsinki.

Sanders, Elizabeth and Pieter Jan Stappers (2008) 'Co-creation and the New Landscapes of Design', *CoDesign: International Journal of CoCreation in Design and the Arts*, 1745-3755, 4(1), 5–18.

Sanger, Mary Bryna and Martin A. Levin (1992) 'Using Old Stuff in New Ways: Innovation as a Case of Evolutionary Tinkering', *Journal of Policy Analysis and Management*, 11(1), 88–115.

Scharmer, C. Otto (2007) *Theory U: Leading from the Future as it Emerges*. Cambridge: Society for Organizational Learning, Inc.

Schumpeter, Joseph A. (1975) *Capitalism, Socialism and Democracy*, New York: Harper.

Seddon, John (2008) *Systems Thinking in the Public Sector. The Failure of the Reform Regime and a Manifesto for a Better Way*, Devon: Triarchy Press.

Senge, Peter (2006) *The Fifth Discipline: The Art & Practice of the Learning Organization*, New York/London/Toronto/Sydney/Auckland: Currency Doubleday.

Shirky, Clay (2008) *Here Comes Everybody: How Change Happens When People Come Together*, London: Penguin Press.

Simon, Herbert (1969) *The Sciences of the Artificial*, Boston: MIT Press.

Staley, Louise (2008) *Evidence-based Policy and Public Sector Innovation*, Melbourne: Institute of Public Affairs.

Stewart-Weeks, Martin (2010) *Government at the Edge: The Emergence of a New Public Sector*, working paper. See also www.slideshare.net/greebo/public-sphere-gov-20-martin-stewart-weeks

Stewart-Weeks, Martin and Paul Johnston (2007) 'The Connected Republic 2.0: New Possibilities & New Value for the Public Sector', Cisco. Available at: www.theconnectedrepublic.org

Surowiecki, James (2004) *The Wisdom of Crowds: Why the Many are Smarter Than the Few and How Collective Wisdom Shapes Business, Economies, Societies and Nations*, New York: Doubleday.

Sydney Morning Herald (2010) 'Ageing, growing population blamed for rise in costs', 26 January.

Tapscott, Don (2009) *Grown Up Digital: How the Net Generation is Changing Your World*, New York: McGraw-Hill.

Tapscott, Don and Anthony D. Williams (2006) *Wikinomics: How Mass Collaboration Changes Everything*, New York: Penguin.

Tempoe, Mahen (1994) 'Organising for Customer Service', in Roger Lovell (ed) *Managing Change in the New Public Sector*, Essex: Longman, Harlow.

Thaler, R.H. and Sunstein, C.R. (2008) *Nudge: Improving Decisions about Health, Wealth and Happiness*, New Haven/Lonson: Yale University Press.

The Guardian (2009) 'Seven ways to protect public services', 16 December.

Thenint, Hugo (2009) *Labs for a More Innovative Europe*, Inno GRIPS. Available at: http://grips-public.mediactive.fr/knowledge_base/view/880/-labs-for-a-more-innovative-europe-workshop-report/

Thomas, David A. and Robin J. Ely (1996) 'Making Differences Matter: A New Paradigm for Managing Diversity', *Harvard Business Review*, September–October.

Tidd, Joe, John Bessant and Keith Pavitt (2005) *Managing Innovation – Integrating Technological, Market and Organizational Change*, Chichester: John Wiley & Sons, Ltd.

Tierney, T. and Jay Lorsch (2002) *Aligning the Stars: How to Succeed when Professionals Drive Results*, Cambridge: Harvard Business School Press.

Time Magazine (2009) *Ben Bernanke*, 28 December 2009 – 4 January 2010.

UK Government (2008) 'Innovation Nation White Paper'. Available at: http://www.bis.gov.uk/policies/innovation/white-paper

Ulnick, Anthony W. (2005) *What Customers Want: Using Outcome-driven Innovation to Create Breakthrough Products and Services*. New York: McGraw Hill.

Ulrich, Karl, with C. Terwiesch (2009) *Innovation Tournaments: Creating and Selecting Exceptional Opportunities*, Boston: Harvard Business School Press.

United Nations (2008) *E-government Survey 2008*, New York: United Nations. Available at: http://unpan1.un.org/intradoc/groups/public/documents/un/unpan028607.pdf

van Wart, Montgomery (2008) *Leadership in Public Organizations*, Armonk: M. E. Sharpe.

Veenswick, Marcel B. (2006) 'Surviving the Innovation Paradox: The Case of Megaproject X', *The Public Sector Innovation Journal*, vol 11, no 2, article 6. Available at: www.innovation.cc/volumes-issues/veenswijk_surve+innovation=paradox.pdf

Verganti, Roberto (2009) *Design-driven Innovation: Changing the Rules of Competition by Radically Innovating What Things Mean*, Boston: Harvard Business Press.

Victorian Public Service (2010) 'VPS Innovation Action Plan'. Available at: http://www.vpscin.org/wiki/index.php/VPS_Innovation_Action_Plan

von Hippel, Eric (2005) *Democratizing Innovation*, Cambridge, MA and London, England: The MIT Press.

von Hippel, Eric, Stefan Thomke and Mary Sonnack (1999) 'Creating Breakthroughs at 3M', *Harvard Business Review*, September–October.

Westley, Frances & Nino Antadze (2009) *Making a Difference: Strategies for Scaling Social Innovation for Greater Impact*, Toronto, Social Innovation Generation (SIG).

Wilson, James Q. (1989) *Bureaucracy: What Governments Do and Why They Do It*, New York: Basic Books.

Wolf, Martin (2004) *Why Globalization Works*, New Haven and London: Yale University Press.

Ylirisku, Salu and Jacob Buur (2007) *Designing with Video: Focusing the User-centred Design Process*, London: Springer.

Zago (2010) *Nine Planets Wanted!* Available at: http://vimeo.com/6851020

Index